D1547167

There Is Nothing So Whole as a Broken Heart is a breathtaking kaddish to everyone living the revolutionary vision that Jewish radicals dreamed was possible. It drives to the heart of a tradition that we must rediscover, a story that is simultaneously particular and universal: we can survive if we do it together.

SHANE BURLEY, author of *Why We Fight: Essays on Fascism, Resistance, and Surviving the Apocalypse*

In this moment of resurgent fascism and authoritarianism, the foundational relationship between antisemitism and anti-Blackness is more stark and apparent than ever. The vibrancy of this collection articulates not only a foundation for solidarity in shared struggles against white supremacy but also the vast imaginaries and world-making potential in the diversity of Jewish cultural expression and radical—specifically anarchist—thought. As a Black anarchist, I could not be more grateful for the generosity, vulnerabilities, and fierce, unwavering love for humanity shared within these pages.

ZOÉ SAMUDZI, coauthor of *As Black as Resistance: Finding the Conditions for Liberation*

A poem and a love note, a prayer song and a protest, an attempt to mend a burning world with the best of Jewish, anarchist, and Jewish anarchist traditions.

DAN BERGER, author of *Captive Nation: Black Prison Organizing in the Civil Rights Era*

As leftist Jewish thought and organizing today witnesses a resurgence, this collection provides an important document of its anarchist current.

TREYF PODCAST

This book asks how modern generations of Jewish anarchists are wrestling with rising fascism, white supremacy, and antisemitism, and lifts up the specific cultural tools we bring to the work of mending (or maybe reimagining) the ever-shattering world. Today the book is a mirror; tomorrow, a new window into the archive of Jewish anarchists throughout history.

EZRA BERKLEY NEPON, author of *Justice,*
Justice Shall You Pursue: A History of New Jewish Agenda

In these times of woe, our solidarity and creativity are more urgent than ever. The texts collected here are striking in their literary richness and emotional openness, awakening both pain and solace, insights and further questions. In the often-fraught encounter between living tradition and radical commitments, each of these voices bravely and sensitively negotiates its unique struggle for meaning. Together, they offer a highly rewarding reading experience that will appeal well beyond the Jewish-anarchist intersection.

URI GORDON, coeditor of
The Routledge Handbook of Radical Politics

There Is Nothing So Whole as a Broken Heart offers an ardent new archive of Jewish anarchism. These voices expand a defiant tradition: they speak of the disruptiveness of care, the labor of grief, and the pleasures of survival. As fascism and antisemitism rise, these poets, rabbis, and organizers urgently reach for another world through this one.

AE TORRES, author of *Horizons Blossom,*
Borders Vanish: Anarchism and Yiddish Literature

THERE IS

NOTHING

SO WHOLE

AS A

BROKEN

HEART

THERE IS NOTHING SO WHOLE

AK PRESS

AS A

BROKEN

HEART

MENDING THE WORLD
AS JEWISH ANARCHISTS

EDITED BY CINDY MILSTEIN

There Is Nothing So Whole as a Broken Heart:
Mending the World as Jewish Anarchists
Edited by Cindy Milstein
All essays © 2021 by their respective authors
This edition © 2021 AK Press (Chico/Edinburgh)
ISBN 978-1-84935-399-1
EBOOK ISBN: 978-1-84935-400-4
Library of Congress Control Number: 2020933560

AK Press   AK Press UK
370 Ryan Avenue #100   33 Tower Street
Chico, CA 95973 USA   Edinburgh EH6 7BN Scotland
www.akpress.org   www.akuk.com

Please contact us to request the latest AK Press distribution catalog,
which features books, pamphlets, zines, and stylish apparel published
and/or distributed by AK Press. Alternatively, visit our websites
for the complete catalog, latest news, and secure ordering.

Cover and interior design by Crisis
Printed in Michigan on acid-free, recycled paper

TO OUR

ANCESTORS

PART II: RESISTANCE AS REPAIR

Together, we will tear it down!
It may take days or weeks or years,
but the old walls will fall, fall, fall,
and a new world will be here!

—"Der yokh," lyrics adapted by Burikes, burikes.com

PROLOGUE

SHADOWS AND MOONLIGHT

CINDY MILSTEIN

On nights like these when the moon's face is obscured by darkness,
much is illuminated: the stars dance a dance over six thousand
years old, and spin tales, new and old, of our collective and
individual futures. Shadows come alive. —*Tohuvabohu* zine

Like Jews have had to do many times over the millennia, I've been struggling for months to re-create life on the other side of a border, thrown into exile against my wishes by a global pandemic, into a landscape so alien from where I came. *There Is Nothing So Whole as a Broken Heart*, so close to being done before COVID-19, was displaced along with me, and it too felt completely out of place.[1] It was as if its dozens of voices were suddenly speaking a dead language, killed off, similar to many tongues before, by the cruel dispossession of a vibrant culture. It was as if its tales of the dynamic reimagining of Jewish anarchism, distinctively shaped by feministic and queer/trans

---

1. The phrase used for the book's title has been attributed to Rabbi Menachem Mendel of Kotzk (1787–1859), known as the Kotzker Rebbe.

sensibilities, were talking not about lived practices in the present but rather forgotten histories, erased by the cold dispersal of joyous communities.

I've never been at home in this world, though. That's why I fight so fiercely for other possible ones. That's why, as both an anarchist and Jew, I've long dreamed of do-it-ourselves, egalitarian forms of social organization—ones in which we're all reciprocally and abundantly cared for, not to mention messy-beautifully whole. Until that time, until we are all fully free, I would "rather stay in the Diaspora / And fight for our liberation," as the punky-klezy trio Brivele sings, even if that entails much pain.[2]

Diaspora has always been bound up with wrenching hardship and yet, inextricably, tantalizing promise. The word itself comes from ancient Greek—a language embedded in a period and region that included diasporic Jews—combining *diá-* ("indicating motion across or in all directions," according to *Webster's*) with *speírō* ("to sow"), thereby creating *diaspeírō* ("to scatter"). As my dear Greek anarchist friend paparouna offered by way of an expanded definition, it originally meant "to disperse, most likely from the act of spreading seeds. I think of diaspora as the spreading of seeds across both space and time. It is a scattering apart, and also a seeding of many places and

---

2. Lyrics from "Oy Zionists," arranged by Brivele, translated by Daniel Kahn into English. The original version was collected by Moshe Beregovsky and republished in Mark Slobin's *Old Jewish Folk Music*. For more on Brivele, see https://brivele.bandcamp.com/album/a-little-letter.

moments. It holds pain, loss, and separation, but hope, growth, and nurturance too."

This anthology was already witness to both ends of that spectrum even before the pandemic flung us apart, for how could it not be? A defining feature of Judaism and the Jewish experience for much of our thousands-of-years' history—and to my mind, a core strength— is the necessity and simultaneous desire to collectively self-organize a rich social fabric, *community*, across and when crossed by borders, in all directions around the globe, without states.[3] Anarchism from the get-go has, of course, shared that same imperative and aspiration. Both share in the bittersweetness of what it has meant to hold tight to self-determined communities, as ethic and ongoing experiments, in the face of empires and monarchies, dictatorships and republics, Christian supremacies and fascistic nationalisms, and now, a modern-day plague.

There Is Nothing So Whole took root several years ago. As a wandering Jewish anarchist, I try to intentionally embrace the doublesidedness of my diaspora: on the one hand, my ancestral trauma compelling motion/flight as protection, and on the other, my ancestral resilience weaving routes/relations of magical, caring spaces as prefiguration. So this curated volume arose, like so many of my labors of

---

3. While it should be self-evident from the subtitle, *Mending the World as Jewish Anarchists*, this anthology and many Jews beyond these pages still hold to a vision of liberatory communities—not hierarchical regimes like states, including the state of Israel—as our paths toward utopia.

love seem to do, from my own broken heart and constant quest to build up elastic scar tissue for the next ache. At the same time, it grew from an increasingly full heart, strengthened by repeatedly stumbling on a delightful surprise: a resurgent Jewish anarchism, queered by those who've too often been made invisible within or left out of Jewish traditions and histories, teachings and rituals, cultures and politics.

In city after city, I saw "shadows come alive"—as anarchists in Jewish spaces, as Jews in anarchist spaces, and as Jewish anarchists reinventing our own spaces. Collective houses were hosting antiracist, decolonial, and feministic Shabbat and Pesach dinners; affinity groups were doing Yiddish and Ladino study groups while also showing up proudly as anarchist Jews at protests and direct actions with their almost-lost languages on banners; anarchistic queer folx were creating a radical yeshiva to study Talmud even as many trans/ queer/nonbinary people were going to rabbinical school and then starting their own alternative shuls; anarchist Jews were researching and reviving cultural forms ranging from song and art to Purim plays and drag, or producing their own radical Jewish calendars, radio shows, and zines; they were resuscitating healing and mourning traditions, or reimagining a nonhierarchical Judaism and connection to god (or not) as anarchists, or drawing on the transgenerational transmission of rebel wisdom to fight today's fascism and antisemitism. Without abandoning the necessity of anti-Zionist organizing and pro-Palestinian solidarity efforts, an anarchist Judaism and Jewish anarchism were blossoming into an expansive ecosystem—a well-spring of all that makes us whole, politically and personally, socially and culturally, emotionally and spiritually.

Jewish rituals, frequently shaped and facilitated by anarchxfeminist, queer, and trans Jews, were pivotal. These sacred spaces, whether in living rooms, the streets, or the woods, exuded what could be described as the best of anarchism and Judaism. Rituals—in the form of attending a yearly anarchist bookfair, for instance, or sharing challah while braided together in blessing on Shabbat—necessitate and solidify communal bonds; they both demand and sustain a deep faith in our communities to mutualistically show up for each other no matter what. They pull from the threads of our nonhierarchical traditions and rebellious histories, ground us in our current struggles, and gesture beyond the present, reminding us of what we're fighting for. Indeed, they revolve around the unyielding obligation we've inherited to do good in the here and now (*doykeit*), as both Jewish and anarchist ethos.

Rituals, too, are moments when we honor our ancestors and their teachings, including by continually revisiting their many legacies within our own contexts. While there are "rule books" for our rituals, most of them, such as the Talmud, consist of interpretation on interpretation on interpretation. We continuously play with the words, knowledges, and other gifts that were passed along to us, and others will do so after us. Within rituals, we lovingly argue out the meanings of what we do, for whom, and why—such as how patriarchy or settler colonialism might be implicated in our practices, or how we can build on already liberatory and ecological impulses—yet with a generosity that welcomes others to join in this endless education and re-creation process.

In these and other ways, our rituals at once prepare us for freedom and set us free, even if only in pockets of time. They are a precondition for and the condition of freedom.

Part of that freedom is our own healing—a multigenerational process involving selves and societies. Jewish rituals contain centuries of somatic practices woven into their very fiber, to borrow an insight from contributor and dear friend Ami Weintraub. There's the gentle rocking motion of davening (prayer), the activating of all our senses during havdalah by, say, smelling spices and seeing/feeling the warmth of flame, or the Tashlich ceremony in which stones or bread crumbs are thrown into a moving body of water as release, among many others.

So it's no wonder that in a time period eliciting trauma responses in most of us, this flowering of a queered Jewish anarchism would be inseparable from collective rituals and/as collective care. After all, for many of us Jews (and anarchists), we only have to turn to our great-grandparents, grandparents, or even parents for their own tales of (or silences about) a long list of still-fresh wounds, including enslavement, forced conversion or conscription, colonization, rape by invaders, dispossession and displacement, bodily assaults, cultural erasure, religious and racial persecution, social and political abandonment, economic exploitation and material immiseration, ghettoization and dehumanization, genocide, and indignities against our dead. Such pernicious forms of violence have touched Jews across the globe—for instance, at least a third of the world's Jews and over two-thirds of Europe's were murdered under National Socialism less than eighty years ago—and are deeply intertwined with how myriad "othered" peoples have been and are treated. Today's rise of fascism and antisemitism, and centuries-old repurposed "conspiracies" that intimately paint Jews as "outside agitators" in league with or manipulating other oppressed peoples, couldn't help but nudge us Jewish anarchists into collective action.

Pre-pandemic, I was increasingly drawn to participating in and helping to hold space for rituals that brought Jewish and non-Jewish anarchists and other radicals together. For example, on the twentieth anniversary of the Montreal Anarchist Bookfair—a space near and dear to my heart, in a city that's long been one of my diasporic "homes"—I decided to add to my duties as one of the co-organizers of the weekend—itself like an anarchist family reunion. With the aid of what has become my beloved Jew crew in Tio'tia:ke/Montreal— noa and daph, whom I initially gathered with for monthly queer Rosh Chodesh rituals in person, and through that, have grown into trusted friends—I invited numerous groupings of other friends traveling from far and wide to all meet up on that Friday night for a potluck, mentioning that some of us would do Shabbat rituals too. About fifty or so Jews and non-Jews came to the space we were squatting: outdoor picnic tables under a canopy next to a romantic, if gentrifying, canal. It felt so beautiful to introduce various friends from so many other places to each other and watch connective conversations drift into the night air.

When we began our short ritual, everyone joined us, and then an adorable queer collective from Pittsburgh leaped into its own weekly Shabbat practice: circling up to sing a capella songs together for hours. The somatics of breaths rising and falling, harmonically allowing people to anticipate each other's desires, converging joys and sorrows into dissonant unity and fierce love, cast a spell. Even a few anarchist friends listening from the sidelines, and who'd long been skeptical of their own Jewish spirituality or the power of queering Jewish space, were mesmerized—and then added their voices. The next day, one of them publicly proclaimed, "Many gods, no masters!" It's less about whether one trusts in a single or many gods, definitions of god that center on the mysteries of the earth and life rather than a divine being, or no god(s) at all, though. We were transformed that evening, a little less broken and a lot more cared for, and nearly everyone who had been at that anarchic Shabbat said it was the highlight of the bookfair. Through ritual and singing, we became a community.

Before the pandemic hit, I danced with the Torah and anarchist Jews in the streets as ritual/resistance for Simchat Torah, clustered arm in arm on a cloud-covered night in a forest for a soothing havdalah during a beautiful yet intense anarchist summer school week, created a banner that displayed our anarchism, antifascism, and Judaism for an immigrant solidarity demo, cried alongside hundreds of Jews, Muslims, Quakers, Buddhists, agnostics, atheists, and others at an outdoor mourning ritual in the aftermath of the murder of eleven

Jews at Pittsburgh's Tree of Life synagogue, and so many more life-giving spaces. Through the best and the worst, I felt fully embraced.

Then lockdown came crashing down like a steel gate, and powerful in-person Jewish anarchist projects, spaces, and rituals came tumbling down with it. This anthology felt like a ghost, as did I, unable to be buried, not at peace, and yet unable to cross the divide into community and thus life again. As I asked myself in an Instagram post on July 26, 2020/5780,

> How does one return from the dead, from the feeling each morning on waking that one shouldn't still be here, when one's bones cry out with the weary pain of ancestors who already said "no to fascism" and yet were burned by its fires? How does one grieve in any way—ways that make one feel whole again, ways that honor the sacredness of life—the mounting ash heap of losses these many long months of pandemic, when one's rituals cry out for communities of beloveds holding each other close, looking in each others' eyes, reciprocally catching the subtleties of how our mind-bodies are reacting while we light candles or sing poignant tunes or recite ancient prayers for the departed, face to unmediated face?

I reflected on how so many anarchistic Jews had pulled from the toolboxes filled by our ancestors over the millennia, and almost immediately as the pandemic physically distanced us, had constructed a robust world of online textual, artistic, educational, cultural, organizing, and most especially ritual space. I realized that of all the failed trial and errors to keep myself going when all that I loved seemed canceled, when I was alone in an eerie new exile, it was Jewish rituals' power that succeeded. It permitted us, as my Instagram post continued, to find each other, outside the disaster of states, capitalism, borders, and other logics intent on dispersing our community and killing us:

One looks backward, into the flames that have engulfed too many peoples, yours included, over too many centuries; into the repeated sparks of resistance and somehow survival, although always at a brutal cost; into traditions that have mutually aided many peoples to bear the unbearable, and still find spaces that make one want to live, even if the world is dying.

In a few days, Jews will mark Tisha B'Av, a major day of communal mourning, the culmination of three weeks and especially nine days of mourning in preparation for what many understand as the saddest day of the year. The reasons for this specific date—and asking that people share the crush of grief—can be and are debated among Jews. Yet one year's Tisha B'Av sticks out in particular: 1492. That Tisha B'Av was the last day of Jews being expelled from Spain, thrown into diaspora, suffering, and/or death again. The harbor was apparently so congested that fascistic day in 1492 that Columbus had to delay his voyage to colonize and kill Indigenous peoples. This same period saw the targeting of Muslims too, witch hunts against women and queers, and the start of the slave trade of Blacks.

How does one return from the dead? After Jews sit shiva—the

seven days of communal mourning following a death—many communities include informal practices, such as walking around the block together, to help them reemerge side by side into the world, with its joys and sorrows.

The same anarchist Jews who'd been creating such powerful spaces before COVID-19, now determinedly reemerged, side by side. I wasn't able to process it for months after lockdown, while this anthology sat gathering dust as if in an archival tomb, but the blossoming of Jewish anarchism had simply formed new buds, new flowers. Our ancestors, in their many times of diaspora and despair, had invented rituals precisely to bravely, communally, withstand and defy catastrophes, even if as messages in bottles in hopes they'd reach those who would outlast them.

One can't return to that pivotal year, 1492, and undo the barbarous theft of lands and lives that followed. And yet we must return to that time, now over five hundred years ago, so as to remember that millions of us were scattered into disposability during the exact same epoch. We share in this trauma, which cunningly took even the memory of our intermingled lives and solidarities, that coldly pitted us against each other in a fight for scraps, in hierarchies of oppression, as if pain were a contest.

If we pull away the mists of time, we see that as peoples dispersed against our wills—Jews and non-Jews alike—we share playbooks not only for survival but also resilience. As varied diasporic peoples, we've long used, for instance, ram's horns or conch shells to call us together; mystical numbers have long spoken to the ways in which we and the earth count, such as the seven-year cycles of food growing, gleaning, and soil revitalization, and the responsibility to seven generations; we've warded off enemies and cleansed our spaces by burning cedar, rosemary, or sage bundles; our calendars have for millennia revolved around the moon, stars, seasons, and cycles of life that swirled around us, nonlinear, contextual, and holistic; we've relied on food and shelter that was easy to make and carry while in rushed flight, and in blessed memory, wove them into our holidays and celebrations; we've knit our communities together around sacred circles with flames and/or sweat, often in communion with our ancestors; we've honored water as life, including in rituals to help our newly dead on their journey; we've used our voices, in songs and storytelling, as carriers of our grief, tenacity, and dreams.

There Is Nothing So Whole as a Broken Heart aspires to speak to all diasporic peoples in hopes that we can remember how much we share—from common foes to uncommonly beautiful lifeways—and not let the profound cleavages of 1492 and other eras win. Or to put it another way, this collection aims to disobey the nonconsensual shatterings of our lives and reaffirm our interdependence. We share not simply survival and resilience stories—tales interlaced into our rituals so that we never forget. We share so much wisdom in already knowing how to do what colonizers, capitalists, and patriarchs have long told us is impossible. Our cultures and communities of mutual aid, collective care, and social solidarity have demonstrated time and again that it's eminently possible and desirable to thrive without a state. Their systems of domination have come and gone, even if others have followed in their footsteps, but nonetheless, we have outlived them. And from our enormous wealth of knowledge about how to do that, we have "dance[d] a dance" together over centuries, all of us rebel wanderers, "spinning tales, new and old, of our collective and individual futures."

This anthology is part of a tradition of storytelling and/as ritual that keeps us alive, that grants us life, because we don't shy away from sharing the whole of our experiences freely with each other. It is a snapshot of a moment in time, too, pre- and now within pandemic, and aims to be a timeless gift, a bundle of touching, vulnerable love letters.

Like a pomegranate, these tales collect many seeds within a single container. Its seeds are at once hard and soft, brilliant and earthy, aromatic and juicy, nestled together in no discernible order or hierarchy other than a circle we can tenderly cradle in our hands, and yet able to be scattered in delicious promise. It is my hope that you'll taste the fullness of these stories, pulling out ripe morsels of what makes Jewish anarchism such a powerful and complementary combination. That you'll see yourself in the bittersweetness of diasporic tales, and savor these stories for the tartness of the trauma within them and sweetness of the hearts that keep beating. That you'll share all the words and images here by questioning, wrestling with, and building on them, using this anthology as fuel to continue reaching toward the stars, guided by the moonlight, as we seek together to mend the world.

> The only writer of history with the gift of setting alight the sparks of hope in the past, is the one who is convinced of this: that not even the dead will be safe from the enemy, if he is victorious.
> —Walter Benjamin, "On the Concept of History"

*

Cindy Milstein would like to thank daph ben david, noah, and Ben Siegel for editing aid on this prologue, and Courtney Remacle and Jordan for heroically proofreading the entire book with me. Milstein is grateful, too, to everyone who enthusiastically shared and responded to the anthology's original "call for submissions," and all who lended much-needed encouragement, wisdom, and love along the way. They offer deep appreciation to all the many Jewish anarchists who came before us; the entire AK Press collective for believing in and publishing this collection; Jeff Clark—under the studio name Crisis—for being a beloved accomplice on yet another book via his exquisite design, which in this case, feels not only sublime but also sacred; and of course, all the many contributors, who generously brought the fullness of themselves to these pages with such honesty, empathy, and courage. If Milstein feels enough of a Jew and enough of an anarchist, it is because of such precious community.

PART I

REMEMBRANCE

AS

RESISTANCE

HOW TO SCREAM,

HOW TO SING

AMI WEINTRAUB

On October 27, 2018, a man came into the synagogue where I work and killed eleven people. This massacre has become part of me—and perhaps it has become part of you too.

My heart broke open the day of the shooting. It cracked along familiar fault lines. I had never been here before, but my bones had, my blood had, my tradition had.

It was months later when the pain started swelling up again, splintering me afresh. I was visiting my parents' synagogue in Maryland, feeling like no one in the congregation knew the weight I was carrying.

I abruptly left the Shabbat morning service halfway through. I wandered through the sunlit hallways to the small library. I mindlessly reached for a book of photos. Flipping through the pages, I realized it was a collection of pictures of pogrom survivors. I studied their wide eyes and gaping mouths, their wails now muted in frozen silence. In their expressions, I saw aspects of my own heaviness. In their bodies, I saw my own reflection.

* * *

After it happened, everyone around me kept repeating the startled mantra, "There isn't a playbook for this." We'd show up to staff meetings and organizing conversations confused and disoriented. There wasn't a playbook, they said over and over. But I kept thinking, "Isn't there?"

When my great-grandmother Anna was a girl, she lived in a small village in Russia. Every time a pogrom burst through her town, she threw her small, nine-year-old hands against the giant wooden shutters of her home and heaved the boards closed. She did this so many times that she came to fear the wooden planks themselves.

I know how she hid, but how did she go outside the next morning? How did she live long enough to give birth to me?

I imagine that morning after.

Everyone lying in bed, on floorboards, in piles of broken glass. They wonder what to say, what to do, on another morning like this. Then the practiced words of dawn prayers drift down onto their tongues. They remember their obligation to begin each day with gratitude for life.

"Elohai N'shama Shentatabi t'hora hee." Oh my G-d, the soul you've given me, it is pure and it is free. These words remind them that they are human. That they are worthy of life even when the world tries to convince them otherwise.

I imagine men rushing by the destruction in the streets, crowding into the *shtibele*, that little synagogue, for Shacharit services. They convene together in uproarious prayer. The vibrations of their songs settle their writhing bodies.

While the sun rises, the women and queer folks roam the alleys, meticulously collecting the names of the dead. They feel the day get hotter as they pour dripping, white wax into well-used molds. They make a Yahrzeit candle for each lost soul.

That night, the whole town gathers at the shtibele for the maariv prayers. The kids, normally nudging and whining, sit in solemn attention. They need this too. One by one, they light the blessed candles. They watch as the smoke curls up to the sky. They whisper about the gray trails. They tell stories about the smoke reaching the souls of the recently departed, building a ladder to connect the world of the living and world of the dead. They pray that angels and blessings might travel along this corridor to find home among the inhabitants of both realms. On their lips are the Aramaic words of the Mourner's Kaddish. The same syllables and sounds that I recite today.

With my Jewish practice, I share customs with people now turned ghosts. Through our common motions and songs, I can see their lives more clearly and learn from their wisdom. This fantasy may be all that I will ever know of my great-grandmother's world. But it has taught me to believe in Judaism's power to free me.

* * *

Judaism contains tools for surviving violence and trauma. Yet so many of us are scared to acknowledge the medicine embedded in our tradition. Doing so makes us feel vulnerable. It makes us admit that we have pain we have never talked about.

Acknowledging Judaism's ability to mend trauma forces us to

admit that we are not the smiling, well-adjusted, middle-class folks that US society has told us to be. That we do have a playbook for this, because it has happened before.

We are from somewhere before the United States, before so many other places. The harm done to me on other lands does not know the definition of borders. It follows me. I try so hard, but I cannot forget how those places hurt us so deeply. We are hurting so deeply. Our home, this current one, is hurting us so deeply yet again.

Who forces silence over our wounds? Aren't they healthier left open and oozing? Who is scared of the pulsing, unhealed flesh, rotting in my body? If we felt our wounds, we might awaken to the cruelty of what was and is being done to us. We might become dangerous, wanting retribution or revenge, or we might stop you from telling us how we should feel and behave.

I want us to feel worthy enough to fight for ourselves, to care enough for our bodies that we believe we too deserve true liberation. I want to turn on the world that has been built from our submission. I want to love our tradition enough to let it make us feel whole.

If we were allowed to apply our own salves to our traumas, we might finally be able to remember them all.

* * *

It's hard to write. I've been spending my time checking over my shoulder when I sit in the synagogue, fantasizing about exit plans in my Hebrew school classroom, bracing for death when I begin to pray.

I want to lie in the long grass at summer camp again. I want to fear the passing heat of the sun.

Instead you ask me to be brave. You ask me to plan a rally or organize a vigil. But we argue, argue, and argue. Is this tragedy or simply adulthood?

My body keeps whispering to me—lay down, sit, eat. Let seven days, a month, or a year give you the space to let this story become part of you. Rest feels distant when I have to work and organize and write. In the first year of mourning, as I struggle to formulate this piece, I grieve for a world that would give me time to sit with my new body.

* * *

When my mind wanders, I remember the little girl at Hebrew school. She ran out of our classroom a few months after the shooting. She hid in a stairwell, and when the teacher found her, she yelled so loud that people came running. I don't know exactly why she was upset. I just know that her body needed to scream.

"You can't yell like that anymore!" the teacher scolded the crying child. "After this October, people will think something horrible happened to you."

Something horrible did happen, months before. The child still needed to scream. I still needed to scream. Yet we have learned to fear the power of our bodies. And the desire for normalcy causes us to mute our racked bellows.

I don't want my screams to become frozen in a book of pictures that my great-grandchildren find. I want my howls to reverberate across generations, releasing the weight I have been carrying for hundreds of years.

* * *

The mending and resistance starts to mix so thoroughly with the pain. I try to pen something beautiful. The words keep hurting me. Instead I simply bleed onto the paper, holding up my burnt offering for you to read.

* * *

I went to the funeral at the Jewish Community Center and the havdalah gathering in Squirrel Hill and the march down Murray Avenue when Donald Trump came to Pittsburgh. I was searching for life in the overwhelming shadow of death.

I watched people wrap around the corner of the Jewish Community Center all the way down to the intersection. Mourners filled the auditorium and then the lobby, until over a hundred of us packed into the overflow gym. We watched the cantor speak on a giant screen while the audio cut in and out. We prayed out of sync with the lapsing projector.

I remember the line of cars in the funeral procession. I waited on the street for what felt like half an hour as car after car rounded the corner. At the rear, a group of Hasidic families walked behind the procession, pushing strollers and holding toddlers by the hand.

We drove by more funerals at a synagogue down the street. Throngs of people in black moved like phantoms from the steps of the shul onto the cool October asphalt.

This happened for a week. At the funeral parlor, the synagogue, the community center. Multitudes gathering and missing work. Lines of cars stopping traffic. Religious families trailing behind.

Every night for a week, eleven houses filled with people bringing food and the will to keep going. This is the care work of rebellion. My community's ability to sit for seven days, block the streets with cars, and skip work to attend funerals was a protest against a life that tries to kill us all.

I learned to trust that our own tradition can beckon in great acts of liberation.

The night of the shooting, the high school students shook me from my stupor. "Meet us in Squirrel Hill," they posted on social media.

As the sun set, over a thousand people trickled onto the sidewalks of the Jewish neighborhood. There were so many of us, we spilled into the busiest intersection in Pittsburgh. In our public grief, we shut down the city's main artery.

The news had fixed me in place. I no longer knew what to say or how to move. I simply came to gather. All the eyes around me were wide saucers ringed with red. Slowly, the tortured expressions became faces I recognized.

And then, without plans or meetings, we knew what to do. This Shabbos had made me fear myself. But it was ending, as all Shabbos days do. The teenagers who called the gathering lifted up a havdalah candle to mark the close of Shabbos. Hundreds of people lifted up havdalah candles. They lit the braided wicks, turning them into small, glowing flames. We became a sea of fire.

We brought our bodies back to earth with the taste of wine, smell of spices, sight of light, and touch of shoulders brushing against one another as we rocked and prayed.

"Blessed are you who separates the holy from everything else," we sang out in Hebrew. Blessed are you who sanctifies separating, cracking, and breaking. Blessed are you who creates a distinction that today was just one day. Tomorrow will be another day. We will continue to learn how to parse beauty from pain, to break from the constriction of this sorrow, crack the ice from our bodies, so we may live and fight again. Blessed are you ancestors who pass down the motions of havdalah. Who through these ancient gestures, teach me how to connect to my body so I may melt the panic inside me and feel human again.

Amen.

How do we keep living? By enacting the practices that we use every week to awaken our aliveness. The songs that hold life-giving power. The words that help us receive a second soul on Shabbat.

It was Tuesday afternoon. Trump was coming to town, and I was marching behind friends shouting, "Safety in solidarity." I could feel the anxiety pulsing through the crowd. We were nervous until someone started singing. "Lo yisa goy el goy cherev, lo yilmadu od milchama. Nation will not lift sword against nation. We will not study war any longer." I felt an exhale from those of us marching, calmed by the collective outpouring of this tune.

It was a song I had learned lying in the long grass at Moshava, my Jewish summer camp. On Shabbat, we would join together to overcome our fear of the July heat in Bel Air, Maryland. We would hold hands and walk in a grapevine motion to a clearing of trees. With these words hanging in the air, our breath created a breeze, and we watched the sun set while we waited to bring in Shabbat.

We resist by remembering these songs when it feels like we are so far from a world that wants us alive. We commit to creating beauty and care even when the motorcades arrive. Even when the man comes to take pictures in front of the suffering he has helped to create.

* * *

I can't help feeling like I am writing a playbook for when this happens to you.

* * *

Jewish practice does not need death to reveal its radical nature. Our tradition is not worthy only when we are in pain. Judaism's rebellious nature is clear whenever we use it to bring life. But my life-giving tradition is handed to me in pieces.

Why did you break it?

I ask this of my parents and grandparents. I ask this of my ancestors.

I ask this of the people who have always hated me and my family.

A Jewish teacher once told me not to ask why our aggressors tried to destroy us. There is no reason besides their own choice to hate.

Yet some of the antifascists I've met want to have a reason. It's economics, it's loneliness, it's the internet. They want to believe there is something new about this moment that makes people turn on me.

But viewing antisemitism as a problem of the present erases the historical legacy of hatred against Jews. It washes away antisemitism's foundational role in the nation building of Europe, emergence of fascism, and maltreatment of other groups of marginalized people.

From the beginning of the development of Christianity and expulsion of the Jews from Jerusalem, Christian Europeans have defined themselves in relation to their Jews. The first Jewish ghetto, the first pogrom, and the first blood libel united Christian Europeans. They had a shared identity as those who were different from and ultimately against their perpetual outsiders. If Christian Europeans were civilized, holy, and pure, they had to turn Jews into the total opposite either by rhetoric or a change in the material conditions of Jewish people.

Europeans could then apply this belief system to other groups of "outsiders" they encountered through colonization and migration. This is one of the reasons understanding antisemitism is important for all of us fighting for the liberation of marginalized people. To my mind, the way Europeans treated Jews was the foundation for Europeans' treatment of other colonized people throughout history. It became the playbook.

Fascism continued this two-thousand-year-old legacy. It created a shared sense of peoplehood based on how societies dealt with the Jews among them and eventually all whom they saw as outsiders.

When those in power import European ideologies like fascism to the United States, we must understand that they are also importing antisemitism as a keystone of their dogma. This antisemitism primes people to turn on other societal outsiders as well, which explains why fascism needs antisemitism to exact its well-known racism and xenophobia. Hatred toward Jews is not a secondary result of the rise of the alt-right. It is not a result of economics, loneliness, or the internet. Hatred toward Jews is a crucial element of fascist thinking and will exist wherever fascism is allowed to prevail.

If antisemitism is only seen as a contemporary problem, Christian Europeans will never reckon with the ways antisemitism is deeply rooted in their culture. They will never understand how antisemitism has enabled them to turn on other groups of marginalized people. Non-Jews will be able to avoid accountability for their role in the historical displacement and murder of my people. They will pathologize the pain I've inherited as merely anxiety rather than the remnants of state-sponsored violence and expulsion.

I will feel so alone.

Do they want a reason because these people are their neighbors? Their friends? Their siblings? Is it because they weren't taught to be as scared as I am?

* * *

"It's shattered, all shattered," my mother cried on the other end of the phone when she heard the news. But I could still see the glass room where I helped teach Hebrew school. The eleven-year-old who drank strawberry fruit juice. The ten-year-old who missed class for theater tryouts.

I could still peer into the lobby of the Tree of Life from our glass bubble. The tan, marbled floor. The small staircase leading to the library. The courtyard where we ate apple slices in our sukkah just weeks earlier. Sheltered by a roof of leaves, we invited our ancestors to join us as we celebrated our fall harvest festival.

While my mom cried on the phone, I was lost in memories of lifting kindergarten students up to the mezuzah in the lobby. "Kiss it," I said, as they touched their small hands to the wooden box and then their lips. It was a week before the shooting, and we were kissing the doorways of this hallowed building. "We do this to remember we are Jewish even during times of change, so we never forget our connection to these walls."

I could still see the enormous sanctuary glowing yellow and red under the colorful, stained-glass windows.

Hours away, my mom could already see the jagged shards. But just fifteen minutes from the synagogue in Pittsburgh, my heart was only beginning to fall apart.

One month after the shooting, I learned that our classroom had been boarded up. All the brilliant glass had been scattered.

* * *

The summer after the shooting, I cupped my fingers in front of my eyes, drawing in the light of the Shabbat candles. Three repetitive motions invited in the familiar glow, asking the power of the flame to fill our small room. I looked at my fingertips, surprised. Resting in my palms were the ancient hands of the women and queer folks who continued to light candles after it all.

Our practice teaches us to fill our cemeteries with rocks.

I want to take the pebbles that we set on graves and join the children who throw stones at the men who murder in my name. I want to throw them at the men who want to murder me too.

We arm our dead with weapons of resistance.

I imagine running into Jewish graveyards, fleeing from the hatred that haunts me. And even when death surrounds me, I find the tools I need to stay alive.

*

Ami Weintraub is a Jewish educator and anarchist living in Pittsburgh. They help organize Ratzon: Center for Healing and Resistance, a place for queer folks, youths, Jewish folks, and those from marginalized backgrounds to mend their jagged edges. Ami is a contributor to Rebellious Anarchist Young Jews (RAYJ). They would like to thank their ancestors for surviving and teaching them how to remember. Ami would also like to thank their friends, who help them believe that another world is always possible, and their family for always, always being there.

TEN NIGHTS SINCE
THEY KILLED GEORGE

MARK TILSEN

Somewhere between sitting vigil and shiva
I sit and watch
call and text
did you make it home yet
are you okay
they're shooting people on Live
Lake Street is burning
From DC to Boston
Chicago Minneapolis Austin
Denver Oakland SF and LA
Waiting for people to get out of jail to check in
as if worry had its own gravity or power
I see the hot takes and counter hot takes
movement critiques
I feel the smallness of my opinion and I'm grateful for the awareness
I stand down when I can hear the morning birds sing
whispering my heretic prayer for my friends and loved ones

live
live
live

*

Mark Tilsen is a Lakota Jewish poet, educator, water protector, and sommelier of memes.

THE MILK POT

XAVA DE CORDOVA

A hot summer breeze coasted through the barn, dragging in recollections of the fire. Shoshana felt a warm trickle of milk run down her sleeve when she forgot to aim. The copper-haired goat huffed impatiently. The goat knew by long experience that Shoshana's daydreaming could drag the milking routine out all morning. Shoshana resumed her steady rhythm of squeezing the soft teats with alternating, calloused hands and let the half-formed memories kicked up by the warmth of the day settle down, like windblown leaves, into the undergrowth of her mind. The steady ceramic splashing sound of milk flying into the pot helped draw her thoughts back to the grim business ahead of her.

The milk pot was a heavy round thing made of red clay, glazed and then burned to black, and cracked on its bottom edge. The lid had a pristine and glossy pattern of *alefim* stamped into it that had survived, undamaged by the flames that had scorched the base. The mark could easily be mistaken for a common crisscross motif, but Shoshana had been educated by her papá in reading holy tongue. She knew that *alef* was the honored first letter of their alphabet, repeated again and again. It was a consonant with no sound of its own, but one that could stretch to hold any vowel that needed to flow through a word. It was the written embodiment of the silent canvas on which all words are drawn. It was a symbol of emptiness, and it whispered to her heart that she could always begin, again, from nothing. She found the pot in the ashes of their home, after mamá and papá were taken to the church in the city for their auto-da-fé. They'd converted during the first riots, trying to survive by choosing to change to fit the times, yet that didn't keep them safe from neighbors who thought it was still a bit suspicious that they kept getting their meat from the Jewish butcher.

After she pulled the final squirt out into the pot, the milk's white-on-white ripples settled into glossy opacity. She wanted to put a curse on this milk. She heard Dama Alvarez finally stirring inside the *kaza grande* and clenched her teeth. Last night, Friday night, the lady had caught her lighting the candle stubs that she'd scavenged. There were angry crimson welts covering her back where the willow switch landed. Dama Alvarez took Shoshana in when she had nowhere to go, plucking her out of the ruins like a misplaced bauble, but she had done it to get a servant who would never be able to demand pay. The lid clicked delicately as she put it in place, taking care to do it gently despite her shaking hands.

* * *

Hatred was bubbling up in her for all those gullible men and quiet women who'd been whipped into a mob. They had taken her parents from her without a care for what would happen to the girl left alone in the blank hole of their absence. That was what she felt most when she tried to think of her parents: a hole, a harsh lack of the closeness and warmth that everyone around her seemed to have grown up with. That mob had convinced the king to expel all her people from Sefarad, as if their ways were a nuisance, a stray and coarse hair to be strained out of the pure cream of burgeoning empire. She would put a spell on this milk for them. Not the deadly, sickening, poisonous curse lurking behind her teeth, making them ache with rage. There were a few souls in this town who didn't deserve that. The burden of living out the rest of their years here would be lightened by forgetting about her. She didn't think it would really work, but words had power, she knew. She'd spent all last night listening to the wind and letting it bring her those words.

She sang the spell under her breath in a whispering moan. The tune was too wild and wandering to quite be a melody, but came out something like a crow's warble when it imitated a person:

I was turned out of my home, so you will turn me out of mind.

Our houses of meeting were torn down, so you will tear the memory of me away.

I've been forced from here, so any thought of me will be forced away from you.

For all your days and mine, amen.

* * *

Letting Roza off the stand where she had been impatiently waiting since the milking, Shoshana's molten anger cooled into a hard iron lump of despair. She felt its weight in every step. She could convert, shatter her own stubborn heart by bowing to the same power that stirred up the crusades and purges, or leave on a journey to a port. She would be lucky to make it alive. At least this way, the kind ones wouldn't have to worry about her, and the vicious ones wouldn't remember to wonder how easy it would be to take advantage of a girl on her own on the long road, with no family left to ask after her. She let Roza walk beside her, without a lead. The goat's dusty cinnamon back was already growing warm with the morning sun where Shoshana rested a free hand on it. She took the full pot of milk out of the barn and began the long walk through town to seek out her regular buyers.

Her first customer lived in a scrawny white stucco house at the end of the lane that lead to Dama Alvarez's estate. "I see you coming, and I'll tell you now I don't want any!" Gustavo said, poking his head out the door.

"Dama Alvarez beats me when I don't sell it all, you know." She never bothered to tell anyone this, since they probably already understood, but today was her last day in this miserable village and that had her feeling a bit outrageous.

"What problem of that is mine?"

"Just take a little." Shoshana raised her eyebrows knowingly. "The baby needs it; your wife needs it."

Gustavo's mouth turned into a tight line, but he mulled it over. He resented her for reminding him of his own troubles when he would rather feel superior contemplating hers.

"Ay, if you're going to badger me all morning, it's worth it just to be rid of you."

Shoshana painted on a smile and took his few thin coins, doling out part of the morning's work into his outstretched cup. He never invited her in. Not that she wanted to be in the dangerous position of being alone with him. His eyes slid over her body leaving a cold, vile feeling like snakeskin wherever they looked. Next was the widow, Devorah.

Her shack was set back from the other houses, though just a little way down the path from Gustavo. "What a blessing, Shoshana, to see you this terrible morning. I don't have money, but I have challah left over from this Shabbat."

Shoshana knew that Dama Alvarez would never let her barter for bread rather than coin, but for Devorah, she would risk it. Besides that, she would probably never have to face the consequences.

"A blessing for me too, since no one will make such bread here anymore, and another blessing since I'll need bread today. Why is this morning any more terrible than any other, *avuela*?"

She sucked her teeth and made a crossed-finger sign against bad luck. "Because today, I go to the church."

She spat the last word out like a seed from a rotten part of an apple that had turned her tongue. Shoshana looked down, a spear of ice gliding through her heart, but she didn't say anything.

"And what will you do?" the widow asked.

"I don't know, I don't know. I suppose I'll find a ship."

Devorah flinched. "And who will protect you on the way? Don't be so proud, girl. The *hambradas* are out there. The red women will get you, if bandits don't. And with what money will you pay for such a passage?"

"Pssht. That's just an old story. There are no witches waiting to snatch me up. I'll find money, somehow. Don't worry about it."

"I used to see their tower myself, in these same hills. Yes, in this place, when I was young, they were known to come down every new moon. In those days, they might give us a cure or some medicine. But now it seems it's only curses coming down."

Throughout this harangue, Devorah had been rooting around in her dark, tiny house for the loaves of bread. She handed them over to Shoshana. They were slightly stale yet had beautiful glossy crusts and were elegantly braided. Devorah would probably never braid her loaves like that again. She would need to be cautious not to be seen as anything but a penitent, enthusiastic new Christian.

"I'll be careful. Don't let me keep you all morning," said Shoshana.

With a final sharp meeting of their eyes, she withdrew and didn't look back. Devorah was going to be part of a new world now. A world that had no space for girls who were too stubborn to convert and too poor to sail away. Better to keep her heart guarded, to make space between herself and that strange society coalescing around her.

She made her way down the dusty road with slow purpose. The dry street sent up clouds of dirt despite her efforts toward gentle steps. They hung around her and settled on her skirt, staining its bland tan with vibrant ochre. Last on her list was Senyor Flores, the mayor. His house was wooden, with two stories, whitewashed and gleaming in the sun. It had a short staircase leading up to a small covered porch, topped with ruddy tiles that twinned those of the main roof.

As she got closer, she could see that he was somehow already waiting for her, slouching unkindly in the shade. Her hands trembled.

"Don't come near this house," he said, when she had made her way to stand with weak knees in front of the stairs.

"I only wanted to see if you wanted any milk, senyor."

"Don't pretend to respect me! You call me senyor, but your kind has never respected us!! Or our ways!"

"Please, it's just, … I'm taking the journey to a port. Today, tomorrow, at the latest. I need everything I can get."

For a moment, he was still and silent, surprised, or maybe just satisfied to know that his kind had won. Then the sudden calm passed.

"Out, out, damn you!" He kicked at her milk pot with a wild smile that went all the way up to his eyes. "I don't have to let your kind pollute this place anymore! I said out!" The pot flew from her hands, drawing a long arc against the pristine blue sky before it crashed to the earth and shattered. Milk pooled on the ground for a moment, until the thirsty ground turned it into sticky mud. The shards of the thing lay where they had fallen, so that you could still almost make out what the pot had been when it was whole.

Vibrating with restrained tears, Shoshana turned her back on Senyor Flores, knelt, and picked up a single scrap of the lid. Its molded *alef* was still intact. Its edge was sharp against her palm. The mayor stood silent, again, chest heaving, but he didn't look away. Drawing the relic of her milk pot across her hand, she opened a bright crimson gash that ran from the base of her pinky to the start of her thumb. She didn't know why, but she felt that it was right; it was what she had to do. She rubbed her hands together until both were slick and wet, her eyes now vacant, though inside her thoughts roiled.

Stomping up the stairs toward the door frame, she saw the mayor hadn't moved. He stood transfixed. Reaching around him so that her face drew close to his, she planted her hands on the whitewashed wood of the doorposts, leaving two perfectly painted handprints in crimson. They would never wash off. She knew that those marks would stay there, indelible, precisely as stark as they were now, until this house aged and rotted into ruin. People would see them and gossip. They would wonder what kind of wickedness must have gone on in that house. Everybody knows evil leaves a mark wherever it finds a home. As surely as the foundation of the house, the foundation of the mayor's power and wealth, his good name, would crumble under the constant pressure of these suspicious and stubborn folk. She tucked the shard of pottery into the canvas bag at her hip, where it rested alongside the few coins that she'd gotten out of Gustavo and the fluffy loaves of challah from the widow. Her hand wasn't bleeding anymore. Shoshana finally realized where there might be a place for her now.

She walked past each house where she had delivered milk, but no one peered out from the shutters or watched from their open doorways. No one took any notice of the girl with a dress wet with milk, dry blood on her palms, and iron in her eyes. Her gaze was fixed on the hills, dotted with oaks and wild persimmons. Above those branches, reaching up as if in prayer, she thought she could see the tip of a tile roof sitting atop a rose-tinted stone tower. Shoshana walked away from the town, like thousands of others doing the same. Only she walked not to a port or church but instead into the hills, where people said the red witches dwelled.

*

Xava De Cordova is a Jewish educator, Talmudic scholar, future rabbi, neo-xasidic Svaranik, and writer living in Providence, Rhode Island. She would like to thank her loving community, especially Binya, Beverly, Violet, all her xevrutot, and Benay, for teaching her to expect more from her tradition.

GHOSTS OF LUBLIN

MEMORY AND GRIEF

ALI NISSENBAUM

It's the first day of the Lubliner Reunion, and also my *aba's* first time in Poland. My father is walking around slightly dazed, as if he can't quite grasp that this is a real place, with roads and buildings and cars and graffiti. He keeps asking me, "Can you believe this place used to be 50 percent Jewish?"

For lunch we go to a Jewish restaurant in the Old Town. It's a cavernous space with a domed plaster ceiling. The wall is painted with a mural of dancing Hasidim. The decor is Judaica kitsch— old-fashioned menorahs, candleholders, and silver goblets like the ones you fill with wine and leave out for Eliyahu on Pesach. The menu, we're told, is based on prewar Jewish recipes, and includes Jewish "delicacies" like matzo, pickled herring, and chicken soup.

"Do you think this is how Palestinians feel when they go to a restaurant in Tel Aviv?" aba wonders.

We order the vegetarian option—hummus and falafel. "Just like *bubbe* used to make every Shabbos back in the shtetl," I joke.

I wonder what my *saba* would think if he could see us now. His son and his granddaughter, all the way from Australia (me) and Norway (aba), eating hummus in the hometown that he left behind when he was conscripted in 1940. I wonder if he ever imagined his descendants returning to Poland.

Growing up, my dad never heard about his father's life before the war. Saba would talk about his old army buddies, his time in Anders' Army, and deserting the army to settle in Palestine in 1944, but the time before then, his family in Lublin, that was a chapter he'd sealed shut.

Growing up, I never heard about my grandparents' lives in Europe. I didn't even know where they were from. When I began researching my grandfather's side of the family, I realized that I'd never even known his real name, just the nickname that his wife had given him.

* * *

Once, after a talk I gave at a Palestine solidarity forum, a woman raised her hand and explained to me and the rest of the room that "Jews just need to get over the Holocaust." I didn't respond. I didn't want to derail a conversation meant to be about Palestinians by making it about antisemitism instead.

Anyone who knows anything about Israel, intergenerational trauma, and the contempt for diaspora Jewry in general, and Holocaust victims specifically, that runs through Israeli society, can see that trying to "get over the Holocaust" is exactly the problem. The pain and fear and trauma get pushed down, sealed behind locked doors. We look forward to a future where we are strong and independent, where we have an army and navy. We don't talk about the past. We try to forget about it, and in the process, we forget what it is to be oppressed and dispossessed.

* * *

The first session of the reunion is about historical research and genealogical databases. An archivist from Jewish Records Indexing explains the various records that are available if we want to research our family tree: births, deaths, and marriages, rabbinical records, passports, newspaper articles, and notary records. Somehow it never occurred to me that all these written records had survived. I'd assumed that the Nazis destroyed all evidence of our existence. I guess that we're lucky to have so many written records and so many databases that collect them. As well as Jewish Records Indexing, the archivist mentions Yad Vashem, the US Holocaust Memorial Museum, JewishGen's Holocaust database, and the various DNA testing services that exist now.

I have never heard somebody sound so chipper while lecturing people about the genocide of their ancestors.

The second session is about Grodzka Gate, the organization responsible for this reunion of Lublin's Jews. Before the war, Grodzka Gate marked the boundary between the Jewish and Christian quarters of the city, although some Jews lived on the Christian side too.

In the 1990s, the NN Theatre moved into the building, and because people kept visiting to ask questions about Lublin's Jewish history, it started researching and recording that history. It's built up an impressive archive, all of which is online. The NN Theatre has recorded a lot of oral history—people's memories of Jewish life in Lublin—and used old photos to map the 1940s' Jewish quarter and animate a 3-D model of the wartime city. It's also digitized thousands of photos of Jewish life before and during the war. Some of these photos were found in the roof of an old house, wrapped up in newspapers. Everywhere in Poland is an archaeological site.

Afterward, aba and I sit down with one of Grodzka Gate's genealogical researchers. We don't have much for him to go on, but I do have a digital copy of saba's birth certificate, and his father's birth certificate too, from the Jewish Historical Institute in Warsaw. Both documents are handwritten in Polish cursive and completely indecipherable to me. The researcher spends over an hour with us, yet we don't find much of anything new. He has a few leads, including the military archives, and makes some phone calls on our behalf.

* * *

In Uri Orlev's *The Island on Bird Street*, there's a passage where one of the characters says that after the war, they should never talk about anything that happened; they should erase all records and wipe that period from history. I love this fictional ancestor for his compassion, for wanting to spare his descendants the painful knowledge of what the world can do to us. But I can't allow myself the luxury of forgetting because this isn't only about the past. It's about the present. I need to know how this happens to a society. How do people become so compliant and cruel, so submissive and racist, so gullible and selfish? What is the process that leads from here to Auschwitz?

When I read Hannah Arendt's *Eichmann in Jerusalem*, the parallels between 1930s' Germany and contemporary Israel were impossible to ignore. Right now, after Donald Trump's election in 2016, after Charlottesville and Brexit, it's not just Israel. It's the United States and United Kingdom; it's Australia with its offshore concentration camps. The whole world is going to the fascists, and I am afraid.

* * *

That evening, we attend the reunion's opening ceremony at the Lublin Castle, which is now the Lublin Museum. It's mostly the usual uninspired self-congratulatory speeches. But then an elderly Jewish man gets up to speak. He tells us that it's against Jewish law to hold children responsible for their parents' crimes, that we mustn't be angry at Poles for the past, that Poland was always a safe haven for Jews, and will be again in the future if we need it to be.

I wonder if that's true. When the Israeli state finally ends and the inevitable exodus of Israeli Jews begins, will Poland be willing to welcome us back?

* * *

On the second day of the reunion, we go on a walking tour of the Lublin Ghetto. We begin in Zamkowy Square, a parking lot built on the ruins of Jewish homes. It's right near the Lublin Castle—prime real estate in the most touristy part of the city. Directly below the castle, behind some bushes, two plaques (in Yiddish and Polish) commemorate the Maharshal synagogue, built in the sixteenth century and destroyed by the Nazis in 1942. This must have been where saba had his bar mitzvah. I wonder how much of his youth he spent here, in this same spot where I'm standing now.

We visit the Jewish orphanage on Grodzka Street. Our guide tells the story of how German police murdered over a hundred children and their adult caregivers—the entire orphanage—in a mass execution on March 24, 1942.

We also visit the building that housed the office of the Jewish committee from 1944 to 1945. It was in charge of helping Holocaust survivors. The committee collected testimonies, and founded a Jewish school and newspaper. It made Lublin the unofficial Jewish capital of Poland for a while.

When we get to Lubartowska Street, our guide helps us find the corner where my great-grandfather once lived. The building is long gone, replaced by a computer repair shop. It's nice to have this tangible connection to the past, however tenuous—a tether to time, to history.

* * *

After the tour, I go to Chewra Nosim synagogue, where a member of the congregation tells us stories about her father, Nuchym. He grew up in an Orthodox family in Warsaw and joined the Polish Army at the start of World War II. When the Nazis took Warsaw, he escaped to Soviet-occupied Poland, and from there was sent to Siberia. After the war, he settled in Lublin and became an umbrella maker. My favorite story is about his time in prison, after he was arrested for helping someone buy foreign currency. Two of his fellow inmates were medical students who'd been caught vandalizing a statue of Joseph Stalin. They were expecting a life sentence, but Nuchym suggested a defense strategy that saved them: they explained to the judge that they'd drunkenly climbed the statue because they wanted to kiss Stalin and sadly his head broke off in their arms. They were released from prison, and both graduated and became doctors.

* * *

I hadn't realized that Jewish life in Poland continued after the Holocaust. I thought that anyone who survived ended up settling in Israel, the United States, Australia, or some other colony. The version of Jewish history that I grew up with consisted of two thousand years of exile, during which Jews were powerless victims of persecution by Christians and Muslims, followed by Theodor Herzl's world-changing epiphany that Jews should have a state, culminating in the creation of the state of Israel, the one true home and safe haven of global Jewry. It's a Zionist narrative that I rejected as an adult. I've seen how it's used to justify the colonization and ethnic cleansing of Palestinians.

In Poland, I see a different version of our history. Most Poles I talk to insist that Jews are part of Polish society, Jews and Poles coexisted happily for a thousand years, and the Holocaust was an aberration, a result of German occupation, not Polish antisemitism. Still, it's always Poles and Jews, not Jewish Poles and Christian Poles, or Polish Jews and Polish Christians. They see Jews as guests who were welcomed into Poland, but were never really Polish. Although there have been Jews in Poland for as long as it's existed as a country, to Christian Poles, we are not really from Poland; we're exotic visitors from the Middle East. It makes it hard for me to believe this account of peaceful coexistence.

I want a different future for Jews—one where we don't accept being treated as outsiders or less than equal, and we don't oppress and exploit others either. We are neither singularly oppressed nor uniquely incapable of being oppressors. Acknowledging that we aren't the only ones who are victims of racism and religious persecution doesn't mean we have to ignore the ways that others have hurt us. We don't have to be separatists and atomize ourselves from non-Jews. We also don't have to give up our traditions, languages, festivals, and stories. I think the socialist Jewish Labor Bund had it right: we can build a future together with others. We can defend our own people against oppression and be solid with others who are oppressed—even when their oppressors are Jews.

* * *

The next day I get a private tour of Grodzka Gate's sister project, Dom Słów—the House of Words. It's part studio and part print museum. In the nineteenth century, the building housed Lublin's first public library. In the 1930s, it became a print shop called Popularna. When the Nazis invaded in 1942, they commandeered the shop and forced the printers to work for them, printing travel permits and other documents. The printers took advantage of the access this gave them and began producing counterfeit papers for the resistance. They were betrayed by a friend's daughter and executed only a few days before the city's liberation.

Some of the old printing equipment is still here. Dom Słów has an incredible collection of metal and wood type in Hebrew, Polish, Russian, Greek, English, and German black letter, reflecting the city's linguistic diversity.

There's also an exhibition about underground publishing under the Soviet regime. One of the items is a printing press smuggled to Lublin by a touring theater troupe. It was purchased in France and then delivered to the troupe's hotel room in London. The set designer had one night to learn how to disassemble and reassemble the machine. He coated the parts in engine grease to make them look old, wrapped them in old Polish newspapers, and stashed them in the bottom of his toolbox so that customs agents would think they were old bits of junk. The cylinder was too large to fit in the toolbox, so instead he wrapped it in twine and decorated it with random objects to disguise it as a stage prop. After successfully smuggling the press into Poland, the first book that Lublin's underground publishers printed was *Animal Farm*.

* * *

These stories of resistance help me appreciate what Polish people went through in the twentieth century, surviving both Nazi and Soviet occupation. It makes sense of Polish nationalism. In a way, it's just a mirror image of Zionism. Both are reactions to oppression by an external power, a force that's perceived as outside the nation. Both use a narrative of victimization to justify racism and violence. Both are reinforced by prejudice. When Poles complain about "anti-Polonism" from international media, they sound an awful lot like Israelis who think any criticism of the Israeli Defense Forces is anti-semitic.

I don't think anti-Polonism exists any more than heterophobia or reverse racism do. It is true, however, that Western countries treat eastern Europeans with a kind of contempt, an ingrained assumption that everyone from former Soviet countries is conservative, violent, racist, criminal, and untrustworthy.

I also see the hypocrisy in countries like the United States demanding that Poland pay reparations to Jews, while refusing to pay reparations to descendants of African people abducted and trafficked into slavery in the Americas.

I wonder if the defensiveness I sense from Poles when I criticize their country comes from a feeling that they are being unfairly singled out. I want to explain that I don't think Poles are bad people. I don't think that the Polish state is uniquely evil. I have no criticism of Poland that I wouldn't also make of every country I've lived in: Australia, New Zealand, the United States, and Israel.

* * *

It's day four of the reunion, and we are on a guided tour of local shtetls. First up, Zamość—birthplace of socialist author and organizer Rosa

Luxemburg and Yiddish author I. L. Peretz. Zamość was founded in 1580 by Jan Zamoyski. At first Jews were banned from the town, but in 1588, Zamoyski decided to invite several Sephardi families to settle in Zamość in the hope that they would aid economic development. In 1610, these Jews finally got permission to build a synagogue out of stone. The Jewish community grew in the seventeenth century as increasing numbers of Ashkenazim settled in Zamość, and by the start of World War II, almost half the population was Jewish. Zamość became an important center of Jewish intellectual and religious life, influenced by both Hasidism and the Haskalah (the "Jewish Enlightenment"). When the Nazis invaded in 1939, thousands of Jews escaped to the Soviet Union. The rest were murdered in Belzec, Sobibor, and Majdanek.

At the Zamość synagogue, a member of the congregation shows us remnants of a prewar Torah that's been recovered and preserved— saved by a local Christian, who found it after the Nazis looted the building. I remember a school field trip when I was seven to Kfar Chabad in Israel. The Chabadniks taught us about the proper burial rites for a damaged Torah. This Torah here, an artifact from the Jewish past, is too precious to be buried.

Our next stop is Szczebrzeszyn, famous for being the setting of a Polish tongue twister about a beetle. There are records of a Jewish community here as far back as 1524. Before the war, this was a hotbed of Jewish political activity. Various Zionist organizations had branches here, including Betar, Hamizrakhi, Hakhalutz, and the Marxist Poale Zion. There was an active branch of the Jewish Labor

Bund as well as Jewish members of the Communist Party. In 1939, the Germans invaded the town and burned down the synagogue. By the end of 1942, all the Jews of Szczebrzeszyn had either escaped, been killed, or been sent to concentration camps. Only one Jew returned— a man named Yakov Grosser, who lived alone until his death in the 1970s.

The synagogue is now a council-owned community center. Our guide assures us that although it's not a synagogue anymore, "it's still being used as a place for people to come together." Inside, there's an exhibition of medieval-style Christian icons.

From there we walk to the Jewish cemetery. Unlike the synagogue, the cemetery is neglected and overgrown with weeds. It's a jarring contrast, and it bothers me. If the local community is using the synagogue, the least that it could do is look after the graves, right?

Our last stop is Józefów. It's a small town, established in the early 1700s, and used to have a huge Jewish population. For a while, publishing was the main industry; people worked at the paper mill, or as printers or booksellers. They used to export Hebrew books to the rest of Europe.

Józefów is infamous for the massacre committed by the German Reserve Police Battalion 101. On July 12, 1942, the police loaded over twelve hundred Jews—those deemed unfit to work—into trucks, drove them into the forest, and executed them point-blank.

There's no Jewish community in Józefów anymore. The synagogue is now a public library. We don't go inside, but we do stroll through the cemetery. Then we sit on some park benches while our guide tells us about an annual arts festival. The festival is dedicated to Yiddish author Isaac Bashevis Singer and takes place in the towns that populate his stories: Józefów, Biłgoraj, Lublin, and so on. Artists are invited from around the world. The wall behind us features a mural of Saint Jozef, the patron saint of Józefów, painted for a previous festival—Christian imagery to celebrate a Jewish writer.

* * *

On the last day of the reunion, I attend a facilitated discussion titled "Who Should Protect the Jewish Heritage?" The room is full of Jews from outside Poland and a handful of non-Jewish Poles, including the moderator.

"Whose responsibility is it to look after Jewish cemeteries in Poland? The Poles or the Jews?" she asks us, as if it goes without saying that Jews cannot be Poles. Several people reply that it is a Polish responsibility.

"Then who should pay for it? The government or local councils?"

I want to yell *I don't care! That's not my problem!* I'm trying extra hard to keep my mouth shut.

"Let me play devil's advocate for a moment," she says. "Why should Polish people have to pay to maintain Jewish graves? If I move overseas, I wouldn't expect other people to look after my family's graves."

"Jews didn't choose to leave Poland," I point out. "We were ethnically cleansed."

She doesn't seem to understand that for the Jews in the room, this is personal and sensitive, not an abstract philosophical debate on public funding.

A non-Jewish Polish guy suggests that perhaps this disagreement is due to cultural differences. He explains that Jews come from a community-oriented culture and see maintaining graveyards as a collective responsibility, whereas Poles are Western and individualistic, and that's why they view it as an individual responsibility. I struggle not to laugh; all the Jews here are from the United States, Sweden, Israel, and the United Kingdom. We're way more Western than him.

There's a question no one's asking: Who has benefited from the absence of Jews? The Holocaust was perpetrated by Nazis, and the Jewish exodus from Poland after the war can be blamed on the Soviets; Poles can avoid feeling responsible for what happened. Yet there's no denying that Poland benefited materially from antisemitism. The Polish economy benefits from the Jewish tourism industry as well as unclaimed Jewish property. The parking lot below the Lublin Castle, on land that used to belong to the Maharshal synagogue, is an obvious example. The synagogue in Szczebrzeszyn is another. If Poles get to benefit from Jewish property, is it that unreasonable to ask them to reciprocate by looking after Jewish cemeteries?

It's getting tense, and I have a strange sense of déjà vu. I've sat through this same conversation a hundred times. Usually I'm on the other side; I'm the settler colonist sitting across from Palestinians, Māori, Torres Strait Islanders, and Aboriginal people, all of whom are justifiably hurt and resentful.

I understand what it's like to feel defensive when someone is criticizing you for acts committed before you were born. I understand feeling as if people are irrationally angry at you when you're just trying to support them—when you're one of the good ones. I've been that person, and I've been fortunate that so many Indigenous people have treated me with patience and generosity. My frustration with this discussion isn't because I don't understand the Polish point of view; it's because I understand it too well. Jews are not the indigenous people of Poland, and we weren't colonized there, but we were dispossessed and ethnically cleansed. I just want Christian Poles to understand that it's not Jews' responsibility to shelter them from our trauma and rage. We can't make them feel better about what happened to us, and they can't expect us to be grateful to them for having good intentions.

* * *

That evening, we attend Kabbalat Shabbat at Yeshivas Khokhmey Lublin, now a fancy hotel as well as an Orthodox synagogue. Actors from the Jewish Theater in Warsaw lead a sing-along of Yiddish classics. A few people get up and dance a hora around the tables.

It's been a long emotional week, and I'm exhausted. I'm struggling to make sense of the last few days. I can't articulate exactly what's on my mind, but it's got something to do with the Polish and Zionist narratives of Jewish history, and the ways that they diverge and overlap. It's about the dynamic between Jews and progressive Poles, and the ways that it mirrors the dynamic between Indigenous peoples and progressive colonists.

I don't know what the future holds, but I know that I don't want to repeat the past. I don't know what to do with trauma and anger, but I know that we can't just put it in a box and ignore it. I don't know how we protect ourselves from antisemitism, but I know that it's not by oppressing and dispossessing others. I don't know how to build a better world, but I do know that it's not through nationalism, states, and borders.

*

Ali Nissenbaum is a third-generation settler colonist in Palestine and first-generation settler colonist in so-called Australia. She's also an anarchist. This chapter was written on the land of the Wangal people of the Eora nation; they have never ceded their sovereignty. A sheynem dank to the Grodzka Gate–NN Theatre for organizing the Lubliner Reunion.

ON BEING A DECENT PERSON

MATYLDA TZVIA JONAS

My family and city were broken and nearly annihilated in the Shoah. Being born and raised in the city of burned books and souls—ghosts you can still feel in the empty courtyards of tenement houses, and the synagogues turned into stores or storage spaces—has a profound impact on both the community and an individual. This sense of loss, after decades of healing, is still a bruise, like a slightly darker place on the wallpaper where a painting was once hanging but is no longer there.

When I was twenty, I watched an interview conducted with my grandfather by the USC Shoah Foundation. When it was filmed back in the late 1990s, I was around two years old, and lived with my parents and grandparents in Warsaw, Poland. My grandfather was born in the Warsaw Ghetto—a fact that shaped our family and continues to do so to this day. He survived in hiding and was saved by an incredibly courageous young Polish socialist, who took him in like he was her own until the war was over. She was just twenty at the time, the same age as me when my mom decided that I should watch the interview.

At the end, the interviewer asked my grandfather if he wanted to include a message for the future me, when I would be old enough to see the tape. I was his first grandchild. Through this time capsule manifested as a VHS cassette, my grandfather sent me a simple message: whatever you do, be a decent person.

There is a line from the Torah in Deuteronomy 16:20 that not only makes me think about about my grandfather but also guides my life as a Jewish queer anarchist and feminist: "Tzedek tzedek tirdof" (justice, justice you shall pursue). I'm by no means religious, yet I find comfort in words that likewise guided generations of Jewish radicals before me, and that I now understand to be at the heart of my political and ethnic identities. Fighting injustice is not only my obligation as an anarchist; it is also my duty as a Jew.

Every day I am reminded of the courage of that young righteous woman who made it possible for me to walk this world. Every day I think about the lives lost to fascism, not only in the Shoah, but in every genocide that happened before and after it. Every day, all I strive for, is to be a decent person.

*

Matylda Tzvia Jonas, born and raised in Warsaw, graduated with a degree in Jewish studies from the University of Warsaw. She now lives in Malmö, Sweden, where she's studying international migration and ethnic relations. Matylda is active in feminist and anarchist circles, and copublishes a zine titled Books and Bricks *with her dear comrades. This piece is for her late great-grandma Bronka, a Holocaust survivor and mensch.*

DIALECTICS OF MOURNING, DIALECTICS OF BRICKS

MOIRA LEIBOWITZ

One summer in Los Angeles, you arrived at a factory with the expectation of a job. The character of that job had been obscured, but you were, of course, characteristically broke. With the cost of your recent name change as heavy on your mind as the lightness of the name tag hanging from your neck, you couldn't care less why you were there. When a woman met you at the entrance to the factory, however, you put on your best mask and held your head high.

The woman—whose ID named her as "the Historian"—squinted as she read your name. She held your ID and took a long glance at her own. She compared the two side by side. She scrutinized you from head to toe. With every shift in her expression, you felt the terrible accuracy of her assumptions. Finally she said, "Again, they sent out the wrong ID?"

You shrugged a pleasant acquiescence. "Bureaucracy, am I right?"

The Historian nodded slowly, betraying her fondness for bureaucracy. You could see her assumptions blooming. She understood the entire history of your name: that it was not the Hebrew name you were given, and that perhaps you never had one. These two possibilities, the many names and wounds, you had hidden, buried, or bandaged over.

"Thank G-d for contingency," she said as she handed you a deck of cards. As you shuffled through them, you noted the descriptions written on each: *The Writer. The Faggot. The Survivor.* The truth in each one was somewhere between an archetype and personal attack. With a flourish, the Historian said, "Pick a card, any card."

Eyes closed, you picked one.

"I suppose I'm the Scholar," you, the Scholar, said, as you offered up your name.

"The Scholar! How very in character." And in an undertone, she added, "We've been waiting for you. Certainly you understand the art of waiting, but have you considered the other side of things? I mean, considering your history, how many you've left waiting."

"Call me out, why don't you?"

"Now, now, no need to be salty. I'm only here to historicize, and the dialectics speak for themselves. You're late, and we have so much to do. Your lateness may be essential for you, but our task here is *critical* to the world. Meaning, of course, that we are here to critique."

"So we're the kvetching contingent?" This the Scholar said with some relief, as she had carefully studied the art of complaining her entire life.

"Rather, this is a matter of dialectics. You should understand the context of our work." She beckoned the Scholar to follow her into a white corridor that stretched to meet a white door on the far side of the room, identical to the one they stepped through.

"This is a factory. You may have detected what you think is the smell of paper, yet I assure you, it's anything but that. In this room, we have white walls. And if you will follow me into the next room, you'll see we have more white walls. But if you look into this next room," gesturing grandly into a white corridor that stretched to meet an identical white door, "we have a room with more white walls."

"It's white walls all the way down, then?"

"You would think! But look closely at this wall," the Historian said as she raked her acrylics along the white paint to reveal a number of thinly threaded, rainbow lines. "This is reminiscent of the fringes on some tallitot, not that I ever wore a prayer shawl. If we continue past this room, we'll find another corridor with white walls stretching to meet an identical door. And behind the white paint, you will find the felted black wool of LA's own Hasidic community. The room past that one is also white, and the doors are locked. Behind the paint, the room is on fire, referencing the Triangle Shirtwaist Factory fire. And behind the locked door in that room, well, that's hardly our concern. But over here, through this door . . ."

She gestured to another door, and behind it another white room stretching out to meet a cross-legged human seated on polished concrete, blockading an identical door on the far side of the room.

"The Scholar, the Theorist. The Theorist, the Scholar. And now that you're acquainted . . ."

The Theorist looked up from a ragged hardcover. They gave the Scholar that unmistakable new-queer-in-town once-over, but they made no gesture of recognition to either woman. Rather, they held up a single finger and said, "The ethical discourse will not cease to speak to us, not of essences, it speaks to us only of power, that is, the actions and passions of which something is capable."[1]

"Very true," the Historian said. She turned away from the Theorist and rolled her eyes. "Have you ever heard such nonsense? A thousand quotations and not a single one useful." And with a look of disgust, she added, "I hate to step outside my discipline of pure science, but I've had to make, G-d forbid, some theories of my own. Now we were hired on as attendants, correct? You remember the job description? Attendants. From the French *attendre*, 'to wait.' And that's exactly why we're here."

* * *

"And what are we waiting for?" the Scholar asked.

"Moshiach," the Historian said.

"The Rev?" the Scholar said.

"The end of exile," the Historian replied. "The end of work. A minyan."[2]

"A minyan?" the Scholar asked.

"A minyan."

And to the Theorist, the Scholar whispered, "Why are we waiting for a minyan?"

---

1. Gilles Deleuze, "On Spinoza," January 24, 1978, University of Paris, https://bit.ly/39eLpMp.

2. A minyan, meaning "to count" or "to number," is the ten-person quorum necessary for Jewish communal worship.

Work is a matter of retreating into your body and waiting. It is always waiting, and that waiting is always a mystery.

For the past decade, the Scholar's mystery of choice had been the art fair circuit. Every summer, before trimming weed in the fall, she had labored in convention centers across "America." She built labyrinths of backdrops, snaking prefabricated half walls through cavernous arenas, work pants covered in spackle, tape, and white paint. The respirator hanging from her neck, wrists, and hands throbbing with pain, she built walls that would stand for a few days to hang priceless, eternal art.

This factory was not her first job, like a fist print in a white wall in the last hour of a sixteen-hour day. It was not the first time that she covered up blood dusted from her knuckles, whitewashed with lime and forgotten, thinking about how they normalize the walls around you and paint them white. Like every other job, it was a mystified process, an exchange of time for money. And here, after the end of it, she sat on polished concrete in the labyrinth and laid her head down for just a moment. Then she woke up on the bus—lights, camera, action.

The dawn's violence broke in sunrise on car horns grumbling from the freeway. Her phone, a vial of lightning and smog, was instinctively in her hand, one arm of her glasses between clenched teeth. Her friends' Instagram posts blended together with early morning ads for stimulants and pinkwashed Birthright trips.

It was a long bus ride from North Hollywood to Echo Park. She'd lied her way onto the lease of an apartment that she couldn't afford.

It was classic LA, intensified after years of exile. The whitewashed stucco of new cafés. Fewer pawnshops lining the streets and more tents under the freeway. More police and more white faces in this historically Chicanx neighborhood. On the flight to LA, she had worried that the body memory of returning to her childhood home would be too much to handle. She knew better now. What memories could survive this world? Or, she wondered, were memories all that could survive it?

In her apartment, she looked at her life's work. She called it a thesis, as though the name could change what was a glorified think piece. All those words about the broken vessels of light and *tikkun ha-olam*, "making whole," and the two intertwined in a brick thrown through a police car window became another brick encased in concrete to build a border wall. She tried to write, but her fingers refused her. She was faced with a wall of text, as impenetrable as any other, and like other walls, not a single brick made her feel safe.

* * *

"I'm tired of waiting."

"Is that the best critique you have?"

"It is tiresome, isn't it?"

"That's besides the point. Now of course, once we have our minyan, there will be no need to kvetch."

"Critique."

"But what will the world be without waiting, and what could waiting be without kvetching?"

One evening it was Shabbat, and after the Historian said Kaddish, the Theorist left long cuts like pipelines down their arm. They were wounds on a body like the earth hemorrhaging oil, delicately bleeding, like spilled ink, a tenuous calligraphy on cold concrete.

The Scholar closed her eyes and opened her mouth as if to speak. She knew that she should say the Mourner's Kaddish, but she didn't know the words. She thought that she should sit shiva. She jealously thought that the Theorist would know what to say, but the Theorist was silent, and the Scholar couldn't live up to her name.

You, however, had seen this before. You wrapped the Theorist's wounds in torn flannel. You pulled them to their feet and led them to the first doorway you could find. The Historian, freed from the rigor of waiting, caught up with you and started tugging at the makeshift bandage, saying, "You can't just do things! We're here to wait."

"What exactly do you call bleeding to death, then?"

"I'm not sure, and this is no time for jokes. I told you that we couldn't trust the Theorist—always trying to prefigure reality. We're here to wait, friend, and they've already put in their notice."

The Scholar ignored her. She took the Theorist by the hand and led them into the labyrinth. Walking through it, ignoring the echoes of dripping blood, she realized that it wasn't really a maze. There wasn't an entrance or exit, just a thousand self-similar rooms with strings of choices between them. Each one led somewhere, though not necessarily the somewhere that you meant to go.

The doorway she opened was an empty closet. In the dark, a dangling light switch compelled her. She turned around into a cold, blue light, but there was no doorway behind her and no Theorist.

It was an empty closet. Where the doorway had been, there was a fist print—first, like the handprints on Hollywood Boulevard, and then like a hole painted with blood. She hit the wall again and heard the Theorist say on the other side, "You are losing your historical friends. / You are still in the ghetto. / Why don't we get out of there together?"[3]

She punched the wall again. On impact, she remembered that as a child, she had raged against the universe. She put her fist through a bathroom wall. The two moments zippered together. She wiped the blood from her knuckles, the broken capillary walls, the drywall dust.

There was another wall behind the first. It was less matte eggshell and more crumbling stucco, or classic dingbat apartment. The thought written on her knuckles was that every wall is mortared with blood and every wall deserves its holes.

As a child, the Scholar's mom gave her one task: patch the wound that she made in their apartment. "We need the deposit back," her mother said.

The Scholar allowed herself another task: patch the wound inside her. Where her blood met the hole in the wall, she reached in. She pulled at the cracking plaster, her tiny gay hands groping through a gaping wound, running on adrenaline, unsure of what she was trying

---

3. Houria Bouteldja, *Whites, Jews, and Us: Toward a Politics of Revolutionary Love* (Cambridge, MA: Semiotext[e], 2017), 72.

to find. She kept digging, and the hole grew, until she hit water or blood. Searching, she whipped the dust to mud, thick as *charoset*, the same color and just as sweet.[4]

Years passed, and she tried to patch the holes in the walls around her. She bored in and filled up on blood and dust. Behind the wall, darkness, and behind the darkness, other walls. Some were felt more in the heart than in the hands. Some were invisible, even in darkness, or were only visible in the light of the dark. Behind this wall and every wall are the walls of the ghetto, camps, grave, Temple, and body.

Waking up on the other side of a wall, the Theorist pulled the Scholar to her feet and led her by the hand into the labyrinth of white walls after white walls, the scratches as windows into other worlds. They wandered holding hands, not speaking. They wandered for forty years or maybe forty minutes. Twenty-six hundred years. Past the end of history, where there is nothing but walls.

"I'm tired of waiting," the Scholar said. "I'm tired of wandering lost in a desert to come, with less than nothing to look forward to."

"Theory is more a map than a set of directions: a survey of the terrain in which we find ourselves. ... Theory is a map produced by the lost themselves."[5]

When you wandered, you thought about rent. You thought about

---

4. Charoset, a sweet mixture of fruits and nuts, is typically eaten during Passover to symbolize the mortar used by the Israelites when they were enslaved in ancient Egypt.

5. Jasper Bernes, "Logistics, Counterlogistics, and the Communist Prospect," *Endnotes* 3 (2013): 174.

waiting. You wondered when you stopped dreaming. But then you, the Scholar, said instead, "Weren't our languages supposed to be bridges across borders? Now it feels like I have to time travel into books and stories just to feel that distance close. I don't even know if it's working. It feels like our languages are a wall, and I'm on the wrong side of it, or all of you are. We were supposed to talk across borders, but now the borders run through our bodies. Israel is the new ghetto, but so is the atomization of living in diaspora. How do we bridge our differences when all we have are stories colliding against each other?"

The Theorist held up a fourth finger. "If myth is the language of naturalization, then narrative might be the language of connection. Like infrastructure, narrative ties together discrete elements, producing a consistency that gives a form to the present."[6]

* * *

"Why are we waiting for a minyan?" the Scholar asked.

"Because in the Diaspora, it can feel like it's DIY or die," said the Historian.

"Then why are we waiting for a minyan?"

"Because there is always a third option. Because however you feel about Hillel and Talmud, tikkun ha-olam doesn't happen alone. Because study always happens in *chevruta*, 'friendship.'"

---

6. Nabel Wallin, "What Would It Mean to Walk Away from America?," *Mask Magazine*, August 2018, https://bit.ly/3l3Zmz1.

* * *

If you are tired of waiting, you can always leave. And if you do, suddenly the workplace dissolves. No longer a worker, do you wonder what that place could be? Who you are to them?

Characteristically broke—more in character than ever before—the Scholar arrived at the factory to pick up her paycheck.

The Historian greeted her with new assumptions gracing her face. "You're here for a tour of the fact-ory, aren't you? Putting the finishing touches on your thesis?"

The thought had not occurred to her, but this, it seemed, was the truth. She nodded and held the affirmation in her mouth, adding another truth: "I do need my paycheck."

"Of course! We wouldn't want you to wait for that. But while you're here, let me tell you about the fact-ory and factory."

"Do I have a choice?"

"Many misunderstand the fact-ory in light of the Jewish garment industry. The etymological conflation of *textile* and *textual*. It's true that we make things here; we're not *just* killing time. Both word and cloth are closest to our skin; we spin yarns and weave tales. We bind spells and books together."

Where they used to wait, where they made Shabbat, and where the Theorist cut their wrists, there was now a knitting machine. As they passed it, the Historian threw a basket of fabric into the hopper. She pressed a button and closed her eyes to meditate on the whirring contraption. When the machine stilled, the Historian took a manuscript from the other side. She lost herself in the text, mouthed the words aloud, and watched them disappear from the page. When the page was clean, she tore it out of the book and into shreds, letting the pieces settle in the basket of textiles.

"But what do they make here?" the Scholar asked.

"Facts. Now, I see your consternation."

"Vexation is the word."

"And I know what the Theorist would say about Nietzsche and truth. But forget that for a moment. Remember, we're talking about facts, not truth. Things not concepts. About *what is*, regardless of how you feel about it." She gestured to a wall, as white as the others. The walls touched others walls, and the other walls touched other walls. The walls made a room—without doors or windows, but a room nonetheless. Here the Historian made an annunciating gesture, arms outstretched.

Eventually a text fluttered out from a gap beneath the wall. It caught on a gust of reprocessed air, as if it could escape into the world before the Historian caught it, though she caught it with reverent fingers and handed it to the Scholar. Written there was a single word in Hebrew that she couldn't read.

"And here, our midrashes, our commentary," the Historian said, "in which some rabbis say that this is how the world keeps going, that on the other side of this wall are written the parts we're meant to play. Some others reject this and say that we're afloat out here, that the horizon is without end. And still others will say that by the time we come around again, betrayed by the curvature of the earth, maybe the stories that we've written don't fit us anymore, or maybe we weren't the ones who wrote them. Here, maybe, are written the stories that *could be*. This is chance and luck and how we know ourselves, and how in knowing ourselves, we find where we can break through the stories that are walls."

* * *

You arrived at the factory to pick up your paycheck. You ran into the language barrier, harder than you meant to, when Human Resources handed you a series of documents and forms. All you could see is that they were written in Hebrew script. They were forms in Arabic and Aramaic, Bukhori and Hebrew, and Ladino and Yiddish. You could read none of them, never mind filling them out. When the Theorist came in, you handed them your papers, and in each box—for a name and date—they left single dissociated words culled from countless texts, but the office bureaucrats refused them. Through the barrier, you landed a promise: they would mail you the paycheck you'd been waiting for.

When you left, you walked sweating and sunburned, through North Hollywood, West Hollywood, and a world filled solely with bougie boutiques. For each store you passed, the Theorist handed the Scholar a single sheet of paper, each one with a single word, each word a "stone" or "brick." For a moment, the Scholar wished that the Historian had come with them to explain the context of their journey—what did this mean in that mythology of wandering Jews?—but holding the paper, balling it up, and considering the living death of capitalism, you listened to the stories written in the passage of time and the movement through the freeing, suffocating air of the world. The Theorist held up all five fingers of their right hand, curling them into a fist. "Haunting... can be construed as a failed mourning. It is about refusing to give up the ghost or—and this can sometimes amount to the same thing—the refusal of the ghost to give up on us."[7]

Remembering then that capitalism is already dead, remembering to throw paper into the clatter of breaking glass, remembering that we grieve and celebrate with bricks and rocks through windows—we leave our rage as stones on the grave of this world, as stepping-stones and bridges to the world to come.

*

Moira Leibowitz currently lives on Unceded Dxʷdəwʔabš (Duwamish) Territory, also known as Seattle. When they aren't organizing around a collective anarchist bookstore, they explore written and auditory art as a means of building proletarian dignity and minoritarian historical memory for these challenging times. In addition to leading workshops and doing readings throughout the so-called Pacific Northwest, their writing has appeared in the Doykeit *zine and* Resilience Anthology *of trans writers. In writing this, Moira wants to acknowledge the Indigenous people and spirits of the land on which they are a guest; their ancestors and their difficult choices; and their* haverim—*friends, or comrades—for their endless work and depthless joy.*

---

7. Mark Fisher, *Ghosts of My Life: Writings on Depression, Hauntology, and Lost Futures* (Alresford, UK: Zero Books, 2014), 20.

AND YOU SHALL LOVE

ALICE ROSS

In 1991, a girl was born.
    (I don't like to write the next part. I will do it this once.)
    Her heart didn't work.
    She lived for one day, then she died.
    She was my sister.

* * *

That was the story of her life.
    One day, spent in hospitals.
    In 1991, I had been alive for seven years and three months.

* * *

In the mornings, my father would wrap an assemblage of leather straps and boxes around his body, connecting his head to his hand to his heart, and all three to the world. My father would repeat ancient words, offering thanks to God for taking away sleep from his eyes and giving strength to the weary.
    In those days, my mother often stayed in bed.
    I asked my father about God and he told me, "When we go to sleep

in the dark, trusting, believing that the sun will rise the next day and that we will wake up in the same functioning bodies we know, with our own minds and memories, that is faith."

He taught me the Shema, which tells us to place words on our hearts, and the Shehechiyanu blessing, about being grateful for the universe and everything that gives us life.

* * *

In 2019, I met a Zen monk.

He had an infancy and childhood and past, and a heart that worked, and a path that led him to a monastery on a hill.

The monk said, "I've been thinking about this recently because, you know, the girl with the heart in a backpack died."

I didn't know.

I asked him to explain.

* * *

In 1994, a girl was born.

She had an infancy and childhood, and a heart that worked and carried her through every day until 2017, when it broke.

A doctor removed her broken heart and gave her a mechanical one, and she carried it in a backpack.

* * *

The girl with the mechanical heart in a backpack continued with her university studies.

In an interview, she said, "At no point did it ever occur to me to give up. Even if it is hard for me, it will then be easier for the next person."

In the monastery on the hill, the monk read these words and remembered them.

In another interview, she said about her operation, "I was terrified, but desperate to live."

She said of her hopes to have children and travel the world: "My dreams have changed."

I only found all this out later.

* * *

In 2019, the girl, now a young woman, with the heart in a backpack went into a hospital again to have her mechanical heart stopped and a new, human heart put into her body instead.

It didn't work, and she died.

* * *

In 2019, a few weeks later, the monk was talking to me about the bravery and importance of being prepared to do things that aren't conventional or easy, and living, fully aware.

I had been alive for thirty-five years, four months, and one week.

* * *

I have a human heart that works and keeps me alive, and it has done this every day for all those years.

I have the opportunity to experience everything in the world.

I have been to the monastery on the hill, surrounded with soft green moss and daffodils coming up through the crisp, shining snow. I have been to the orange and red rock canyons of the desert, glowing fiery in the light of the setting sun. I have been to the blue mountain by the tranquil lake surrounded by golden grasses and crimson autumn leaves.

* * *

I have sometimes worried about being too big, too small, too quiet, too loud, and about loving too much or not enough.

I have worried about allowing my body to be seen or known, and about wanting to change it. I have made it change in many ways.

I have worried about being too sensitive, about being too careful or careless, about being in places early or late, about showing my emotions, about being heard, about taking up space.

These concerns seem ridiculous.

I have people who love me.

I have loved, I love, and I shall love.

I have a human heart that works.

I think about it all the time.

*

Alice Ross is a linguist, photographer, model, painter, and reader in Scotland. She is a member of a feminist art collective as well as the diverse and defiant gathering of anarchist Jews in Scotland known as IRN-JU. Alice is inexpressibly grateful for her living siblings, Sam and Helena, and the sisters whom she never knew. She would also like to thank her parents, Lin James and Benny Ross; Peter Hellsten; Matthias Ediger; IRN-JU; Lighthouse Books in Edinburgh; Cindy Milstein; and countless others who nurture kindly and thoughtfully, and who love fiercely and fearlessly.

AND YOU SHALL LOVE

I WILL NOT

FINISH GRIEVING

DIANA CLARKE

Grieving brought me to the movement. By movement, I mean action, or more precisely, doing something about what hurts. Part of the doing, I hate to remember, is just letting the feeling move through me.

Grieving itself, I am learning, is a kind of movement. How it crashes and recedes, wells up unexpectedly and gathers suddenly at the surface of my body. I go running, and the breeze hits me; I make the breeze with the movement of my body, and the breeze makes me weep. Again and again, in Pittsburgh, I cross the Bloomfield Bridge, climb a slant that overlooks the city, little leaning brick row houses, and the holler thick with green. It's knotweed, invasive and reviled for it, but also one of the few plants known to help in treating Lyme disease. Sometimes there's a salve where I wouldn't even think to see.

Jewishly, I know about mourning. My *bubbe* and *zayde*, both past ninety, died within a few years of one another when I was in my early twenties, and I learned the ritual of shiva the common way, by attending to my grandparents' deaths: seven days shoeless for the mourners, who shouldn't even have to fix their own plates of food or ask for the care they need, and a minyan required in the shiva house three times a day. I learned how to practice, but I had not yet learned how to weep. Still, I understood that it was brilliant of Jewish tradition to create material voids for the community to fill: ten Jewish adults are needed for each minyan, and someone else to make and pass the plates of food. People like to feel useful, and in the first wave of loss, a mourner should never be alone.

I have spent so much time alone.

In my family, I was taught the rites of mourning and yet I did not know how to grieve; none of us did. I now know that our ignorance itself was an expression of grief unfelt generationally; when had it been safe to stop doing and cry instead? Which is to say, I did not know how to feel, how to stay open to and through what I was losing, how to be in community with what goes away from me, or how to be loved when it goes. Often I still don't know, but now more frequently I know that I don't. Every single thing that I do know about grief I have learned in community, which is to say family, so much of which is Jewish, but not like the family into which I was born. So much of what I know about community I have learned in Pittsburgh, in the movement, which has such deep roots here and has offered me a way to make a home in this place by making myself useful to it, as if the city itself were a mourner (living means living with ongoing loss, ongoing grief) and I were tending to it, tending my partner the city itself, a partner with whom I share care and responsibility among anarchists and trans people and Jews—like me.

⁂

Late in summer 2019, I was newly twenty-eight and my heart ached, so I decided to make myself useful. Shiva teaches me that it is medicine to be of use. On the invitation of a friend I'd cruised on Instagram and then met in person that spring holding a line against the police, I drove from Pittsburgh to Harlan County, Kentucky, where miners who'd worked for the Blackjewel coal company before it declared bankruptcy and denied them back wages sat on camp chairs on the train tracks in Cumberland and blocked the coal that they had dug without pay from getting shipped away. A blockade means stopping, sitting still. The miners mostly played cornhole and drank Red Bull; they didn't move much from the rails.

My friends, encampment veterans and trans anarchists from central Appalachia, one of whom grew up just across the mountain in Letcher County, had been at the blockade for weeks—only one day less than the miners themselves. They'd set up the camp kitchen, made food runs to Walmart, watched the miners' babies, and with consent, talked to the media. I arrived at camp and did the same thing that I always do when I'm new somewhere and don't know what to do with my body: I washed dishes, cooked meals, picked up trash, and put things in order, and then later in the day did it again.

Late at night, I listened. An older woman told me that her husband had been in the mines his whole life; now the two of them sat all day, holding hands in silence. Heading home from camp in the dark, the woman turned to the circle of queers sitting in folding chairs, declaring that she wasn't used to receiving handouts and had never had to do this before. Another man who lived down the road in Sand Hill Bottom and had been out of the mines since 1999 with an injury came through to share stories, getting weepy and showing off his gun. He joined our circle of young trans people, and the fiftyish-year-old career strip miner told about his love life and asked about mine. He had recovered when the woman that he thought would love him forever broke off their marriage at twenty-three. He'd been married twice more since, but couldn't imagine starting a new kind of work after all those years.

It was a kind of shiva that I hadn't anticipated. Grief for lost pay, lost work, lost love. Grief for the story that came with a job underground in Harlan County, with its labor and strength and solidarity, with its century of mine wars and blood. Mine work means self-sufficiency, self-respect, and a middle-class life, yet that became unsustainable with the loss of even a single paycheck. Jewish practice taught me how to sit with the miners; the movement, though, taught me how to feel with them, and how to stay.

I grieved again when the miners failed my friends, refusing to kick out the Three Percenters who showed up at camp as part of a crew of Teamsters from New Jersey. The Far Right militia and paramilitary group said that it wanted to offer solidarity. Suddenly, the Jews and trans people were a target, and my friends who had helped set up the blockade and stayed there for a whole month were now harassed for how they'd handled money, raising funds not just for the mostly white miners' bills and camp supplies but also specifically for reparations, two thousand dollars for the Eastern Kentucky Social Club, which serves mostly retired Black miners in nearby Lynch. It's a different kind of grief to lose something without the finality of death. To feel undermined and betrayed and still refuse to quit.

* * *

So much of the movement is mourning. So much of it has been so for me.

A year after I moved to Pittsburgh, on Juneteenth 2018, a white police officer in the borough of East Pittsburgh, Michael Rosfeld, shot a seventeen-year-old Black boy named Antwon Rose II in the back and killed him. White supremacy is murder.

What I didn't know was that when Black women led a march and blocked the Parkway the night after Rose was murdered, people standing on the asphalt would open up their bags and share snacks with each other. They would hold each others' babies. I remember someone passing me water, chocolate, and beef jerky. I had been taught to believe that I had to earn care, to deserve it, and here it was being freely given by strangers amid the big care work of joining together in protest and grief. The march where I met my Instagram crush in person was organized by Pittsburgh students who walked out of class the Monday after Rosfeld was acquitted. You see why I had to go to Kentucky?

Three nights after Antwon Rose was killed, people marching on the South Side passed boxes of pizza through the crowd, wiping the grease on their own clothes as the riot cops tried to hem us in. When

I say that I grieved, I mean I learned to use my body to mark my anger and sorrow, and for a purpose: to help stand between mourners and the police. In movement, in movement, I learned something about feeling, about not going numb.

Three months later, on Shabbat, Robert Bowers brought an AR-15 to a shul in Squirrel Hill, Pittsburgh's Jewish neighborhood, and killed eleven Jews in a building where three different congregations were praying. This murder too was white supremacy, but because the Pittsburgh police viewed most Jews through the lens of whiteness, they didn't agitate and harass and intimidate us when we mourned in the street. It was a shiva obviously. We wore black and sang for a long time into the falling dark, blocking the road. We had a table of food on the sidewalk, and no one moved it. The police left us alone, no matter that Rose and those eleven Jewish people were all killed by white supremacy.

The day afterward, another student brought snacks to the class we had together because she had heard me say in a speech that Jews feed each other in mourning as part of shiva. I see my friends check up on each other. I see the ones who held it down at the Blackjewel blockade posting reminders about paying reparations, holding me and helping me weep in moments when my heart feels like a column of ice.

* * *

It is 5780. It was Yom Kippur, and now it's not, and I am still grieving. It feels immovable. It is relentless. I am numb again, heavy, not present enough to feel really moved. There were two shootings outside synagogues in Germany. Turkish president Recep Tayyip Erdoğan, on a genocidal mission, is sending troops to Rojava because US troops pulled out. How many more griefs will accumulate? I cannot catalog them all.

This morning I stopped at a friend's house to drop off some political flyers, and he saw that I was sad. His sadness recognized mine, invited me in for tea. I ate toast with black raspberry jam that his partner's father had made. This afternoon I talked on the phone with another friend while picking seeds out of a sunflower. When we got off the phone, she texted me that it seems like all my "griefs are connected, that they reinforce and regrow one another. And also maybe that grief keeps transforming." When will there not be more grief? And wouldn't it be something to grieve over too if these griefs were not connected, if we were somehow trapped each in our separate sorrows?

After seven days of shiva comes the funeral, and then the mourners reenter the world with torn clothes, visible in their grief. The first month of a loss is another period of mourning, and the first year, and then each year on the anniversary. In this life that I share with others, however, loss is constant. Will I live now always in those first intolerable seven days?

Ongoing grief also means that the work of care is ongoing, that Jewish ritual gives me a shape to imagine how I might practice care with the ones I love. Sitting shiva helps me understand, materially, what mutual aid can look like: our ongoing grief means that our care must be ongoing too. Jewish ritual gives me an image of how I might care for loved ones and others, but not the skills of how to do that in practice. When my family showed me how to mourn, they did not show me how to grieve. Living in the movement is what shows me how to uncontain my emotions, how to build the kind of intimacy that allows for real grieving, and that in its excruciating truth, helps me find space to keep myself from freezing, helps me know that I am connected to struggles, griefs, and joys far from me. When I use my body as I am able to care for others, it moves me, and so I move with and through my grief.

After the synagogue shooting, I saw some Pittsburgh Jews who hadn't taken white supremacy seriously before now finally believe in its deadly nature, and begin to act on that belief, which they would not have done had we not moved through the streets. My Instagram crush who is now a dear friend once called the movement their primary partner before they fucked me. This weekend a lover held me, and my body remembered how to weep. Grief teaches me to love, so long as I bring movement to my grief.

*

Diana Clarke lives in Pittsburgh on traditional Seneca, Osage, and Haudeno-saunee land. Their writing has appeared in the Village Voice, World Litera-ture Today, *and the* LA Review of Books. *They have loved Yiddish for ten years. Diana is grateful to Anna Elena Torres and Kenyon Zimmer for inviting them to think on Jewish anarchist histories, presents, prefigurations, and futures, to their movement people, friends, and chosen family in Pittsburgh and upper Appalachia, and especially to GG, BC, and HMH, big thinkers, comrades, lov-ers, and writers in the work of it all.*

AS THE SEA COMES

CRASHING DOWN

STEFANIE BRENDLER

It was not yet Pesach 5778 when seventeen Palestinians in Gaza were killed. On this day, thirty thousand Palestinians approached the border between Gaza and Israel in a protest/celebration of Palestinian Land Day. And in a hallucination of my own imagery, as they approached the border, the chain-link fence parted, the razor wire parted, the concrete wall parted, the sea of Israeli Defense Forces parted, the bullets parted, and the smoke and shrapnel parted. The people of Gaza could once again move freely through the world—to visit family and loved ones, attend university, receive medical attention and health care, fish and farm, and trade resources freely and amicably.

But this is the dream of a Jew. A Jew living far away, in the United States. Who am I to project my own vision onto another people, in a place where I have never set foot? How does freedom of movement appear to the people of Gaza? To Palestinians in the West Bank? To Palestinians within Israel's 1948 border?

When I realized that I was dreaming, the death toll had risen to thirty-one. Palestinian lives had come and gone; Pesach had come and gone. The anniversaries of the expulsion of Jews from Spain (1492) and the Warsaw Ghetto uprising (1943) had come and gone. The Israeli occupation of Palestinian land continues. In the ongoing siege of Gaza during this particular week, more than fourteen hundred Palestinians were wounded by Israeli state violence. We have, in some respects, come so far, and we have simultaneously learned nothing.

Shema, Yisrael! Hear, oh Israel! Dear Jews in Diaspora!

As the sea comes crashing down, filling the space from which we walked, as we seek liberation from the narrow places within which we dwell, from the open-air prison of the Gaza strip to the shackles of our minds, and as we walk forward out of enslavement in Mitzrayim—this time, we are taking everyone with us. Everyone. For if we should leave anyone to fall into the sea, we too should fall.

*

Despite the constant toil under capitalism, heteropatriarchy, and nationalism, Stefanie Brendler's art reflects the joys of life as a queer Jew, musician, and crafter. Stefanie is a multi-instrumentalist, composer, visual artist, poet, and storyteller, with East Coast yikhes and West Coast chutzpah. Active in Seattle's music community since 2004, Stefanie is the founder of the klezmer brass band Shpilkis, a member of the Yiddish antifascist band Brivele, and aspires to make diaspora a threat again.

THE OTHER SIDE

BINYA KÓATZ

they used to light them up, two by two, for the honor of the day

each witch like a shabbes candlestick
with warped glee in the match lighter's hand
as they offered our mamas as unwilling incense
to a god who hated the smell,
the children covering their eyes like
kadosh, kadosh, kadosh
holy, holy, holy

we break bottles now at weddings because of the mamas who broke
 them on cop windows,
Compton's
where Hashem's word cracked through the windshield like the
 heavens
where we found revelation standing on police cruisers like
 mountaintops

my *tateh* throws me bread across the shabbes table
like Miss Major threw that stiletto, that brick addressed:

"NYPD"
like my *mameh* throws salt over her shoulder,
get rid of that devil,
same words that they screamed:
"Get rid of that devil!"

we stand on the shoulders of giants

what a sin this *would* be
—pride—
without the humility to know
that nothing over which we are proud is our own

without remembering
that we aren't shopping a "gifted" pride
but an earned one
not received, but excavated

one we got clawing through dirt 'til the nails came unglued
and the paint got chipped
and with mangled paws we rose panting and holding the gem that'd
    been hidden away
the compressed ashes of offered-up mamas,
turned diamonds over the centuries
that's what we keep around our necks, adorning our tiaras

every high note karaoke hit
—is a reclamation of a mama's shriek

every
beat mug at the ball
is Brandon
is Matthew
—a beat body

and what about her body
Queen Marsha
floating down the Hudson like Moses in the Nile
whichever city agency fished her out:
did they see a prophet like pharaoh's daughter did?
did she rise from the reeds to lead her people again?

and if not, why not?
and if not, *will we*?

we stand on the shoulders of giants
every inch of height
a fossilized leather boot heel caked over vinyl pumps
walking us through this wilderness on these ancestral clown stilts
for however many years we're given to wander

today is the day we commemorate the days when so many of those
    journeys ended

BINYA KÓATZ

76

when our *doyros* laid themselves out
exhausted, bruised,
covered in glitter
an offering at the foothills of the promised land[1]

the inches that their bodies tallied lifting the soles of the next pair
    of chucks
and in the ancient ritual, they prayed,
let these ones be the ones
let these ones be the ones
that take us over, to that other side

*

Binya Kóatz is a transfemme, sefardi-ashkenazi, diasporic daughter-of-queens, from Queens, New York City, living on Ohlone land in the Bay Area. She dreams of a flourishing galus, lived in our mother tongues and deep service to Hashem. This poem was written for Pride Shabbat for her local gay shul. More writings can be found at binyakoatz.com.

---

1. *Doyros* is Yiddish for "generations," meaning, in this case, "ancestors."

LOST AND FOUND

LEIGH HOFFMAN

My walls speak Yiddish better than I do.

What would my bubbe think? Would my grandmother be proud of who I have become? Would she even understand?

Two nights and one weekend morning throughout my childhood was spent learning to manipulate my mouth in twisted formations to spell out the curved script of prayer books.

Every Thursday, my too-many-generations-Canadian-to-count friends played soccer after school. I looked on longingly; my mother reminded me with her eyes that her parents' families had not died for soccer. I climbed into the family car, off to Hebrew school, heart heavy with the haunting of ghosts whose names I never learned, strong from the sense of survival.

At my bubbe's funeral, I laughed. I imagined her rolling over in her grave, blood barely cold, at being buried in the labor section of the cemetery. She was a right-wing nationalist—anything but a socialist.

I wondered if this possibility ever crossed her mind, as she pretended to be dead on the streets of the shtetl in 1940. Lying next to her murdered family, warm blood bleeding out of her knee, could she have imagined that her fascist, Zionist training in Beitar would help her survive the war, but that she would end up next to the socialist Bund?[1]

I have had a recurring nightmare since my earliest memories. Running. Sweating. Silence. Desperately gasping for air under strained and muted breaths, only to find a large rock in an empty field. I crouch and hide. And I feel my heart calm, as booted men kick at trees and brick walls, but never find me.

My bubbe's voice through the phone, held unsteadily to my ear, told me that while we might disagree about some things, at least we know what is right. We love each other, and we both love Israel. I felt the warm Mediterranean air softly brush against my legs, as a shiver crawls across my thigh. I glanced across the land, at the Jewish com-

---

1. Beitar was a Revisionist Zionist youth movement in Eastern Europe (it is still active in Europe, North America, and Israel). It saw Jewish nationalism along with military training as means to achieve and sustain Jewish national independence. Beitar was the precursor organization to the Irgun, the right-wing Zionist, terroristic paramilitary organization that operated in Mandatory Palestine from 1931 to 1948. The Bund was a secular, anti-Zionist, Jewish socialist and labor party in the Russian Empire, the precursor to the International Jewish Labor Bund.

mune where I've been living for the last five months in Israel, and
cried silently.

She needs to be proud of me. She needs to know that she survived
for something.

I tell my mother that I am going to Palestine. I tell her that Palestinian activists in the West Bank have made a call for internationals to come and support them, using their privileged passports to de-escalate the violence. For too many years I supported the national colonial project of Zionism, and now I need to support the Palestinians' right to self-determination and decolonizing the land.

She sighs just like my bubbe did—a deep guttural release that fills the whole room with cold silence.

The next year, in preparation for our family's Passover seder, she calls to gently remind me that "we disagree on some issues, and perhaps the seder is not the best time to bring them up." I clarify that she is asking me not to bring up Palestine.

My bubbe never made it to the Holy Land. She had to find her sal-vation in her only child, in the poverty of being a refugee immigrant, in the cosmopolitan antisemitism of Montreal in the 1950s.

Her Promised Land became Notre-Dame-de-Grâce, nicknamed NDG, with its tree-lined streets symbolizing freedom from the pol-luted air of the Plateau's factories in the city's center. She always stood by the window as we drove away, peering from behind the cur-

tains, and I wondered if the trees, crowding her scope of view, made her feel safe. Hidden.

The year before I moved to Montreal, on our annual family trip to visit bubbe, we went for smoked meat sandwiches at Schwartz's Deli in Montreal's Plateau. We always brought an extra suitcase with us on these trips to fill with Mrs. Whyte's Original Brine Kosher Dill Pickles, a brisket, and bagels. My mother and her mother whispered to each other in Yiddish when they didn't want me to understand. My Jewish sense of wonder and guilt still smells like smoked meat.

Over black cherry soda and rye bread, my bubbe jokingly mused with me that perhaps I will live in this neighborhood when I move to Montreal. My mother rolled her eyes, settling in for a story of the early days of her life, the family's early days in Montreal, in the decrepit tenements of the Plateau.

My first month living in Montreal, my bubbe died. I filled my hip new Plateau apartment, mere blocks from the fading Hebrew script etched in stone across from Schwartz's, with her dishes, tacky wall paintings, and Judaica. I lived in the smallest room in the apartment; her decades-old things, my new things, took up the whole room.

A francophone woman I'm dating is committed to helping me learn French. She asks how my family can be from Montreal, how both my parents grew up here, and yet I didn't learn French. When I respond in broken grammar, she compliments my pronunciation of the letter *r*, how my tongue curls perfectly for its guttural French roll. I kiss her and think of the smooth curves of the Hebrew letter *resh*, my tongue curling in her mouth as it was trained to do when reading words that I never understood.

My bubbe learned nine languages. She used her tongue to blend in, assimilate in appearance, to survive. She used it to live in hiding, speak to Nazi guards, illegally cross borders, and help run her husband's business from behind the scenes. She never learned French.

My collective house in Montreal hosts a backdoor klezmer concert. My room, being the largest, serves as the coatroom. Guests drop off their bags next to walls covered in posters juxtaposing the "Queer Intifada" with Yiddish lyrics for "The Internationale." We line our backyard with chairs, and open the concert with a territorial acknowledgment that we are on stolen Kanien'kehá:ka (Mohawk) land.

In the Plateau, the neighborhood that my grandparents tried to so quickly escape, we have built a diasporic home. They may not have chosen it, but this is my choice. A commitment to diaspora, a commitment to the nonnormative within Jewishness, to queerness, home on my own terms.

And yet I am mourning. Mourning the deep loss that reverberates in my bones. The culture destroyed, the family that was murdered, the embodiment of Jewish life lost that I will never even know.

Mourning the language lost through the killing of its speakers and colonial project of Zionism—my mother's mother tongue, of which I speak none.

My mother winks at me as my childhood lullaby, the only song that my mother ever sang to me, melts out of the lips of the duo playing on my porch.

Tumbala, tumbala, tumbalalaike.
Tumbala, tumbala, tumbalalaike.

Girl, girl, I want to ask of you,
What can grow, grow without rain?

(What would my bubbe think?)

I am free. Free in ways that my genocide-surviving ancestors could never have dreamed possible. Yiddish words and the melody of fiddles float into the Plateau's alleyways, suspended on the densely humid summer air, on the thickness of reviving a language in a neighborhood historically dense with Jewish joy and pain. Free when I am read as white before being read as a Jew, benefiting from the shifting construction of race only when it serves the powerful—a privilege taken away as quickly as it is given. I am free from being a target of the state structures of violence by appearance alone.

I am scared. Scared of the rise of fascism, the rise of racism, and the contemporary repetition of state strategies that were used to murder my family. Scared of the swastikas that I see spray painted on the city sidewalks, for the bodies and minds and cultures and languages that are already the targets of social and systemic violence, for my friends, for those whom I have never even met. Scared for when the boundaries of race shift; when the boundaries become lines that separate us through violence; when those lines become ever-expanding targets that include more and more of my communities, of me. Scared to see the conditions that led to the genocide of my people and so many other peoples being reenacted.

Tumbala, tumbala, tumbalalaike.
Tumbala, tumbala, tumbalalaike.

What can burn and never end?
What can yearn, cry without tears?

(Would she see me? Would she be proud?)

I am proud. Proud of the work that my community is doing to revive something that was almost destroyed, to be a part of a reclamation of Yiddish and Judaism and art that is political, that is labor conscious and antifascist and diasporic, proud to see the fusion of queerness and anti-Zionism and truly embodied Jewishness. Proud of my home for the work, aching, messiness, and tension, and the deep joy, of all that we have done to host this event for three years, when my backyard overflows with people. Proud of having ragtag Shabbat dinners

as if the frayed threads of the garments my bubbe sewed in her basement are being mended, led by women and nonbinary folks, the
chorus of our stumbling voices singing together over all the loss it
took us to get here. Proud of the lessons that I have learned from anarchist community: that boundaries and lines serve the powerful, and
we deserve to create (and destroy) our own. Proud of the annual seder
that we host, honoring the inheritance of liberation from bondage
through discussions of how we are both bound in enabling and hurting from the ropes of today.

Living in diaspora, as a queer person, as a Jew, living under capitalism, with fragmented community along with the threat of economic and ecological collapse, I am lost. My body aches with pain, the
kind that leaves me breathless, and the tension of living between
worlds. Living between the past that I have inherited and the present
that I am building. Aching between the survival and loss, between the
freedom and grief. Living between the present that I am told to live
in and the present that I am building on the margins. I am lost; finding home on stolen lands, while knowing that my ancestors' homes
were never really theirs.

I am longing. I am yearning for all that could have been different,
all that I wish I could be, all the ways that were taken from me before
I even had a chance to touch them, held just out of my reach. And yet
I have hope. Of a dream, a tomorrow where freedom is not merely a
concept but instead something that rings deep in our bones. I am
honoring all that came before me, all that I have inherited (both
power and suffering), and all that we are building. I strive for liber-

ation, truly embodied freedom, and all the connection and solidarity that it requires.

Pain transforms you, if you let it. Into longing, a combination of mourning all that is lost with yearning for all that could be. With love and care, pain heals into a dream. A dream that we can choose our own path, acting as individual agents within a collective whole.

My walls speak Yiddish.

*

Leigh Hoffman is a Jewish, punk, polyamorous nursing student, community builder, and socialist living in Tiohtià:ke (Montreal, Canada). They are passionate about youths, tackling structural power that impedes access to health (services), lovingly calling out bullshit, and giving people a fucking break.

A N T I S E M I T I S M   H U R T S

CINDY MILSTEIN

Hurt: still. We are moved because it hurts still.
We are not over it; it is not over.
—Sara Ahmed, "Feminist Hurts / Feminism Hurts"

One pond, two ramshackle farmhouses, ten acres, and some eighty anarchists, miles from anywhere. Tucked away on the hill where they'd pitched their tents, hoisting up red and black flags, they felt miles away, too, from the cares of the world. They were transfixed by fireflies in the tall summer weeds and marveled at all the stars in the clear deep sky. They felt the flames within themselves reignite again as they circled around a campfire, ashes and embers, banter and laughter, floating into the night, reverberating throughout the valley below.

Sometimes, during those ephemeral moments that you want to last forever, it feels like "there is a crack," as Leonard Cohen wrote, "a crack in everything (there is a crack in everything) / That's how the light gets in." You look around at all the faces, flushed with a radiance that only comes from creating something magical together. You see old friends, new comrades, people who've inspired you, or who you've learned from and been challenged by, helping you grow strong like the vegetables thriving in the garden on this land.

"Jews control the world."

He'd made a beeline for you. His nose is several inches from yours. You can smell that he's drunk. You think he must be joking.

"All Jews," he emphasizes, leaning in even closer. "*All* Jews!"

You can now almost feel the hairs in his nostrils. You can smell that he's adamant. He spews out a monologue that could have been lifted from *The Protocols of the Elders of Zion*, barely skipping a beat to hear your objections, until out of the corner of your eye you can see four or five other anarchist Jews crowding around him. "Us too?" "Yes, *all* Jews! You *all* control the world!" There's suddenly a cacophony of loud voices, overlapping. He stays nose to nose with you, the only Jewish co-organizer of this weekend bringing "prominent" anarchists from across the continent to one place, as if that in itself is confirmation of your global domination. You remember little of what you said, though at one point recall gesticulating wildly, likely affirming his notion of "the Jew," as you ask him, "If all that's true, if we have that much power, why wouldn't all of us anti-Zionist Jews here free the Palestinian people?" He remains unmoved.

Later, under an expansive night sky, some friends made excuses for him, saying "he drank too much." Others at this do-it-ourselves theory conference preferred to abstractly debate the meaning of the terms "Semite" and "antisemite." Most simply ignored the whole incident, as if it didn't even register.

Only the anarchists who were also Jews came to your aid.

CINDY MILSTEIN

* * *

Your father just died, and your mother will follow him soon. You've been caring for them both and now need to dismantle the five-bedroom home they lived in for some four decades. Neither of them could throw anything away, and everyone in your family was fond of dragging free stuff into the house. It's a huge task, or mess, depending on your perspective.

After a few days of packing up a box of mementos for yourself and similar boxes for your three bio siblings, your anarchist ingenuity takes over. You turn the whole space, from basement through first and second floors up to the attic, into what becomes a "really really free market": a make-an-offer yard sale, from zero dollars up.

For a week, you let people dig through the home you grew up in while you hang out in the living room. Folks bring you an individual item or create a pile of things. They feel awkward about naming a price, and you suggest "free." All you see are memories via association with objects you'd forgotten about. Then, touchingly, you get to hear folks explain the ways they're going to give their finds a good, new home.

You are, in essence, sitting shiva, though you only realize that in hindsight.

During those seven days, you're surrounded by a constant community. Each person asks why you're emptying out the house alone and giving everything away. They pepper you with questions—this is the chatty Midwest after all—and really listen. They come back another day to help with cleaning, or bring and share food. Almost everyone has hard-luck tales—this is the economically devastated Midwest after all—and so they tell you their stories of loss. You end up holding space for others' grief stories along with your own, as you gift the entirety of life in this home to others until only the bare walls and some dust bunnies are left. For you, there's deep truth in the phrase "May their memory be a blessing"—not their things.

Still, things matter to others.

More than a handful of folks—all at separate times over the seven days, and none of whom know each other—come rushing to you in the living room with a concerned look on their face. "Do you know there's a *Jewish thing* in the family room [kitchen, bedroom, ...]?" They are clearly trying to protect you, as if a Jewish thing stealthily crept into the house and bodes ill. "Yes, we're Jewish," you reply each time, as nonchalantly as you can, curious as to the response, which each time is the same. Incomprehension that someone, or you, could be a Jew, that Jewish things are in people's home in this midwestern town, and that you don't seem to be worried too.

* * *

She was the only other person in the ancient-looking basement locker room. You had that in common. You both swam laps, and at the precise same time. There was that in common too. And you both always awkwardly smiled at each other, until you broke the ice almost at once. It was then that you discovered you shared something else: the ability to speak German, though hers was mother tongue exacting, and yours was rusty *schlecht*. Or *shlekht* in Yiddish, which you should have learned from your dad, but you only heard it used when his mother, your *bubbe*, "spoke" to him, always kvetching and screaming, as she transferred a lifetime of trauma onto her son.

Your pool pal was visiting the States from Berlin for a couple years while her partner studied here. You'd spent two years in Berlin with your former partner while they studied there. This commonality forged an empathy, not around that German city—she loved it, and you felt nothing but the unquiet dead blurring with the continuity of hate or exoticism toward the few remaining Jews—yet instead around how it feels to be away from home with no real purpose. You remembered swimming laps regularly in Berlin, especially at the first pool that Jews were banned from in Nazi times; it still boasted a 1930s' fascist-realist sculpture carved outside its entrance, only a few blocks from where Jews were deported to death camps.

For weeks and then months, your friendship grows, always in this locker room. Time stretches out between when you arrive to change into your swimsuits and when you actually stop talking to get into the pool. Some days, you chat so long that you miss the allotted lap time. You share what seems like everything, from politics to ideas, from joys to hardships, and no matter how tough the emotions, she maintains an upbeat spirit. You realize how much you look forward to seeing each other—so much so that you finally begin speaking of getting together outside the dank basement, including visiting her when she returns to Germany. Autumn turns to winter turns to spring, as both your relationship and the locker room warm up.

"It's hot as a gas chamber in here!" she exclaims one day, smiling, with a big wink of camaraderie.

You've never been good at hiding your feelings, which in split seconds appear on your face. From the way her face reacts, you're sure you have no need for words. You have none.

She repeats it, smiling more broadly, "Hot as a gas chamber, right?" A silence fills the space between you.

"It's just a saying. You know. You have sayings here too, yes? It's a saying we use in Germany. It doesn't mean anything."

The locker room walls close in. Her smile is gone.

"I grew up saying it; my parents said it. I've used it my whole life."

She starts swimming at a different time and never speaks to you again, even though you never found the words to say something, anything, to her that last day, even—although you know it was clear— "I'm Jewish."

* * *

The Signal thread is abuzz with shared intel.

A Confederate flag spotted on the back of a truck driving through town. "Some of us are heading out to keep an eye on him and get his license plate number."

Rumor of another white supremacist coming to do a public event. "Can we put pressure on the venue to cancel? If not, we'll need to ramp up our organizing."

Anti-Black graffiti on a Black person's front door. "There's going to be a rally and wheat pasting to counteract this racist shit. Let's reach out to see if the person needs other support."

The Signal group is a hodgepodge of progressive, lefty, socialist, communist, and anarchist folks. It's held together not by shared politics, other than the glue of antifascism, but instead a shared spirit of solidarity, in theory and practice.

Since you walk a lot, you're often the first to see white supremacist "street art." You snap a photo, upload it to the Signal chat with the location, and try to disappear the propaganda. It helps that you carry an array of stickers and a Sharpie; your keys will also do. And when something is too high, you know one of your fellow Signal pals who's good at climbing will deal with it soon, and others will then keep an eye on that general vicinity in case new racist materials go up. It's all quite cooperative, amicable, and efficient.

One day, you spot an image of a skull. There's a hammer and sickle in one of its empty eye sockets, and a Magen David, or Star of David, in the other. The sticker bears the name of a group known for its explicit antisemitism: Blood and Soil.

When you send the image to the Signal thread, rather than the usual emojis of support, self-described white allies urge caution. "Maybe we shouldn't be taking down anti-Black stickers after all?" "What if Blacks don't want us to?" "What if removing such stickers means that these racists will take it out on Black people, maybe even with physical violence?"

Never mind that there are Black members of the Signal chat whom these allies feel compelled to speak for and that "Blacks" are suddenly now allegedly opposed to us taking down racist literature, with no mention that some Black people are thrilled to help smash such symbols. Never mind that no one raised these concerns about any other instances of white supremacist materials, or that a Jew had spotted, shared, and said it felt scary awful to see this skull—threatening even—and yet it had felt super empowering to remove it. Never mind that no one thought to ask if "Jews" would feel endangered by fascist literature being trashed, or comforted that others would want to trash it.

It was almost as if no one saw what was right in front of their eyes: a simple six-pointed Jewish star in the hollowed-out eye of a dead person.

* * *

It's your birthday, which you've never liked and typically spend alone, trying to ignore the trauma that it brings up for you. You're driving between Michigan and Wisconsin to visit a sister. On impulse, you decide to mark this day after all by stopping halfway on the outskirts of Chicago to honor your ancestors—some anarchist, some Jewish, and some Jewish anarchists. It feels right on this day when usually everything feels wrong.

At the Waldheim Cemetery (now anglicized to Forest Home), you first pay homage to the Haymarket martyrs as well as Lucy Parsons, Voltairine de Cleyre, and Emma Goldman, all lying near each other. The tree branches are bare, the sky gray, the mementos that other radicals have left lie withered in this wintery-deserted graveyard. As is your ritual, you pick up the first stones that call out to you, and with intentionality, place one on each tombstone or monument. There are already other stones, especially on the granite markers of the Jewish anarchists. You feel in good company with recent comrade-visitors and your rebel predecessors.

Then you head over to the Jewish Waldheim Cemetery, or what more precisely could be called a shtetl for displaced persons who tried to make Chicago their home. Its unkempt two hundred acres contain some 175,000 Jews in what are actually almost two hundred associated cemeteries (apparently Jews couldn't agree on anything then either, but also couldn't imagine being without each other). The burial ground follows the history of Jewish refugee/undocumented waves, bookended with its start in the 1870s and tapering off by the 1950s. As Jewish mutual aid societies faded away, and tight-knit Jewish immigrant communities dispersed or died off, Jewish Waldheim nearly perished too. These days, it gets relatively few visitors, much less new occupants. It's now more of a time capsule, filled with those who escaped pogroms, forced conscription, the Shoah, and other surges of genocidal violence.

There's something so schlepy-beautiful about this place, though. For one, there's no rhyme or reason for gravestone placement; the cemetery instead mimics the bustle of an overcrowded, congested nineteenth-century city. Many of the gravestones also boast little porcelain or tintype photos of the deceased, who by white Christian supremacist attractiveness standards might be considered disheveled, peasant-like, frumpy, but who stare out at you as if worrying, "Have you eaten? You look so skinny!" And the way you find a particular person's grave is a complex, nonlinear, always-in-need-of-reinterpretation system that would warm most Jews' hearts. It involves seven or more layers of numbers and letters that don't correspond with what you see on the tombstones, because the system relies on scraps of paper taped or glued like post-its to the graves, and thus are prone to falling off and composting with the dead below.

The first time you came here to find your great-grandparents' graves, it took you about two hours of fruitless wandering—even though they were supposedly right in or next to a socialist Jewish workers' section. You then spotted the only other person around for miles, a groundskeeper with a huge cross around his neck, and the two of you wandered for another hour or so. Once you found their graves, the groundskeeper decided to stay with you for an additional hour to chat about the history of this place and honor your great-grandparents because "I never see anyone coming to visit their people anymore."

This time, it again takes you about an hour. Numbers and letters have disintegrated even further, and there's no groundskeeper, but you know you're looking for two stones, side by side.

Then you see them: one gravestone upright, and the other knocked over.

Your great-grandfather is flat on his face. All you can see is his back, the smooth-gray rear of his stone, which is the height of a person, lying as if murdered. His porcelain photo—his head—has been smashed to the ground. Your great-grandmother's porcelain-photo face—the woman who died just before you were born and so you were given a middle name to honor her (Bracha, meaning "blessing")—seems to be contorting with sorrow.

Your body feels as frozen as the January soil. Your mind transports you to the numerous Jewish cemeteries you've visited across eastern Europe, with most of their stones also knocked over, also smashed, broken by generations of antisemites, and yet somehow you are right here, wondering how out of the nearly two hundred thousand Jews, the fascists knew which were your great-grandparents, because plainly they're after you—a living, breathing anarchist and antifascist. They're probably still here, hiding behind trees, waiting to attack you, but how did they know you would come here today? You feverishly survey the area around your great-grandparents' stones: six or seven others are toppled in an intentional pattern.

Through fear and tears and confusion, you do a ritual for your great-grandfather. You tell him that you'll right this wrong, gently touch his cold "body" in goodbye and comfort, place a kiss on your great-grandmother's face.

You trudge through as many acres as you can on this bitter-cold birthday to see if there's more damage, and find two other spots where some half-dozen graves are kicked over. As you walk, thousands of sad, wise-old porcelain eyes tell you that they've seen this before.

Later, when you go to the 1950s-looking cemetery office to see about having maintenance raise your ancestor's stone from the dead, the woman behind the desk instantly nods her head as you say, "My great-grandfather's tombstone was knocked over ..." and completes your sentence "... by fascists. Such are the times. Again."

* * *

On October 23 and 24, 2018, you visit dear friends in Pittsburgh at the tail end of a monthlong book tour about loss and mourning.

At social centers, free schools, and radical bookstores, you've held grief circles. You've witnessed, time and again, people making themselves bravely vulnerable in front of others, sharing stories and tears that they've never expressed. You're always struck by how much two seemingly simple acts—naming and talking about one's deepest hurts and absences, and giving oneself permission to be fully present with whatever emotions arise—have the capacity to aid people in giving meaning to and bearing pain. There's a reason that Judaism structures how we grieve so as to not leave one alone; so as to be in community.

Your body has become a container for these stories. It's an honor. And it's a lot. So it feels good to be in a warm circle of friends, sharing a meal and laughter. It's what you need, you realize, to wholly integrate the stories that people have entrusted into your own body memory.

As the first evening with your friends winds down, one of them asks if it's OK to share a dilemma they're facing and, of course, you all say yes.

Just before you got to Pittsburgh, swastikas were painted on two anarchistic spaces, both of which include volunteer staffers and many visitors/users. Both spaces decided to cover up the tags and not tell anyone.

Your friend is distraught. Why, at a minimum, didn't the collectives alert folks coming into the buildings so that they could fully consent to the risk that fascists targeting spaces might imply? Why didn't they share photos of the graffiti widely with media or public calls for community self-defense? Shouldn't this have been a rallying cry for collective outrage as well as solidarity against antisemitism and white nationalism? Isn't it a big deal?

Your friend is doubting the pain that their ancestors transmitted to them. How can a swastika become so detached from the targeting of Jews? How are we able to forget? You again witness the power of storytelling. You're distraught too.

So you and your friends devise a plan that respectfully but firmly demands that the collectives respond. The idea of action offers some relief to your friend. In hindsight, it's clear this was less about organizing a response than the comfort of what was, essentially, an informal grief circle—for yourselves and your ancestors.

The next day, your Jewish anarchist pals urge you to stay through Shabbat that weekend, not merely to keep processing the antisemitic incident but especially to partake in the delight of radical, queer Jewish rituals. Stay, they nudge, to light candles, sing a capella songs together, and break communally from the time of capitalism for twenty-four-plus hours, moon to moon.

You're torn. You'd promised to do one last book event in nearby Toledo on Thursday night. Maybe you should cancel? It was a last-minute addition, and you're emotionally exhausted. Your Jewish guilt wins out, and you head northward, first to Ohio, and then home to mid-Michigan. Some twenty-four-plus hours later, you hear the news. In Pittsburgh, a white supremacist who hated both Jews and immigrants walked into the Tree of Life synagogue, a place where Jews engaged in immigrant solidarity, and murdered eleven people.

Symbols have a history, a weight. They flag meaning. They carry warnings.

They are deadly serious.

* * *

Antisemitism hurts.

It hurts in the innumerable ways that other racist logics or patriarchy hurts. Deep-seated, pernicious ways. It hurts in everyday ways, like a leaky faucet.

Drip ... drip ... drip ... Slow, steady, persistent.

Drip ... drip ... drip ... Torturously louder with each drop.

Drip ... drip ... drip ... Impossible not to hear, impossible not to go crazy.

The faucet appears fine to everyone else, no matter how many times you drag someone over to look at it. "See? See! That bit of moisture there in the sink? Look closely!" It's hard to explain. It seems so trivial, so microscopic. What harm could it do? There's a drain, after all.

Drip ... drip ... drip ...

"It's just a little drop of water. What's the big deal? Actually, is it even dripping at all?"

Each of your anecdotes is just one more *drip* until the sink is overflowing. The room is flooded. You are drowning, gasping for breath, in a pool of water no one will admit that they see. A repair person who told you "don't Jew me" when they handed you a bill. One of your best friends repeatedly pushing Christmas on you, even after you mention that antisemites used to burn Christmas trees in village squares to scare your ancestors, and one time they put your kin in a synagogue and torched it. Supposed comrades telling you to "go back to Europe" although the last town your relatives escaped from before coming to the United States was razed to the ground and all its Jews killed by the Nazis, and you've no idea all the places that your ancestors had to flee over the centuries and across continents due to inquisitions, empires, colonization, and notions of blood libels or racial purity. People being appalled by QAnon yet omitting the Jewish conspiracy bundled at its core, or back during Occupy Wall Street, ignoring the thinly veiled antisemitic conspiracy theories related to "finance capital." Radicals forgetting that the concept of "outside agitator" has long included Jews too. Or the man who pulled out a loaded gun, waved it in the air, and told you that he's going to kill all the Blacks and Jews that get in his way.

Antisemitism hurts, too, even in the most beautiful of moments, like the first time you visited the city of Chana on Crete. It felt instantly, inexplicably, like home. Not a home in the present—though it felt that way as well—but a home you had come from and long lived in. A home where you wanted to stay put. A home torn from you—the "you" that is made up of your ancestors.

You're standing outside the most dreamy squat you could ever imagine. It's perched on the highest point above the ocean, with an expansively breathtaking view, including toward the old city across the harbor. The squat is not only a vibrant social center but also a collective home for Greeks and folks without papers from other lands, and you're there at a gathering with hundreds of anarchists from across the Mediterranean, listening to their conversations about solidarity networks without borders for so-called immigrants and refugees—whom they see as only fellow humans. The building is enormous, with a gorgeous interior courtyard and regal exterior; it's been home to monarchs, military, secret police, and fascists, with a prison in the basement. Now, in a flourish of poetic justice, it's in anarchist hands.

One of the local anarchists is standing by your side. "You're Jewish, right?" he asserts more than asks, followed by, "I'm sorry."

He points across the harbor, its waters dancing in the sun, at a tourist-romantic ancient neighborhood. "That was the old Jewish quarter. I'm sorry. We tried so hard to save you. We resisted the Nazis so hard in Greece, harder than most other places, and especially in Chana. But we lost. You were all murdered. I'm sorry."

His "sorry" is personal, to and for you, collapsing time. It's as if he can see into your bones and knows that this was in fact your home, many generations ago. That despite being alive, parts of you have always already felt dead. That you are one of the ghosts receiving this apology.

You're sorry too—that at some point your ancestors had to make the Sophie's choice, the impossible yet necessary nonchoice, of staying put or leaving. Some must have left, venturing north to places where they ultimately wouldn't be able to stay either, or you wouldn't be here. But you want to be here. Again. Still.

Antisemitism kills.

*

Cindy Milstein writes, agitates, and rages, while holding firm to love and solidarity as verbs. They are especially proud of having crafted numerous magical, caring spaces out of "nothing" with and for others, from anarchist summer schools, bookfairs, and social centers, to curated anthologies like Rebellious Mourning: The Collective Work of Grief *and* Deciding for Ourselves: The Promise of Direct Democracy. *Shout-out to Wren Awry, Shane Burley, and Ami Weintraub for their insights on a draft of this essay.*

OF PERFORMING MITZVAHS

AND TOPPLING KINGS

STEPHEN GEE

I didn't realize that anyone believed in God until I was about ten years old. I had gone to temple all my life on the High Holidays and, when I had to, for Shabbat services. I had been in Hebrew school three days a week since age seven, learning prayers, history, and culture, but it always seemed to me more a thing of tradition, a series of ceremonies and rituals we all did to remember our heritage. I would walk home from services laughing with my brother as we sang our silly approximation of the cantor's prayers. I didn't really enjoy any of it, whether sitting through the seders, waiting for the blessings to finish before being able to eat, or having to go to services. But I thought it was mostly just a casual hobby for everyone. I didn't imagine anyone took it seriously, especially the idea of an all-knowing, all-powerful entity in charge of everything.

So when I started asking people if they believed in God, I was somewhat shocked to find that most people did. Not only that, but millions of people dedicated—or even sacrificed—their lives to this belief. I realized that all of it, the Hebrew school and hours-long services, wasn't really for us and our ancestors. Rather, it was for the reverence of a supernatural being who I didn't even think was real. This revelation turned me off to the whole thing.

So I resisted going to temple. I tried my best to get kicked out of Hebrew school, mostly just by acting up in class and frustrating the teachers. My mother got herself elected chair of the board of education there to prevent it. Of course I was the contrary child at Passover when it came time to read the four questions.

None of this is to say that I resented or was embarrassed by my Jewishness. In fact, I've always taken great pride in it. Our long history of overcoming insurmountable odds, our ability to survive and often thrive, despite our enemies' best efforts, is nothing to be even remotely ashamed of. But during my formative years, I did not look to Judaism for guidance or direction. Even today, I shy away from Jewish-oriented spaces and practices, both in the organizing I do and my personal life.

Looking back, I can trace the person I became to three main influences. The first is the comic strip *Calvin and Hobbes*, from which I learned how powerful an imagination can be, and to distrust and rebel against my immediate authority figures, such as those at Hebrew school, or any school really. Calvin regularly questioned his teacher or parents about everything from the effectiveness of memorization-based educational techniques to why his socks needed to match. Calvin's father would rail against consumer society, and the tiger Hobbes would lament the destruction of nature by humanity's recklessness. All this served as a baseline of values, easily sliding me toward anarchism.

The next major influence was the rock band Radiohead, which I discovered around the time that I was getting bar mitzvahed. I drank up the sweeping melodies and complex rhythms, the wailing vocals and syncopated bass, and spent hours researching the band and its members. When I read in an interview that lead singer Thom Yorke thought all of Radiohead's fans in the United States should read Noam Chomsky, I did just that. I bought several of Chomsky's books, and learned about the brutal history of the United States and equally brutal functioning of the institutions that rule the world. Radiohead's music is rarely explicitly political, but I heard the lines "Riot shields, voodoo economics / It's just business, cattle prods and the I.M.F." in its song "Electioneering" so many times that ten years later, when I faced those riot shields as I was protesting the International Monetary Fund, nothing could have seemed more natural.

The third and largest influence on my worldview would be my parents. My mother, who grew up in one of the only Jewish families in her midwestern hometown, and my father, who was raised a secular Jew in Brooklyn, instilled in me a deep empathy and kindness for others. Through their encouragement, it became instinct to offer assistance whenever I could and give without expecting a reward.

They always were so shocked when I merely did what they taught me. When I was about six, we were on an airplane, and a woman sitting near me was having trouble dealing with the air pressure changes, and her ears were hurting. This was something I had dealt with before, and my parents often had me chew some gum, as it can help make your ears pop, equalizing the pressure between the inside of your head and the plane's cabin. I had gum, so I offered some to the woman. The only reason that I remember this simple gesture is because it made my parents so proud and astounded them so much (even though they likely would have done the same thing if *they* had had some gum) that now, almost thirty years later, they still tell this story to friends and whoever else will listen.

Thus prepared, when I happened on a book by Peter Kropotkin in a library at age nineteen or so, and therein was described a philosophy of mutual aid and questioning precepts at every level, I took to anarchism immediately. I studied anarchism for years as though it was the Talmud. I put it into practice in ways that I thought Calvin, Thom, or my parents would approve of.

Imagine my surprise, then, at how my parents reacted when I first told them that I was an anarchist. In my mind, I was telling them that I would dedicate my life to fighting against oppression like the Maccabees or Yael from the Torah. I was saying that I would always treat others fairly, and be generous with and grateful for what I had. But to hear that their nice Jewish child from New York, instead of going to college and becoming a lawyer or doctor, would embark on a project of undermining the dominant society, well, they weren't pleased.

Yet embark on that project I did, and that instinct to help others, which they helped instill in me, held so fast that enacting it has made up the bulk of my activity as an anarchist over the years. For several winters, I helped coordinate an anarchist snow-shoveling project for elderly and disabled folks. Over Christmastime, being the only Jew in the group for awhile, if it snowed I would shovel the couple dozen or so houses alone, as everyone else was out of town or with family.

When it snowed on Christmas day and I made the rounds, people would come rushing out of their homes, overwhelmingly grateful, offering me cookies and tea, which I accepted, and sometimes money, which I refused. For many, it was difficult to get out of the house due to mobility issues, and they never imagined someone would come on Christmas of all days to help them out. Of course I did. What would my mother say if I left these people stranded?

And when there was an obstacle to our project of empowering our community and bringing people together on the basis of mutual aid, we toppled it. Over the warmer months, when we weren't shoveling people's sidewalks and porches, we would organize an event in a public park where people could give away items as well as share skills and whatever else they so chose, as long as everything was free. No buying or selling, no barter or trade; only gifts. The event was fairly popular, bringing several hundred people into the park. Older folks and children, punks and hippies, most of whom all lived nearby, would come together for a few hours. They would bring things to give away and take whatever they wanted. Furniture, TVs, books, clothes, tools, instruments, and anything else you could imagine were redistributed from people who didn't need them anymore to people who could make use of them.

A local landlord, a person who owned a good deal of commercial and residential property in the neighborhood, and lived across the street from this park, apparently didn't like the event, though. Not only that, but through their control of neighborhood organizations, they were able to gain the ears of the mayor, chief of police, and permits department. Anyone who wanted to do an event in this park couldn't get a permit without this person's go-ahead. We didn't bother to get a permit, knowing that we didn't need one to do this type of event in a public park, and not being interested in getting one even if we did.

Over the course of a summer, more and more police would show up each time we did this event. But our support from the neighborhood was strong. After all, we were the same people who shoveled their neighbors' porches over the winter and helped them get a free wardrobe in the summer. The police presence didn't keep people away, and each event continued to draw hundreds. Eventually this culminated in the whole park being taped off, all the items that people brought to share being thrown into police vans, and one participant being arrested. As soon as the police cleared the park, however, people poured back in with more to share, and the event continued. The city knew it had no real case against the arrested person and dropped the charges. The next time we held the event, there was no police presence at all, and people and groups continue to be able to use the park for most anything they want, free from harassment from powerful local interests that want only to control everything around them.

Through this organizing, I've come into contact with many people who are different than myself. Like the elderly Catholic couple whose back walkway always got icy, or the estate sales agent who was seriously concerned about what we would do if someone took "too much" stuff that was being shared. We made sure that the couple didn't need to worry about slipping, and showed that sales agent how much could be achieved through the power of the gift. We did this by focusing our efforts on what was immediately around us and within our reach, and not limiting our activities to only ourselves and people like us but rather everyone who lived in or interacted with the places we called home. If the people we found were friendly, we worked together. And if they were hostile, we dealt with that too. In this way, we were able to have a noticeable impact on where we lived, our neighborhoods and communities, our neighbors and ourselves.

The work I've done as an anarchist has largely been centered on aligning myself with like-minded people, generally other anarchists, and organizing to build or deconstruct power in ways that directly affect our lives. I organized with people I lived with or near, and centered what we did in the neighborhoods where we lived. Those sidewalks we shoveled were the same ones that we walked down daily, and the park where we opened up space to share was a place that we interacted with all the time. This way, what I did as an anarchist remained grounded in my everyday lived experience instead of combating some abstract enemy.

In recent years, though, perhaps because of the political climate that arose starting around 2015, with a marked increase in white supremacist, fascist, or otherwise antisemitic activity, and more so after the synagogue shooting here in Pittsburgh in October 2018, I've begun to reexamine my Jewish roots and what it means to be Jewish as well as an anarchist. I long suspected that there was a connection between the lessons I took from my disparate sources and tried to enact through activity as an anarchist and the lessons imbued by my heritage.

The prayers from Hebrew school didn't really stick, but the history and culture largely did. I remembered the story of the Maccabees, who rose up against the Seleucid Empire, and the revolts against the Romans after that. I remembered Yael, who showed no mercy to the oppressor Sisera. But there always seemed to be a bit of a divide in the telling of our people's history. We speak little of the time when we ruled an ancient empire, yet speak and learn a great deal about our time as an oppressed people. We speak of our exile from Egypt and the pogroms that my parents' grandparents fled. At my Hebrew school, we met Holocaust survivors, and looked at pictures of lines of our people, starved to nothing and seemingly walking themselves toward death. It is a shame how much harder it is to find stories of Jews who fought back against the Nazis than it is to find stories of Jews who simply went along with the wave of horror as it came—a wave of horror that could always reappear.

There is a tendency in Jewish thought, mirrored in anarchist thinking, to see ourselves as perpetual victims, as a people on whom history has trod, and not as masters of our own fate. Even now, similar to when I was growing up, there lingers in me an aversion to ritualized Jewish spaces, where this tendency is often on display. After all my soul-searching, my renewed pride in my heritage, I still don't really enjoy Passover seders, or saying the blessings over wine and bread. And I find that when I'm in spaces with Jewish friends or family where these things are practiced, I look at my feet, smile, and follow along, and wish quietly that we could just eat, drink, and not make a thing of it.

I find myself uninterested in political organizing that is specific to my Jewish identity. I worry that to organize that way would needlessly limit what I could do. When I've dipped my toes into that world, I've felt that bent toward victimhood always lingering, sometimes on full display. That same insistence on seeing ourselves as an oppressed people, and little more, that was there through Hebrew school, is all too present as well in the work of those of us interested in liberation. This effect also lingers within anarchism, with a focus on our defeats and seeming desire to sometimes re-create them rather than push further. I worry that this can create barriers to performing the types of actions and kinds of relationships that are necessary if we are to find a way to live opposed to and apart from the forces that dominate the world. If I base who I am on an inherently oppressed identity, how does that leave me empowered to take personal responsibility for dismantling those powers and defending my communities from attack? How does that help me build relationships of mutual aid with people who do not share that identity?

Still, it is hard to escape that feeling that we *are* victims, or at least potential ones. So many times we have been targeted for destruction, what else could we think? It was drilled into us, at Hebrew school, at home, in temple. They've come for us before, and will likely come for us again. And "they" could be anyone, or even each other. We learned of the Nazis' rise to power, the way that many Jews of the time reacted, and the passivity of the gentiles. We learned how to spot fascism in its infancy, and I think for this reason I, or I should say "we," because I imagine the same could be said for many other Jewish people, have a heightened sense of rising fascist threats. We always learned to say "never again," but also that it is always our own responsibility to make that true, and not just for ourselves.

Personal responsibility appears baked into my Jewish upbringing in other ways as well. I was taught in Hebrew school that while Christians had to go to church and see a priest to connect to God (apologies to Christians for any inaccuracies; I never understood your religion), we Jews believe that each of us is connected to God personally, and praying in the middle of the woods is just as effective as praying in the holiest synagogue. And since that connection is implicit, we alone are responsible for what we put into the world, good or bad. We are encouraged to do good deeds—mitzvahs—and own up to our misdeeds.

There is no talk of an afterlife in Judaism; the focus is on what you do while you're alive. This is a distinctly anarchist idea too. We want to live our best and fullest dreams as well as desires now, not after some long-foretold coming or in a promised paradise after death. The anarchist movement has always been full of people trying to live without authority in their relations to others now, in the present, even when the whole of society tells us we can't. We take action directly to accomplish our goals, uninterested in appealing to those in power or their representatives. To hark back to my park example, who would demand a permit to share? Only the same people who would demand a permit to love.

And what of my penchant for disputing all authority—that most anarchist of instincts? Jewish teachings are rife with rabbis arguing among themselves. The Talmud reads as though it's a roomful of Calvins, endlessly taking issue with each other's ideas. Traditions, teachings, and established customs are always up for debate. And this isn't even to mention all the literal revolts throughout Jewish history, from the aforementioned Maccabees to the Warsaw Ghetto. Further, how many times throughout history did we have to hide our practices, such as those in Spain during the Inquisition who defied the law, risking torture and death to keep their traditions alive? If Jews were expected to always follow the rules, we wouldn't be here to argue about it now.

The more I look, the more I find Jewish practices, history, culture, and teachings that can easily run parallel to my practices, history, culture, and teachings as an anarchist. Perhaps this is because of all the debating that those rabbis have always done. The Torah and Talmud are so open to interpretation; some rabbi somewhere at some point likely agrees with whatever your view is. Obviously, this also creates the possibility of Hebrew teachings being used to justify some heinous acts, as the brutal enactment of the Zionist project clearly shows.

To remember these practices, history, culture, and teachings is to remember that Judaism is old indeed. Perhaps, after nearly six thousand years, after ruling a mighty kingdom and being cast into diaspora, after being made refugees and nearly being wiped out, and arguing among ourselves about all of it the whole time, a kind of consensus arose within Judaism. That for a people to survive, they must be able to adjust and reinterpret themselves at times. That there is no one right way to be Jewish, just as anarchism teaches us that there is no one right way to live. The important part is that we each get to choose for ourselves. For what is anarchism but the universalization of Hillel the Elder's ancient wisdom to do unto others what you would have done unto you?

So perhaps I was right to begin with. Going to temple, learning the prayers and history, and taking part in the various rituals, maybe none of it was really about showing reverence to an almighty creator. It's about us. It's our temple, prayers, history, and rituals. And the ones that don't serve to empower us to live more freely and fairly? We can toss those out, and still gladly declare that we are Jews. The anarchist project of storming heaven and bringing paradise to earth can also be a Jewish project of performing mitzvahs and toppling kings. Nothing, I think, would make our ancestors prouder.

*

Stephen has worked on several anarchist print publications and is a longtime anarchist organizer, participating in projects in Pittsburgh, Syracuse, and elsewhere across the northeastern United States. His day job is in childcare, and he is honored to have a place in this anthology.

HERITAGE AND DISCONTENT

BREZINSKI ASZ

During my youth, my father was one of the few parents I knew who even discussed racism. I think that I learned to hate Nazis and fascists even before I understood "the birds and the bees." My father adored taking me to see *Saving Private Ryan* and *Schindler's List*, regardless of whether other people in the theater were shocked by the sight of a child watching these films. I remember when the Klan marched in New York City in 1999; I never felt uncomfortable cursing in front of my father again.

Still, he was a classic reformed Jew. He hated Nazis, loved Israel, went to temple for Yom Kippur (rarely making it through the fast) and maybe Rosh Hashanah, and was discreetly atheistic yet openly savored Chinese food as if it was a staple of his Judaism. And he didn't challenge the view of the United States as some sort of salvation for the modern Jew (never mind that Russians, not US soldiers, freed my grandfather from Auschwitz).

My father didn't question capitalism or the state in any sense either. He certainly never could have expected that through his inspiration, I would not only carry on his legacy of a deep animosity toward Nazism but also expand that abhorrence, applying it to the broader logic of authoritarianism—a passionate recognition of the struggles remembered in my DNA. In fact, my first fight with my father, and the only physical one, was when I declared my opposition to Israel in 2001, following the 9/11 attacks. I explained to him that as a Jew and enemy of fascism, it was my responsibility to oppose not only this medium for US intervention in the Middle East but every nation-state in existence too.

Growing up, other children viewed me, pejoratively, as a fat Jewish kid being raised by a low-income single mom, and thus someone who wasn't worthy of respect (which in a predominantly Catholic town, led to some traumatic incidents indeed). I wasn't accepted much by other Jews, since my mother had converted, and I wasn't accepted by Catholics, because she had converted and married (and then divorced) a Jew. Christmas stirred up classroom humiliation. My classmates would draw and flash swastikas at me, hoping for an awkward laugh. They were basically instructing me to be afraid and insecure, and in some cases, pushing me to hide my Jewish identity. I only found myself welcomed by others who were also excluded: lower-class whites and black or brown people. These experiences contributed to my understanding that "Nazism" was not the result of "human nature" but rather part of imposed and learned social structures such as racism. The Holocaust wasn't a finite event in human history; in big and small ways, heinous ideologies seep into everyday life, compelling people to choose a side.

Armed with my father's reminder that the kids bullying me weren't in the right, however, I turned my fear and anxiety into a self-defense mechanism, learning at an early age to give up trying to adapt and fit in. I wasn't swayed by the pep talks of creepy principles and coaches to simply go along. I didn't dismiss racism or classism by labeling them "bullying." Instead of brushing off or ignoring my experiences, I saw them as introductions to an authoritarian society that we are told and often forced to accept. Somewhat inevitably perhaps, my attention was grabbed by tendencies and cultures that celebrated the refusal to acquiesce, and opposed conformity and submission.

The first action that I ever took against racism must have been when I was twelve years old, in the early days of the internet. I made a fake online profile, based on real-life personal information, for a rich kid I knew who used the N-word, intending to ruin his young life. Then I messaged as many students in our school as I could through his false account, asserting, "I'm a racist rich kid and like to say the N-word!" I got caught. My mother was threatened with a lawsuit, and I was almost expelled from school. Yet this act was only a beginning. Shortly afterward, I refused both aliyah to Israel and a bar mitzvah as well as the notion of god. While Christianity was more prevalent behind the ugly faces of the youthful racism and general oppression that I witnessed in my school and town, organized religion in general and all its fallacies seemed to contradict a voice for freedom versus fascism.

I have now been a self-proclaimed anarchist for over half my life.

I have been beaten for it, intimidated and harassed for it, and had my life turned upside down on more than one occasion. I have forfeited ease and stability for uncompromising integrity. The FBI has come to my work and home, and threatened many friends and loved ones. I have been pulled out of lines at borders and interrogated for hours on end. I have lost critical years of my youth inside juvenile facilities meant to crush my spirit and been doxxed by snitches. I have been backed into a corner where cooperation with the state would have been the easiest choice, but decided on the harder route instead, realizing that cooperating with the state would mean abandoning my ethical position as an enemy of fascism in all its manifestations.

In contrast, I would gladly share the clothes off my back with comrades or friends, and at times have done so. I've dedicated myself to schemes and projects that benefit political prisoners, war chests, and anarchist propaganda. But to this day, I am assumed to come from privilege and have been mocked as cheap by some anarchists.

Yet I am a high school dropout with two poor parents, both of whom are now barely surviving through disability payments. To survive, I have chosen an approach of what might be considered crime, financial instability, and the sincere subversion available in the streets. I have never been helped formally by the broader Jewish community, and indeed have been scammed and fired by Israelis—both fully aware of my family's Shoah history. I've donated remnants of the Holocaust from my family to a museum, yet when I asked to explore the museum for free due to a lack of funds, I could feel the judgment in the room. More ridiculously, when a play about a relative of mine was performed on Broadway, and my brother and I wrote to the director about getting complimentary tickets, again due to a lack of money, we were ignored. And when I tried to retain my Polish citizenship through Swiss and German reparations paperwork, I was asked for my grandparents' birth certificates, despite the fact that their homes and belongings were all looted or destroyed. I was told to consult ancestry.com, as if it could magically make their documents reappear. So I reached out to Holocaust descendant groups, and was informed that I could potentially get assistance, yet at a hefty price tag that I could never afford; even in "modern-day" Europe, Polish Jews are unlucky.

In the most critical and scary of times, I was forced to leave everything behind in a process of informal evasion. This has led to the loss of jobs, savings, relationships, and friendships, and most poignantly, the opportunity to say I love you and goodbye to my nana before her final dive into dementia.

The point is simply that if it wasn't for hearing a Jewish voice against Nazism from an early age—my dad's—I may never have been driven to question or react to oppression in the ways that I did. I wouldn't have become and stayed an anarchist.

I know that my position today as an anarchist is without a doubt an extension of survivors' blood flowing through my veins. I know that being told to never forget what happened in Poland, and especially being told who to blame and who to respect, allowed me to react in ways that many other children didn't, and grow into the person I am now. It allowed me both consciously and unconsciously to connect my own traumatic experiences of abuse, feelings of deception, and confusion regarding a normalized world of divisive and stratified suffering to something bigger—recognized through my father's teachings. Whether he could have ever expected to lay the groundwork for my current understanding of the world is irrelevant; he did. So even though I lack faith in all religions, I am a proud Jew. I became an atheist and oppose Israel because of my heritage. I despise all domination because of my heritage. And I warmly embrace the honor of having learned as a kid, unlike my peers, that deadly systems like fascism aren't "just the way it is"; they are the enemy of that which defines me.

Through years of pain and sorrow, I've never given in to fear. Struggle, to my mind, is defined as taking a position regardless of hope in victory (much like those who stood up to the Germans, with no hope of victory, yet no choice but to resist). The people I know and love are extensions of my experiences and principles. As an anarchist, to cooperate with the state or snitch would be a slap in the face to those people and myself, and essentially the death of any life worth continuing.

I'm certain that my grandparents, if they were alive today, could never understand what I'm trying to say here, and that I want to give respect to the Jewish foundations of my anarchism. They would happily watch a Volkswagen car burn for hours, but they wouldn't feel the same about a US police cruiser in flames. Deep down, however, I know that they would be proud of the strength of my integrity and my passion for challenging what I see as the same belief system that led to their suffering. They survived so I could live. And you have to fucking respect such a struggle, not only as an anarchist, but as a human with a heart.

In some ways, the Jewish faith has more of an appreciation for this mortal life than some other religions. Abandoning my values in the face of fear and repression would be a betrayal to my very existence, which includes being an anarchist, yet it could also be seen as betraying my Jewish heritage, the legacy that runs through my blood. Distinct from all books and written histories documenting this religion, Judaism is a culture grown in struggle. Just as the Torah, even though it doesn't speak to me, can be interpreted differently depending on which sect of Jews you ask, there are many interpretations to be made of this Jewish culture. Anarchism is one; it is mine.

*

Since Brezinski Asz has been a target of state threats for some time, they've been relatively broad in their references. If it matters, they only know the Hanukah prayer by heart because of the gifts they got as a kid during the holiday, and while not bar mitzvahed, they did have a proper bris. They are a direct descendant of Holocaust survivors and many murdered by the German state as well as some well-known Jews in history, including a man who participated in postwar partisan revenge and liberation efforts in Ethiopia. Brezinski hopes that this piece provokes some goose bumps of love and solidarity. And while they defy Zionism and its right-wing influences on the modern Jewish community, Brezinski also hopes that if their grandparents were still alive to read this, they could appreciate its affectionate and loving intention.

IN THE WORLD AS A JEW

CHAVA SHAPIRO

It was not on my mind in the lead-up to the Unite the Right rally in Charlottesville, Virginia, that I'd be confronted with my own Jewishness. I had a background in antifascist organizing that was informed by my Jewish lineage and family experience on a metalevel, but my deeper motivation for a counterdemonstration or even disruption was tied to my politics. I felt a sense of duty as an anarchist to participate more than I felt an obligation as a Jew. It was anarchism compelling me to resist white supremacist Richard Spencer's efforts to unite the fascistic Right under one banner.

Truth be told, my Jewishness was a tangled mess before August 12, 2017. I was a Jew doing things in the world, but I was not in the world as a Jew. I loved the holidays, traditions, and *idea* of my Jewishness. I loathed the Zionism, religious zealots, and state of Israel. My Jewishness was a negative project, if it was anything at all. It was a proving ground for "I'm not *that kind of Jew*," and involved checking the box of Palestinian solidarity to make sure that people knew it to be true. At best it was a model immigrant legend and at worst a tale of assimilation into whiteness. My childhood was replete with Ellis Island visits and knowing what New York borough my grandpa once lived in. It was a bat mitzvah and Torah portion long forgotten.

I did not expect to see organized formations of men in white polo shirts march past Congregation Beth Israel, the oldest synagogue in Virginia, early on the morning of August 12, hours before the Unite the Right rally was scheduled to take place. I did not anticipate having to deeply interrogate myself in that moment. The men shouted "blood and soil" and "Jews will not replace us." I knelt down in the grass of a nearby park with my Jewish comrade, and asked if we should stick to our plan or offer our support to the temple. The only people there to defend the synagogue that morning were the rabbi and a hired security guard. Despite the many credible threats of violence made against Congregation Beth Israel in the days preceding Unite the Right's convergence, and a request by the rabbi and mayor—himself a member of the temple—for aid, the police had decided not to provide a contingent for the synagogue that day.

Around forty people had observed Shabbat services that morning while neo-Nazis trooped past. The Jews davened in worship. They sang. They said kaddish, an ancient mourner's prayer, for those who had died.

None of us knew that we'd be saying kaddish for Heather Heyer during the shiva, the communal mourning period, to come.

In the park, in the grass beneath some trees, we chose to stay with our anarchist comrades. We chose to stick to our plan to try to keep the rally from happening.

I return to that moment in the park on a near-daily basis. I hear those men chanting Nazi slogans, marching in military style past a synagogue full of people praying on Shabbat. It haunts me that the

CHAVA SHAPIRO

124

congregation had moved the Torah scrolls out of the building in advance for fear of losing them to an attack on the building. One of the scrolls at Beth Israel had been saved from destruction during the Shoah and then found refuge in Charlottesville. Holocaust scrolls are cherished because they're imbued with the history of Jewish survival and resilience.

I come back to that morning and the decision to stay with my friends, and sometimes I feel certain that I made the right choice. The anarchist in me affirms this commitment to the collective, to the whole. The Jew in me, though, questions what commitment I perhaps should have considered to the Jews davening in that building, to the Jews who once studied that Torah scroll, to the ancestors who fought against Nazis from the ghettos and forests. It is in that instant in the park, in my decision and indecision, that I found my Jewishness. Charlottesville, for all its pain, pried open the space within myself to engage in the world *as a Jew.*

How many different versions of my own experience that summer morning, sitting with the pang of antisemitism, and impossibility of being everything or everywhere at once, have led our ancestors toward their Jewishness?

In the months following Charlottesville, I oscillated between total despair, shaken by trauma and depression, and glimpses of joy. Through it all, I unwaveringly longed for Jewish moments, and fumbled toward cultivating them.

On Rosh Hashanah, I sat by a river in observation with both Jewish and non-Jewish anarchists. We performed *tachlich,* the ritual casting off of the wrongs one has done over the past year, but instead of atoning for our transgressions, we tried to mend our aching hearts. We built a fire by the water, and shared stories and food. I don't think a word of prayer or Torah was spoken, but we created a sacred space together.

The challah we ate that night, braided into a lopsided crown, was the first I'd ever made on my own. It had been a meditative process. The kneading by hand on the kitchen table was a form of release. I hadn't yet learned to let necessary tears flow through me, but I could feel anger move through my body as I pounded the dough against a wood board. Centuries of ancestors had likely done the same as they prepared for other new years, permitting their broken hearts some respite as they braided the bread that their loved ones would share with them in the darkness, illuminated by blessed candlelight.

On New Year's Eve, after journeying on a red-eye bus, I joined friends in New York City for an annual noise demo outside a federal prison. The city was impossibly cold that night, yet without fail, dozens of anarchists, many of them Jewish, and other radicals made as much racket as possible as we attempted to penetrate the prison walls with our solidarity. Many of us wore masks or otherwise tried to conceal our identities; we'd been present in Charlottesville and were now being doxxed by the alt-right.

A comrade began to read a statement, and we all echoed his words, amplifying them to those who were locked in concrete cells. My voice cracked as I yelled the words in repetition, and my body shook from the frigid wind. Suddenly I felt the warmth of tears, running down my face behind my mask and turning icy on my cheeks.

CHAVA SHAPIRO

To many, it feels like we live in a time like no other with surveillance and repression at every turn, but also resistance, rebellion, and open revolt. This is neither the new golden nor dark age. It is simply another moment in time where we can collectively force conflict with a fucked-up system.

Every day there are revolts of varying scale, most of which you never hear about. For those captured in revolt, we come together in protest and celebration. Through the din of revelry and rage, we tie ourselves to those who suffer systematized white supremacy and war against the working class, behind steel bars and safety glass.

You are not alone.
You are not alone.
You are not alone.
You are not alone.

We shouted "you are not alone" into the air, and as I moved back and forth to stay warm, I felt as if I were davening. *Shuklen.* In Yiddish this means to shake. I shook. I shook in spirit and body as I swayed rhythmically, chanting "you are not alone."

The following morning, on the first day of 2018, I went to see the Amedeo Modigliani exhibit *Unmasked* at the Jewish Museum in Upper Manhattan. Modigliani had been my favorite artist as a child, along with Marc Chagall. My sister once told me that I had a face like a Modigliani painting. I've never been certain if she meant that as a kindness or insult.

At the museum, I stood in front of a small piece of paper that depicted a bearded man, with full and rounded features, drawn sparsely in ink with fine lines. The sketch was titled, simply, "Self-portrait with a beard." The image in front of me didn't look anything like Modigliani, who was clean shaven with a thin face. The curated text explained that he was portraying himself as an Orthodox Jew.

While wandering through the show, I learned that during a period of intensifying antisemitism, Modigliani would introduce himself by saying, "I'm Amedeo Modigliani. I'm a Jew." He'd been raised in a home by Jewish parents who followed kabbalah-inspired rabbinical teachings, but chose a bohemian milieu as an adult, turning away from Jewish life and practice. Yet he would recite kaddish to himself as a comfort when hit by waves of depression, and would drunkenly scream things like "I'm a Jew, and you can all go to hell!" when he found himself at parties with nationalists and fascists, who traveled in the same avant-garde circles at the time. He shunned Jewishness for a different world, and then embraced it as an act of defiance and resilience.

Four months after Charlottesville, in front of a triptych painted in hues of blue and gray, at a Jewish Museum in Upper Manhattan, I began to cry again. I was frozen in front of the figures depicted, my tears moving slowly down my cheeks, and when I could finally move my feet again I found myself confronted with the death mask of Modigliani. He'd made a request of his dearest friends: on his passing, he wanted a cast made of his face. I thought of Heather's death, which we'd witnessed so recently. I thought about the death that my friends and I had so narrowly escaped that same August day. I thought of comrades who had died in prisons, ancestors who'd perished in pograms and the Shoah, and anarchists who'd given their lives fighting fascism.

I remembered that indeed we are not alone. We are carrying those lost with us.

It took me months after Charlottesville to release my pain in any productive way. I learned how to daven. Then I learned how to cry. And now, I've learned how to introduce myself to the world: "Hello, I'm Chava. I'm a Jew and an anarchist."

*

Chava Shapiro is a Jew living, parenting, baking challah, davening, and organizing in the occupied lands of the Tohono O'odam and Yaqui nations. For Heather, Chava will continue to fight against white supremacy. For Toor, they will not let despair take hold of them. For their friends, they will never let geography tear them apart. For their children, Chava will try their hardest to ensure that they have something left of this wild world to grow into. For their partner, they'll find the safest place to keep all their tenderness, bad ideas, and hope.

KER A VELT

TURN THE WORLD OVER

ELIUI DAMM

Jewish anarchist and literary critic Baruch Rivkin (1883–1945) wrote about Yiddishland—an anarchistic, borderless, and multicultural land—and *yuntoyvim*—holidays—linking "Jewish time" in his work to the Yiddish language, Jewish holidays, and Jewishness itself as a negation of capitalist time. He did this as an anarchist practice, and I believe that his work can still be used as a tool against our horrible world. Others who have written on the subject of Jewish/Moshiakh/messianic time include philosophers Walter Benjamin (1892–1940) and Giorgio Agamben (b. 1942), contributors to the "journal of queer time travel" *Bæden*, and countless authors and rabbis, including the late Lubavitcher (1902–94). The latter gave a speech in 1984 known as "ker a velt"—a phrase meaning "overturn the world," charged with a sense of immediacy.[1] I was moved by this Hasidic rebbe's words, but still felt that there was more to be said, so I set out in search of the speech I had wanted to hear. Inside myself, I found this:

---

1. For the rebbe's speech, see https://bit.ly/2KH8qxp.

Pawned to an alien time,
I search
For the spoor of days that are blotted out.
—Rachel Korn, "Searching"

The earth still wheels about; and Time has still
No power over lasting memory.
—Avrom Sutzkever, "Spiritual Soil"

I saw it all happen. That is to say, I, the little bird, was there to see it all unfold. After all, there were hundreds of people in that room sweating, packed together like herring in a tin with hardly any space to breathe. But *I* heard it and *I* saw it. After the last rebbe's death, the Lubavitcher, may his soul be resting in *gan eydn*, there was such melancholy.[2] What a mensch he was! Some say he was even a *tsadek*, a righteous person! Such a wise man, I would not be surprised if he hadn't been a *lamedvovnik*.[3] Old in years, he was like a tree, a real Jew of the field. He never appointed a successor, which only aided in his projected venerable title. So we were, then, clearly surprised when we were so suddenly blessed with the *nayer* (new) rebbe twenty-five years later. With such ease he picked up where the Lubavitcher had left off—since not much had changed in the world, had it? The nayer rebbe publicly spoke for the first time in the heat of that 12th of

---

2. Gan eydn is Yiddish for paradise.

3. In kabbalah, Talmud, and Hasidic tales, it is said that in every generation, there walks among us thirty-six righteous people, by whose merit the earth exists.

Tammuz, 5779, in that famous ornate building, simply known as 770, nearly packed to the *ner tamid*, and I was there to hear it all.[4]

Now they say that when three Jews gather to discuss Torah, angels come to listen. Can you imagine now how crammed we all were in there! How stuffy it was in there! My legs were stiff, my tongue parched, my soul yearning, and my stomach awaiting the coming *oneg*.[5] What was I to do *but* listen? No one listens to me anymore, the learned person I am; they once called me *"gaon,"* a Talmudic genius, but now they call me a golem—an idiot, a *feygele*, a queer![6] Well answer me this: Can a golem speak like I do? Golem or not, one must contest with gentile Time just to exist.

Listen, when the nayer rebbe spoke, I could see that ugly, false stifling Time all around us begin to fragment and momentarily float, lifting higher and higher from us to reveal *HaShem's* holy time.[7] Those words that were spoken that day ignited in my heart a breaking of the gentile Time that had formed a crust around my *n'shome*, my soul.

---

4. Ner tamid is the eternal light that is often found hanging before the ark in a synagogue.

5. The meal after Shabbos services.

6. A golem is creature in Jewish folklore, comprised of mud, in the shape of a human, who cannot speak and seeks truth (*emes*). Feygele, in Yiddish, is often pejorative.

7. HaShem, meaning "the name," is one of many terms for God.

It is said too that Talmud is filled with HaShem's time, and when a sage reads Talmud, time becomes tangible, like sunrays that have traversed the cold vacuum of space to touch one's skin. I've felt it before. The Talmud isn't just a book written hundreds of years ago; it's a book of a thousand voices, and when one reads it, it is as if one is conversing with them all. As the nayer rebbe spoke to us, I could see him bend time itself and *d'rash* with the voices of the Talmud.[8] In fact, I bend time myself when I study! I simply close my eyes and see time as it is. It begins to move, a swirling of text that one can hear—not like an echo, but something that one can speak with—and those swirling words create images before my very eyes. Who is better at bending time than a feygele such as myself? It is in between the letters where the boundlessness of HaShem rests. So when the nayer rebbe closed his eyes and bent time, I was there with him. Though he did not notice me, I too could hear all the Talmudic voices echoing there.

Like Jews, these voices ached to tell a good story. There in front of me appeared thousands of people, all speaking—quite a commotion if you ask me. The nayer rebbe, however, focused on only one voice at a time, and first was the Lubavitcher. There they were, two wise men (and me, the feygele) seeking out a space—one that is not contaminated by *their* Time—a room maybe with four walls, a floor, and possibly a ceiling.

---

8. D'rash means to discuss an interpretation of the text.

TIME

The two stood face-to-face in complete darkness. *This is a present,* said the First, blindly reaching toward the other. The Second held the present in their hands, while carefully inspecting it: a small, soft, wooden, warm box with four corners and a rounded lid. The box itself smelled of summer sweetness and *real* time.

"Is this what I think it is?" exclaimed the Second.

"Yes," said the First. "This small container is a box for all the Time that you can steal. It is so small that not much else can fit in there. Though HaShem has left us here all alone, every once in a while the four corners of this little room are graced with its light."

The Second became worried. "If I open it, will the Time escape?"

"No," replied the First, "you don't have to worry about that. Time isn't real."

THE STORY OF THE CHERRY TREE AND THE SHUL

In one of the many shtetls that peppered the highway to Łódz was a young Jew, devoted to his learning and inner peace. Every day he wore tfillin and recited the morning prayer, followed by the afternoon prayer and evening prayer.[9] He fasted; he would even fast on days that required no fasting. Occasionally this young Jew would disappear for

---

9. Tfillin, or phylacteries, a set of small leather boxes containing Torah verses, are worn while saying the morning prayer.

days at a time, walking to the edge of town, through many fields, to sit beneath a massive cherry tree. There he spoke with HaShem. In the summer, the cherry tree would bear delicious fruit and create beautiful colors when the sun shone through its canopy; in the winter, the tree would dance naked in the breeze. Regardless, the young Jew would sit.

It is said, "One must break Time to seek HaShem in all its creation because a Jew is a tree of the field, and it is the life of a Jew that sprouts from the tree." When he closed his eyes beneath the tree, images unfolded before the young Jew, each one piling on top of the other like stacked photographs—all the moments, exile after exile, destruction after destruction. The young Jew had so much reconciliation to ponder in these moments that he no longer heard the outside world.

On a summer day, as the young Jew lay under the tree and spoke to HaShem, a rich gentile baron who owned the land drove by, accompanied by some of his men. He became angry at this *Jew* trespasser who seemed to be sleeping under *his* tree. He bid the driver to stop and call to the young Jew, but the Jew did not answer, so deep in conversation with the Talmud that he barely noticed the shouts. This enraged the baron even more, and he ordered the driver of his buggy to dismount and bring the man to him. The driver, however, was unable to move the young Jew because he was too relaxed to carry and impossible to wake. The baron, having now completely lost his temper, ordered his driver to beat the young Jew. Without hesitation, the driver began whipping the young Jew as if he were trying to get from Minsk to Moscow within the day.

Despite all this, the young man remained in internal conversation. Suddenly the now-bloodied Jew stood up, turning his back to the driver, and began to daven, to pray, with great fervor. Without an order, the baron's driver turned the young Jew toward him and slapped him six times with a gloved hand. The young Jew turned back around and continued davening toward the tree. Baffled by this young *zhid*'s behavior, the baron sat and waited.[10]

After some time, the young Jew picked up his things and approached the baron's buggy. Warmly, the young Jew said, "Good afternoon, brother. I'm sorry, what was the question you asked me?"

The baron replied, "I must ask you only two things. First, why is it that you dishonored me by not answering when I had asked you a question? Second, why do you now call me 'brother' after I had you beaten so severely?"

"Both answers are quite simple," said the young Jew. "I did not answer because I was trying so hard to rebuild the Temple and was in the presence of HaShem, to whom I was accounting my life. And I called you 'brother' because all people were created as the children of HaShem. Thus, we are all brothers."

"But don't you hate me for having you beaten so severely?"

"No. Because I pitied you."

"Why is that?" asked the baron.

"Because you were not beating me, but HaShem, and it was you whom HaShem had chosen to punish me for wanting more to rebuild

---

10. Zhid is a Polish pejorative for a Jewish person.

the physical Temple in Jerusalem than the temple within myself. For that, I pitied you."

These words shocked the baron. "I understand now that you are a pious Jew, and I am sorry for having beaten you. Please forgive me and give me penance."

Hardly understanding the Christian concept of "penance," the young Jew said, "I immediately forgive you. As for your 'penance,' pledge that you shall never beat any other of your siblings ever again."

"What about my peasants? Can't I even beat them?"

"No," said the young Jew. "Not even your peasants. They too are the children of HaShem."

With tears in his eyes, the baron made his pledge, adding, "I will have built a glorious synagogue in the place where you were praying." And before the young Jew could protest, the baron's men were already chopping down the giant cherry tree. When it was felled, the young Jew went home, disheartened.

After some time, the synagogue was finished. Though sound and beautiful, it had been condemned by the town's rabbis as "unholy" because an ancient tree had been felled for it at the hands of Christians, and moreover, the ark faced in the wrong direction. No one came. No one touched it. For it is said, "Do not spoil or destroy My world—for if you do, there will be nobody after you to repair it."[11] Eventually the town nearby grew to encapsulate the synagogue; it became the dead heart of the city. After awhile, time began to erode

---

11. Kohelet Rabbah 7:13:1.

the structure: the roof caved in, and the pillars crumbled. Things began to grow within it. Life emerged within the corpse. Nothing is sacred here; nothing is sound.[12]

DISPARATE TREES

The trees sang, and the Jews, the *yidn*, heard them. They sang from summer to winter, from spring through fall, and the yidn sang with them. Wherever the yidn went, they would hear these songs, find peace, and build their homes near the trees. The trees sang alone in fields under a canopy of stars or in woods so dense that no sunlight shone on the forest floor. For five thousand years, the yidn had done their best to make a home, even when something like a "home" was difficult to make.

With little time to rise, they would leave many things behind, as if in a rush to depart, still praying for a better home. And still the trees sang, and the yidn, like branches of a tree, spread throughout the lands. In one such place, the yidn tried to make a home, even when their neighbors had only contempt for them and even more so for the trees, who sang songs of welcome. Regardless, the yidn kept to themselves. When the war came and the yidn disappeared, the town was

---

12. This story is inspired by a Yiddish folktale about Rebbe Levi Yitskhok called "The Large Stone Synagogue of Berditshev," which I originally found in Beatrice Weinreich, *Yiddish Folktales* (New York: YIVO Institute for Jewish Research, 1988), 339. For another account of this story, see "Jewish Ethnography and Folklore," Berdichev, https://bit.ly/37cbbhT.

quiet. The forest was quiet too. Although the neighbors did not like their new invaders, they did like the new silence. But things were not silent for long. Soon a new song emanated from the trees—one of pain and sorrow—but it was not the trees who were singing. Throughout Polish towns, Polish people could hear the tune they had yearned for since *their* arrival.[13]

OUR NEW HOME

In the town of Safed, Jew haters abounded. Rocks were thrown. Shots were fired. Fires were set. Yet every Friday night, the tables were made and the candles were lit. When looters came, father bade them enter, and gave them *khala* and wine, though he knew they came for our time. Now drunk, they ran amok without care, smashing our glassware, swearing, tearing apart our world, and sparing not even our holy book.

Through it all, Shabbos did not subside; father made the *kiddish* blessing in a dignified voice, and no one cried as mother crooned a solemn *nigun*.[14] Of course, nothing can be perfect. With everything ablaze, the Shabbos candles trembled to mere smoke, and our hearts

---

13. In Buchenwald (Beech Forest), one form of punishment was to tie a person's hands together behind their back and hang them by their wrists from the trees that lined the road to the concentration camp. The prisoners named it the "Singing Forest."

14. Nigun is Hebrew for melody. It is a mystical form of vocal music—without instruments or words—that people sing in groups by repeating a syllable.

nearly choked. We were thrown into the sea, a stream of red marking our trajectory.

Now little fish blow bubbles and nibble my long flowing hair, as I lay next to father and mother in cold, soft, bare sand, and think of my dear friends in the shul and evening prayers that sing "Sholem Aleykhem." And through weightless water I can glimpse the moon in full, to whom I sigh, "How ever will we light Shabbos candles in our new home?" But father and mother do not reply. They only float motionless and stare up at the moon, perhaps pondering a similar question.

THE TZADIKAH OF MOROCCO

As bodies and Torahs were piled high on the other, higher and higher, just like Time (yet not burning anything like Time), the city of Safed was destroyed. In a city called Fez, two thousand miles away, was a young Jewess named Sol. She possessed many strengths. Her family was proud of her, for she was learned in Talmud and Torah, and beautiful too. Yet it was only for her beauty that she was recognized; for this, nearly every gentile man sought her hand. "Such a beautiful treasure," they would say. "It is a sin for such a gem to be in the hands of the Jews." She turned down each suitor, one after the other.

One day, as the sun slipped away, Sol, still unmarried at seventeen, was (as usual) immersed in her studies when her gentile neighbor asked for her hand in marriage. She did not even look up from the Talmud to turn him down. For no reason at all, this rejection proved to be the one for which she dearly paid. It was not long before her neighbor stood before the pasha to falsely report that Sol Hachuel, the beautiful Jewess, had committed an atrocious crime. Her neighbor asserted that although he had converted her to Islam, she had turned back to Judaism. The pasha, accordingly, called for her arrest, even though everyone knew that the famously beautiful Jewess had always been a Jew and never once converted to Islam, yet the pasha too wanted Sol.

She was thrown before him and ordered to convert back to Islam. She indignantly refused. The pasha was enraged by this young girl and her defiance toward him in his court; he was aflame with lust, looking at her. "I will load you with chains," he said. "I will have you torn piecemeal by wild beasts. You shall not see the light of day. You shall perish of hunger. You shall experience the rigor of my vengeance and indignation, for you have provoked the anger of the prophet."

Sol Hachuel replied, calmly enough, "I will patiently bear the weight of your chains. I will give my body to be torn piecemeal by wild beasts. I will renounce the light of day. I will perish of hunger. And when all the evils of life are accumulated on me by your orders, I will smile at your indignation and the anger of your prophet, since neither he nor you have been able to overcome a weak female! It is clear that Heaven does not favor your proselytizing."

And though both her family and rabbi now pleaded with Sol to convert to Islam, she did not relent. The pasha ordered her execution. Thousands of people came to witness the decapitation of the most beautiful Jewess in the land. The pasha ordered the act to occur at the exact moment when both the moon and sun shied away from the earth. This, the pasha understood, is a grave moment for Jews. For them, when day meets night, frightening things abound.[15]

BENYA KRIK

The last time that Benya Krik—the Jewish gangster of Itzhak Babel's stories—died was not the first time that he had experienced death. After dying a second time, however, Benya knew inside that he was in fact dead, though he miraculously still lived. Not being a religious person, Benya was uncertain what to do in this situation. So he made his way through the dark, empty streets of Odessa to the Brodska shul, where he sought the advice of the rebbe there. The rebbe did not at first notice him; sitting in his study, the rebbe appeared to be laughing over a tractate of Talmud. Odd behavior from a rebbe, thought Benya. After some time, Benya cleared his throat. The rebbe glanced up, a pale round, smiling, smooth face, with hardly a trace of beard.

"Rebbe, why is it that you laugh so?"

"Because," said the rebbe, "HaShem has written such a dark comedy."

---

15. Sol Hechuel (1817–34) was a real person, as is the dialogue above. See Eugenio María Romero, *El Martirio de la jóven Hachuel, ó, La heroina hebrea* (Madrid: Impr. á cargo de Diego Negrete, 1838). She is often considered a *tzadiket* (holy woman).

"Rebbe, have you noticed that the sky is empty this evening?"

"No, I have not. That is strange."

"Rebbe," said Benya. "I have died twice over. The sky is most unusual this evening, void of both moon and stars, and I fear that I am really no longer alive. And if I am dead and talking to you, then you must be dead as well."

The rebbe pondered this for a moment. "Yes, you must be right. But look at my room!" The rebbe pointed to his walls, covered in volumes of commentary. "So much to study." The rebbe, unfazed by this new information, went back to his reading, chuckling to himself again after a moment. Benya stood there for a while and then inquired,

"Rebbe, which tractate is it that you find so funny?"

"This isn't a tractate. It is your life," said the rebbe. He showed Benya the cover of the novel that he had never seen, which read, "Odessa Tales." "And what a funny life you have led!"

"But how can that be?" cried Benya, at last upset.

"The first time you died," explained the rebbe, "was also the first time that you were born! When his supposed allies, the Bolshevik secret police, put a bullet in the back of his head, Mishka Yaponchik, the real Jewish gangster of Odessa, was dead, and you were born, Benya Krik, in the mind and pages of Itzhak Babel.[16] To be so lucky!

---

16. After the success of the Russian Revolution, the party cleansed itself of revolutionaries through mass imprisonment and false confessions under torture, leading to executions. This was the fate of Jewish author Isaac Babel (1894–1940)

See, you were born twice, and for that you must die twice, as you have. And yet you still live! Throughout these pages of Babel's stories, you run amok through the lives of these goyim—something that I have relived over and over again, and others besides me. But writing about a revolutionary does not make a long life, and soon the revolutionary police came knocking for Babel, just as they had for Yaponchik. It is in the field, Benya, next to the live oak, that your unburied body rested. Today in the gulag, your blood soaks the dirt. And in these pages, your soul will continue to provoke and delight.[17]

YISGADAL V'YISKADASH

It was in the furthest reaches of the US Jewish diaspora, in a city somewhere far from New York City—the diaspora of the diaspora, one could say—where flickered the last vestiges of Yiddish.[18] As that city's final generation of Yiddish-speaking Jews breathed their last, so too did many Jewish stories: untranslated, forever forgotten.

In a room in this city, a child lay next to a bedside lamp and scoured

---

and countless others. Babel wrote Yaponchik into his stories as Krik. Yaponchik, the real-life Jewish gangster, temporarily joined his Jewish gang with the Bolsheviks and successfully fought off the violent antisemitic White (czarist) Army. He was executed in 1919 as an "anti-Soviet" by the Bolshevik secret police.

17. I was inspired by Nathan Englander's "The Twenty-Seventh Man" when conceiving of the structure for this story.

18. Jews have been in exile for thousands of years. Today, "diasporic Jews" refers to Jews living outside the state of Israel. In this story, the "diaspora of the diaspora" refers to a city outside both Israel and New York City.

the forgotten pages of a Babel story, slowly sounding out each Yiddish character, transforming them into word, action, and thought. Outside on the empty streets below, an agonized group materialized, fraught with a sense of impending doom. A group made up of all the Yiddish greats, who had by that time been dead for decades or centuries: Mendele Mocher Sforim, the three Singer siblings, Kadya Molodowsky and Anna Morgolin, the anarchists like Baruch Rivkin, Emma Goldman, and David Edelstadt . . . too many to name; hundreds of the greatest Yiddish writers. They walked through the streets, marveling at the modern world. For what is even an "Urban Outfitter" or "American Apparel"? They were shocked to see such immodesty displayed behind department store windows.

"What is this dreck!" shouted Morris Rosenfeld.

"Where are we?" asked young Joseph Opatoshu, with wonder.

"Nu, where should one be but Brodvey?" mocked the tall, slender S. Ansky, pointing to a street sign.

"Clearly, I'm no schlemiel," said Opatoshu. "But what city is this, and where are all the people? Where are all the Jews if this is Nu York?"

A baffling silence befell the small but growing group, for they did not know the answers to these questions, nor could they even ask how they came to be in this new, strange place.

In the middle of Union Street and Broadway, they stopped to gaze at the bright digital clock on a bank that flashed "12:01," reflecting on the store windows opposite the bank. It was Sholem Aleichem, a former newspaper man himself, who first noticed the newspaper protruding from a trash can.

"Look at this newspaper," said Aleichem, retrieving it. "We are in Amerika, and this paper is dated 2018!" The group, which now numbered in the hundreds, assembled around Aleichem as he translated the article, titled "Polish Law Denies Implication in Mass Murder of Jews," for his Yiddish readers. "A new Polish law," Aleichem read, "was passed saying that anyone who implicates Poland or the Polish people in the murder of Jews during the Holocaust, over seventy years ago, may be fined and jailed for up to three years. Once home to three million Jews, it is estimated that over 90 percent of Poland's Jews were murdered in death camps in Poland. These camps were operated by German Nazis and Polish collaborators." Aleichem began heaving with sobs. Tears streaming down his face, he dropped the newspaper and fell to his knees.

The group, many having just learned the fate of the world's Jewry, and believing themselves to be indeed the last vestiges of *yiddishkayt*, started to weep and wail, to flail and beat their chests. How could such a fate befall them? Where was the Messiah now! Why has Moshiakh not yet come? Such betrayal!

Although these writers all held conflicting ideas on Jewishness and the modern world, they did hold as common belief that assimilation would end antisemitism. But look where they are now! Such a future—a world with flashy things, automobiles, scantily clad mannequins, and no Jews? Their trust in society to end all sufferings seemed now like naivete. With this realization, the large group's sadness flowed into weeping uncontrollable rage, and the writers attacked the streets.

It was Alexander Berkman who finally began, and with great precision flung his homemade steel-file dagger through the air, shattering the bank's clock facade, sending shards of glass and sparks showering down. Then injuring his fists, Chaim Grade took his grief out on the pavement, which pooled with his own blood and tears. Rachel Korn, a survivor herself, screamed out "My limbs tear loose in wild rebellion; all that was close to me betrayed me!" before sending a piece of concrete raging through the window of a Victoria's Secret. The applause of glass covered the sound of an igniting match lit by Celia Dropkin, as she set the store ablaze (but not without first looting it of scandalous bras and panties, which she used to veil herself).

Avrom Sutzkever cried out in grief, tearing his clothes apart as he walked down the street, punching out every side mirror and reflective surface, leaving behind smears of his own blood. His plight inspired the Singer siblings along with Avrom Reyzen and Itzik Manger to throw stones through car windows, kick in their headlights, jump on and dent their hoods and roofs, slash their tires with knives of broken glass, and with a collective rocking, flip the cars, setting them alight.

Atop one of these wreckages, Margolin stood, arms raised and looking toward the heavens, cursing God. In her deep, smoky voice she howled out, "Ancient murderous night, help me! Beguile him, entangle him, swallow him, beat him to death! And I'll bow to all four corners of space, and sing and sing and sing to life my praise of death," while Jacob Glatstein looted a watch and jewelry store, placing each piece meticulously in a pile before stopping Time with the bottom of his worn loafers. Finally, Rivkin lit several bins of trash on fire to memorialize a people and their many lives lost, weeping the Mourner's Kaddish and then editorializing God for his poor show.

The group trembled through the empty streets, now littered and aflame. And still the child remained in the room, reading, not having noticed the desperate commotion outside their window. But as the Polish, Lithuanian, Ukrainian, German, and Hungarian people await the last of the Shoah generation to die out so they may rewrite their own national histories, one by one each of the raging memorial candles were extinguished along with the authors who lit them and Rivkin's last fading words of "Yisgadal v'yiskadash . . ."[19]

THE VILNIUS CLOWN TROUPE

In my father's home, we were visited weekly by many people. Family and friends came, but more interesting to me were the schnorrers, or beggars: paupers who would tell their tales of misfortune—a sick child, a lost job—and traveling rabbis who came to visit from distant countries, where the small Jewish community was struggling to build a yeshiva or study house. These people would never come on Shabbos, but at other times, late on weekday evenings. My father would always, regardless of what was happening, invite them in and

---

19. Hebrew Aramaic, "yisgadal v'yiskadash" (magnified and sanctified) are the opening words to the Mourner's Kaddish. The Korn quote is from her poem "Searching." The Margolin quote is from her poem "Ancient Murderous Night."

offer them a shot of schnapps. Almost all these visitors came in search of money, and almost all had a story. Although he had little money, my father loved their stories and would give what he could, as my father was a pious man with a wife and nine children. As a child, I would stand behind my father and listen to his conversations with these worldly people as they weaved in and out of different languages— Yiddish, French, Hebrew, Spanish, and rarely, English. Rabbis were my favorite, as they were cosmopolitan and usually full of the best tales.

I remember one such rabbi who was always willing to tell a story. I don't remember his name, but I do recall his round, red face and long, white beard. Having been to my home already a few times, this rabbi would skip the appeals for money to my father and instead catch up on old things. He wore traditional clothing and spoke with a thick accent. On one such occasion, the rabbi spoke of a Jewish Yiddish theater troupe in Vilnius.

"During the dark years of Stalin," the rabbi said, "life for Jews was always topsy-turvy. One never knew when one could trust the regime, but one always knew that behind its back, was the keen-edged dagger of the Soviets."

For a short time, the state allowed the troupe to exist, but before long the troupe was forced to disband in a Soviet shearing of Jewish life. The troupe was greatly disheartened; not only could the actors no longer perform, but their beloved friend and director had been arrested and sent to a concentration camp. The theater troupe in Vilnius was affected, yet so were all, it seemed—Jewish poets, writers, and intellectuals. Dozens confessed under torture to anti-Soviet crimes and were sent to death. People will confess to anything under torture.

"It is said," the rabbi continued, "that there was little protest from Jews, and that is true. What could one do? But in Vilnius, a group of rabid antisemites had made their joy over this persecution known, parading around the city in song. They were met in the streets, though, by groups of Jews dressed in black."

"Dressed in black?" interrupted my father.

"Yes. Head to toe in black. Even their faces, like HaShem's, were obscured. But what I have heard is that Time suddenly manifested, as it does, out of nowhere."

In this case, Time appeared in the form of a line of police between the two groups, their backs turned away from the armed antisemites, brandishing their police weapons toward the Jews. Then something miraculous happened. The Vilnius theater troupe appeared from the crowd of Jews, dressed not in black but instead as clowns.

Full of color and without word, the troupe traipsed and paraded through the crowd and up to the Time of police. With their animated expressions and bizarre gestures, the clowns cut through Time and walked directly into the crowd of antisemites, who became confused by these clowns.

"From nowhere," the rabbi went on, "these Jews produced crow-bars and bats from their baggy clown clothes, and gave those *kha-zeyrim*, those pigs, a great new meaning of piety!"

At this the rabbi threw back his head in laughter. He recovered and finished. "But the troupe was arrested, though I do not know what became of the actors. And the theater was turned into a Catholic church."

My father reflected on this story for a moment, then stood up with a smile on his face, and gave the rabbi a good hug, saying, "Ah yes. The Catholic church—the most drab of all theater."

And the rabbi was at the door, laughing and stepping back out into the cold, brisk night.

THE LAGGER TIME

She worked in a factory, always looking down. The factory wasn't like any ordinary factory—none that she had ever known before anyway. How long had she been there? She wouldn't be able to tell you. For although she worked in a Time factory, the factory, it seemed, was void of time completely. Everything there was like clockwork— everything—not just the coming, working, and going, but the rank and file too were always under watchful eyes. There in the factory, she experienced no past, no present, and there was no sight of the future anywhere. No one knew when the day would be over or if it would just suddenly end early for them—and some, if they knew how, yearned for it to end so suddenly. Like the grinding mechanisms from behind the clockface, she worked. When walking, she walked briskly, always looking down yet never noticing her own two feet, which kicked rocks and snowy ash. If she were to look up, she would certainly be struck down by the horror of her fate mirrored in the faces of passing laborers; she would see the cloud factory over yonder with its ever-smoking, never-ending smokestacks that reached for the heavens, and she would think on her mother and son.

One day, for one moment (for who knows how long), the Time factory unexpectedly halted work. They would someday call it an uprising, but it was more of a beckoning. Across the many fields, at the camp where they slept each night, one of the crematorium smokestacks exploded and came crumbling down. Everyone looked up, including the overseers. She looked about herself and saw time as it was in that moment: its sky was a beautiful baby blue, faded by the casted colors of the rising sun, which complemented the turning trees of the nearby forest, and mixed with the freshly formed gray clouds that emanated from the nearby cloud factory.

With the oppressive Time lifted, nature sifted through its fissures. All the beauty stuck out to her and the others, even the guards, who nervously wrung their guns and looked about in bewilderment. But most of all, she noticed that the facade of Time had been peeled back to illuminate a futureless future, which bored its way into her mind. It did not last long nor did it bode well. With futures turned to smoke, Time is not burdened by her or the others; it merely allocates death without care. Knowingly, she turned toward her own feet and became overcome by the emptiness—a sheen of Time over time, the terror of knowing coated beneath a fabricated future that speaks: *Work makes you free.*[20]

---

20. This story is inspired by an account I read in Serafinski, *Blessed Is the Flame: An Introduction to Concentration Camp Resistance and Anarcho-Nihilism*

As a child I used to walk with Shabbos. Together we would walk side by side, dragging and looking down at our dirty feet—sometimes kicking rocks and dirt—keeping our hands behind our backs or twirling our locks that dangled from beneath our hats. We would talk about worldly things. Sometimes Shabbos would even tell me stories about the universe! Like which planets or worlds were made first, or which was their favorite (which was, in both cases, Pluto). As time passed, others like us yuntoyvim, holidays, came around, and they too met with us to talk about Torah things, to gossip about all that was happening. Our group was becoming ever larger with the passing of time. Mountains crumbled and seas trembled; the world was always changing and so were we. And with that change, some of the yuntoyvim fell to the wayside. People stopped caring or thinking about us, and we became obsolete in daily and yearly practices.

If you listen closely, the evening stars gather too, telling enchanting stories, gossiping about others—rulings, histories, teasings, lustings, and curses (it always seemed that they were cursing, and even making up new curses as if every night the heavens became a

---

(Berkeley: Pistols Drawn, 2016), 60: "On October 17, 1944, Hanna Levy-Hass, an inmate of Bergen-Belsen whose diary survived the war, recorded that her camp was put on severe lockdown and that rumors had circulated about a women's rebellion in the neighboring camp. The only evidence of this rebellion for Levy-Hass was the cessation of all regular camp activity and the glow of the crematorium, which operated nonstop throughout the night."

curse factory). But the light we see and stories we hear from some stars are mere echoes of a time from when that star once existed. There is no knowing which stars are dead and which still live—their light still unraveling to earth, their histories still told in each passing moment. The earth is wrapped in this light and these stories; they are what make us. One can see proof of this in the dancing flames of the *yuntif,* holiday, candles. With the clockwork of Time in motion, it is common now for people to stop listening to the stars, as they once had, and stop thinking of us as we too, becoming lost and faded like the stars.

Now I am old, and yet Shabbos and I still walk along (though there is not much of anywhere to walk to these days), our long locks flowing like the branches of a willow, and we talk of the old days. We try to remember the other yuntoyvim of yore. Shabbos recently said to me, "Six days of toil, but is this the work that HaShem intended for humans?" I did not reply; we merely kept walking the inner lines of the enclosing borders of our home. If not, I thought, then it was surely in Shabbos and the yuntoyvim that the exit from Time lies, into a world of Timelessness, ready to be sought—a gift awaiting acceptance.

THE GOLEM OF TRAVME

Once, when I was ten, my Aunt Sheyna sat me down on the floor of my grandparents' side room to tell me something quietly. For years my aunt, who had not spoken since the days of the camps, seemed to me to be brewing with secrets—secrets that I felt in my bones and made real in my dreams at night. My family called Aunt Sheyna crazy and prevented most contact between us. But like her, I was getting older, and so were all the other survivors. One day, when no one else was looking, we sat together, and with a grave look, she told me, "It's time I tell you about..."

I spoke aloud, "...about the war?"

"No. Not about the war, but about the *after war*—the time when I left the camp."

The after war, I thought. The war had seemed so distant to me then, a thing I could hardly understand, *barukh* HaShem, blessed HaShem. I became lost in my aunt's words. Today her words still echo in my mind, for they were words that I had been taught to fear, a history that I yearned to hear, words that no one had dared to speak to me before.

"On May 8, 1945," my aunt continued, "they announced to the world that the war was over, that soon normalcy would reign again. But as Jews, emaciated and traumatized, we could only set out wandering, many of us with nowhere to go. For us, this 'normalcy' was a cup of poison with two lumps of sugar. The war was not over. For Poland's Jews—those of us who survived, having been liberated from Polish death camps—we came home to find our houses and possessions, even our family heirlooms, taken by our Polish neighbors. They, moreover, threatened us! They asked, 'Why did you return? You should not have.' And many Jews were pogromed. And some Jews, such as myself, young and angry, had stepped out into a world that was no different from the one that I had been forced out of eight years prior; the only thing that I lacked now was my family and friends, leaving me with an emptiness that I filled with an ever-increasing thirst for blood."

"A new type of Jew began to spread across Europe and then the world: a ghost Jew, a dybbuk, a golem.[21] In this new world, I eyed every gentile on the streets, at the market, on their way to work, lying in the grass with a loved one. To me, they were all complicit with the Nazis, my enemy, *our* enemy. If the Poles didn't love the Nazis for invading their country, they were at least grateful to be rid of us!"

"Didn't anyone stop them from killing us?" I interrupted.

"After the war," my aunt went on, "things did not go back to normal as quickly as some politicians had hoped. There was great confusion. No one protected us. It was up to ourselves alone; it was up to myself, the wandering golem—the enraged—to brake Time. I did it all alone, and acted against anyone who I suspected of being complicit. I rarely planned it out. I hardly thought anymore. I would wait for them in the shadows or sneak up from behind—the camps never leaving me; it was a swift movement of the hand, the soundless glint of metal. I would even sit in on trials of people suspected of being SS to make my own judgment. Standing at the back of the mock courtroom, I would glare at the disgusting Nazi pigs. How I hated them! And when asked if anyone could identify the suspect, your dear Aunt Sheyna,

---

21. A dybbuk is a soul in Jewish folklore that has been severed from its body and walks the earth looking for a new one.

like a *meshugene tzadika*, would identify the suspect.[22] Then I would, myself, hang the Nazi pig from a telephone pole, tree, or building awning. I would stand there for some time and watch the swinging body, like that of a pendulum. Other people would watch too. Maybe they admired my handiwork; maybe they, like me, caught by the sight, found themselves back in the camps. I eventually kept a journal of all the Nazis I had killed: their names, the camps at which they had worked, accounts of their evil deeds. My revenge became my hobby."

"You see, my Rivkele, I am merely a golem—mute and strong. I am a creation of revolt and revenge. My thoughts are the words that my mouth could never sound. My flesh is formed in mud. My blood flows tears of the river Travme."[23]

As she spoke, I hardly noticed how tears formed in my own eyes, traversing the angles of my face and narrowly eluding my nose. I had told myself that I wouldn't write about these things anymore, but it lives within me. I can feel it growing inside me and creeping through my dreams.[24]

---

22. Meshugene tzadika is Hebrew/Yiddish for a crazy righteous woman.

23. Travme, in Yiddish, means "trauma."

24. There are many accounts of actions taken by Jews in the after war for revenge in order to stay the hand of additional pogroms, or simply out of grief and trauma from their experiences.

THIS TIME

It was slow. Time crept in as time crept out. Bits and pieces of it slipping away as best it could, only to be caught and brought back in the jaws of Time, as if Time were a real and living thing. It hadn't always been this way. In fact, there was a time when time was unchained and unquantified. It floated freely about, swirling around and shimmering in both the sun and moonlight, flirting about Scripture. Oh, how it would sometimes tickle your nose, time would! But time was capitalized by Time and became restrained, and soon there was plenty of work, which would soon, in a short scale of time, replace time altogether. Soon there was no time at all to study or play. One *had* to work. Because keeping the Sabbath means not working, things became much harder for Jews. It was work under Time that made us miserable—and not just us, but everyone. With the quantification of time came the quantification of our lives. One was forced to get a *job* to have even a home or food. The gentiles took pieces of time and saved them for themselves, and with Time did they build a new world—a world of kingdoms, countries, cities, and such. And they built banks to keep their Time—time prisons. They built real prisons too—human prisons—for people they did not like. This new Time floated, still, over everything so that one could not escape it. But as it is said, "We were forced into these bodies," and even more onto this land—exiled from our body. When the last of us are gone, though, there will be no one to repair what has been destroyed. We are a dybbuk of a diasporic people, and although we tried to keep our traditions, it was not long before Time's traditions crept into our lives.

ELIUI DAMM

There, in a dark room, within the dimensions of an ornate wooden box, hidden between two tenement buildings in Brooklyn, was finally a silence—a silence as if all that were left were the flickering consciousness of our beloved nayer rebbe (and myself, the little bird). He was not aware of my presence, nor were either of us aware of the large crowd that anticipated his wisdom. I saw those first words that he had spoken echo forth from the dark distance, louder and louder, until they retreated back into his own mouth—splitting into thought, breath, and Talmud—and resting again in their respective homes before he shouted them once more. I could see with my two black eyes those words protruding, about to explode from between his trembling lips, but instead of his voice, I heard the voice of hundreds or even thousands from across generations.

Thinking himself alone, the nayer rebbe pleaded with the void in a quivering cry of impatience: "Yidn!" spoke the rebbe, "The relics of light that we see in every evening sky, what we call the night's stars, are like the destruction of the Holy Temple, a great piling up—a burning memory of their own life and destruction. The Rogatchover Gaon says that the Holy Temple's destruction is not a onetime event, for time is a spiral.[25] Take the Holy Temple: every day, every night, every minute, every hour, every second we experience Its destruction as if we were there to see It destroyed. Those who destroyed It

---

25. Rogatchover Gaon, or Yosef Rosin (1858–1936), was a prominent Talmudic genius.

ripped apart Its fabric of existence, and with a fine hand wove their Time over our worlds, constricting us, as if a shroud had been tailored for the world, but one that only fits a young child."

When I heard the nayer rebbe's voice, in my throat I felt the constraint, the impossibility of my own existence—a feygele, a yid. So I closed my eyes to calm myself, but when I did I was struck by the horror that I saw! No, not just the *Beys Hamikdash*, the Holy Temple, in flames, but all the barbarisms of history committed against Jews and others. These images flickered alive like devils in my eyes, licking my skin and singeing my *peyos*, my sidelocks, with the smell of smoke choking my lungs.

"The Temple's destruction," continued the rebbe, "piles higher and higher every second, choking our prayers, as their Time clogs our arteries. It is our time that is like a body—ephemeral and malleable. It is soft and warm; it smells fresh, and it is escaping us. As the Lubavitcher of blessed memory once said, "God forced your soul to descend into your body, as the Mishna states: 'You were born against your will.'" The gentile tradition of Time is killing us. Every day we mourn the loss of the Temple, just as we do the trees and world that HaShem has asked us to care for and pray among. It is our prayers, unanswered, that pile higher everyday too, and still the Moshiakh does not come!?"

The rebbe's words I could hear, and yes, they raised my spirit, but it felt as if my soul had passed the veil and was being defiled by *sheydim* and dybbuks in Gahenna; my soul was being tortured by the sight of Poles, Ukrainians, Russians, French, and German pogroms.[26] Families defiled and slain, babies swung like *Kaporos*, shuls and Torahs pillaged and destroyed, and to see the world treat it as "progress," like it were a symptom of the 1940s.[27] My soul became infuriated, filled with hate for these murderers as well as a love for life!

"As the Lubavitcher once said," the rebbe went on, "'Jews are always expected to live with contradictions.' And we are contradictions. Just as HaShem has forced us into these bodies, gentiles have forced us unto these lands: a diaspora. We live between two worlds, between heaven and earth, this world and the next, the moon and stars. We are perched between the mountain of truth that hides HaShem's face, and the gentile world that both envies and despises us. It is with their Time that they despise us, preventing us from experiencing the holy era of Moshiakh. When Moshiakh comes, then HaShem will build for us a Palace of time—not just for Jews, but for everyone. For now, all we can do is cry out for Moshiakh and build the space for that Palace—the entire world. Look around us. Forced within the imaginable borders of this land, when one looks around, one can still see Its remnants."

---

26. Sheydim is Hebrew for devils. Gahenna is a valley in Judea where Judean kings sacrificed their children by fire; Christians would later interpret this to be "hell."

27. Kaporos literally translates to "atonement." It is a centuries-old tradition, and today controversial, in which a chicken is swung above one's head three times, slaughtered, and then donated to charity.

In imagining the nayer rebbe's words, I found there that boundlessness of Moshiakh, a suspension of Time and breath of air. I feel this unbinding in the lighting of the Shabbos candles. I feel it when my eyes are covered in the silence before the *bruchas*, the blessings, or in the quiet solitude of the yuntoyvim, or when I become absorbed in the text while davening, or in my own thoughts and imagination. I want more of this timelessness, but the smoke and screams clog my lungs, and the images from all time suspend my thoughts. I want to do something, but I find my wings unable to move. I feel I must do something, but what does the Torah of life, of truth, say about such a thing as revenge?

"A thing such as a country," said the nayer rebbe, "is not Jewish, nor are its borders. Nor is a state, law, or social constructs of gender or race. They are only made real by the light of their Time. All that is real is HaShem. We have lived within these confines for far too long and have suffered greatly. And so, yidn, I implore you to rebuild the Temple where you are, together, in our hearts! God has abandoned us, and Moshiakh is still not here. And so, ker a velt!—tear this world apart—as if you were there, as if you were Moshiakh, as if you are standing on the precipice of time, where one can see the destruction of the Temple, the divine body."

"*Ker a velt haynt!*—turn the world over now!" cried the nayer rebbe. "The suffering has gone on too long. Tear apart their world, their societies; tear apart their Time—the Time that chains us and HaShem, that dictates the every movement of our lives. Jews are not beasts of burden. We do not live to work. It is Shabbos and the yuntoyvim that unchain us; it is our Jewishness that frees us. *Menukha* defines and decrees our rest, but it also states that even on the holy day of Shabbos, one can destroy something, so long as there is no element of creation.[28] May we rid ourselves of Time and its traditions! Ker a velt! No more clocks. Toward the Moshiakh and a Timeless world—a world of possibility. It all must be betrayed! It all must be torn apart! Ker a velt haynt! L'chaim! To life!"

In my ears, my heart pounded and my insides were churned into a *beys oylem*, a Jewish graveyard, at the very thought of the nayer rebbe's pleading words. Like a forest fire, it spread throughout my body; those words affirmed my very existence—*an anarkhistishe yid un feygele*—and desire to turn the world over. But my desires had been stifled for so long by the oppressive clockwork of a society that allows for all the horrors to continue to pile higher and higher. Under this crushing heap of "progress," my heart agonized. Within me, I understood what needed to be done. From beneath the heap, I could see others like me, crushed, demanding the same thing of the other: ker a velt haynt!

---

28. "Indeed, according to the Jewish tradition, an act of pure destruction that has no constructive implication does not constitute *melachah* [work] and is not considered a transgression of the Sabbath repose (for this reason festive behaviors, even beyond Judaism, often involve a joyous and, at times, even violent exercise of destruction and squandering)." Giorgio Agamben, *Nudities*, trans. David Kishik and Stefan Pedatella (Stanford, CA: Stanford University Press, 2011), 105. Menukha, in Hebrew Aramaic, is often translated as "to rest," yet it is actually a state of being, not a verb.

*

Eliui Damm lives in the Pacific Northwest, where they strive for the era of Moshiakh and all its potentiality. Author of the zine Tohuvabohu: Chaos and Desolation // *Yiddish and Anarchy,* Eliui *is a writer, teacher, musician, and friend to all cats.*

INTERLUDE

ART OF

RESILIENCE

EZRA ROSE

WE WILL OUTLIVE THEM

The phrase "mir veln zey iberlebn" (we will outlive them) comes from the story of a Yiddish protest song from 1939; over eighty years later, these words remain a uniquely Jewish antifascist rallying cry. The creatures pictured are the Leviathan and Ziz, two legendary sacred monsters that are used here to represent the enduring survival and resilient power of the Jewish people and our stories.

*

Ezra Rose is an illustrator, zinester, and multidisciplinary creator living on a small farm in Western Massachusetts with queer chosen family. Their art explores monsters, magic, queer/trans identity, and Jewish culture, celebrating the marginal, and connecting to the symbols and stories of both past and present. For their portfolio along with links to their online shops and social media, see ezra-rose.com.

מיר וועלן זיי איבערלעבן.

ELIUI DAMM

MOUNTAIN GOLEM

Originally appearing in the zine *Tohuvabohu: Chaos and Desolation // Yiddish and Anarchy* (2018), this papercut was created for the short story "Timtum and the Golem," and included the caption "Inside a mountain, inside a shul—a mountain golem."

TASHLICH

This papercut was made for the zine *Tohuvabohu: Chaos and Desolation // Yiddish and Anarchy* (2018) to accompany the short story "Kol Nidrei," about assimilation and loss. A father and child cast their sins for Tashlich.

TOHUVABOHU

Two cats gaze at the moon before an undefined world and future, beneath branches of cherry blossoms and a banner proclaiming *Tohuvabohu* (chaos). They unknowingly sit, collecting dust, on the mantle of my *bubba* and *zeydy* (grandparents).

SMASHY DREIDEL

This image was borrowed from Andy Warner's "D20 Critical Hit," featuring a twenty-sided die that called to its dungeon master dice slingers, "Out of your basement, into the streets." Similarly, this version pleads with its Maccabean spinner, "Out of your caves, down with the Hasmoneans!"

*

Eliui Damm lives in the Pacific Northwest, where they strive for the era of Moshiakh and all its potentiality. Author of the zine Tohuvabohu: Chaos and Desolation // Yiddish and Anarchy, *Eliui is a writer, teacher, musician, and friend to all cats.*

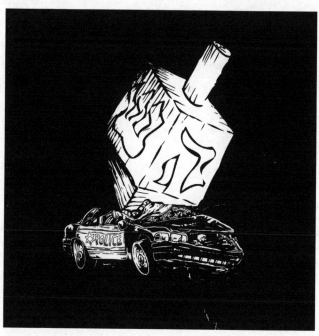

DAISY DIAMOND

DWELLING WITHIN

COILED TIME

In Jewish mysticism, the descriptions of the distinct yet interconnected/interdependent characteristics of G?d give form to why/how chaos and transformation exist in our world. The *sefirot*, the ten characteristics of G?d, represent revealed aspects of the divine. The relationships between the sefirot are impacted by the contradictory, emergent aspects of human relationships. Our relationships can heal/hurt us, just as they can heal/hurt the sefirot. This G?d is actively shaping and being shaped by the world. I draw and surprise myself. I remember what I know about the sefirot, and wonder what this meant to past generations—people who were forbidden from accessing this knowledge due to their gender, age, or lack of education. I visualize a sort of wise/compassionate/accepting "figure" that intuitively understands what is best for the collective rather than individuals/egos. I represent this with witchy/angel creatures of flight, who help me move through the chaos and contradictions of history that also exist within me.

*

Daisy Diamond is a queer, Jewish, reconstructionist arts educator and maker of things currently living in Philadelphia. Daisy thanks the queer, rad, anti-Zionist Jews who have helped them and many others find their way. More art can be found at @daisydiamondart (Instagram).

ANDREA MARCOS

CAN'T HELP BUT WONDER

The streets have probably been cobbled and bombed and cobbled over again since you walked around this city, but I can't help but wonder.

This print emerged from Andrea's search in Germany for their Jewish ancestors.

WITH A THUD

My grandmother died with a thud, feathers and blood on the windshield. A sky hazy and billowing. Orange and dark gray. The smell of burned, wet wood and debris, fresh in the wind. We were quiet, so close to the fire.

Touching on intergenerational trauma, this print revolves around Andrea's German Jewish grandmother.

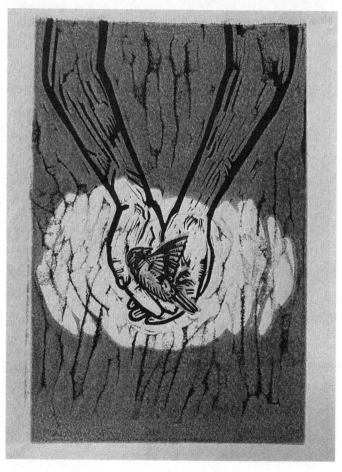

DIE PFEFFERMÜHLE

Die Pfeffermühle was an antifascist cabaret group formed in 1933 with a star-studded cast, including the famous actress Therese Geise along with siblings Erika and Klaus Mann. Erika wrote much of the content, which explicitly critiqued Adolf Hitler and the National Socialist Party. Shortly after forming the cabaret, the troupe fled Germany and was officially expelled in 1935 for expressing anti-Nazi sentiments as well as having Jewish, gay, and/or lesbian members. The group had to move around because its work was repeatedly seen as dangerous. In New York, for instance, Die Pfeffermühle was investigated by the FBI and House Un-American Activities Committee for its alleged Communist connections and sexual identities. This print celebrates queer antifascist resistance by continuing to tell the stories of queer cultural makers and their creative movement work. It honors those who make space for humor, rage, imagination, critique, and community to come together. May their memories be a revolution.

*

Andrea Marcos is a queer printmaker, nerd, educator, graphics maker, aries-youngest-child dedicated to collective liberation and radical imagination, and is located on unceded Duwamish land, Seattle, Washington.

ANDREA MARCOS

AMI WEINTRAUB

WE REMEMBER,

WE RISE, WE FIGHT

I created and wheat pasted this poster in Pittsburgh to mark the two-year anniversary of the shooting at the Tree of Life synagogue. It depicts a tree with eleven leaves falling from its branches to symbolize the Tree of Life and eleven people who died in the massacre. The tree is a papercut, a common Ashkenazi folk art tradition. The main Hebrew and English texts says, "L'dor v'dor [from generation to generation], we remember, we rise, we fight, Aleynu [it is upon us]." The text connects the 2018 murders to the history of oppression and violence that Jews have long faced. The phrase *Aleynu* derives from a major Jewish prayer popularized by the martyring of the Jews of Blois. In 1171, they were the first Jews killed because of the blood libel accusation. The Blois Jews recited the Aleynu while their neighbors burned them alive. Several days after these posters were put up on October 27, 2020, comrades noticed that many had been purposefully ripped, often slashed across the Hebrew, or torn down.

*

Ami Weintraub is a Jewish educator and anarchist living in Pittsburgh. They help organize Ratzon: Center for Healing and Resistance, a place for queer folks, youths, Jewish folks, and those from marginalized backgrounds to mend their jagged edges. Ami is a contributor to Rebellious Anarchist Young Jews (RAYJ).

JB BRAGER

DOYKEIT

The concept of *doykeit*—Yiddish for "hereness"—is taken from the pre–World War II Polish Jewish group The Bund, which believed that Jews have both a right and political commitment to live and work for change in the here and now. This drawing was created for the cover of the first issue of *Doykeit*, a submissions-based zine that speaks to the cross sections of Jewish and queer identification, and how this may inform anti-Zionist or Palestinian solidarity politics—and increasingly, a broader project of dreaming. *Doykeit* is a gathering place, a kind of biannual-ish yearbook. It has been the conduit through which I return to Jewishness so as to build community and affinity after being iced out because of my queerness and radicalism.

DIASPORA

This image was drawn for the cover of the second issue of *Doykeit*, which focused on the theme of diaspora, touching on topics such as home and "homeland," displacement and dispersal, and structural violence and remembrance. Being a diaspora Jew is not in and of itself a righteous opposition. If we are to be opposed to the colonization of Palestine, we must also commit ourselves to decolonial hereness ("doykeit"), to live and work for the decolonization of places like the United States, Canada, and Australia in particular.

*

JB Brager is a QT nonbinary femme, Jewish, Lenapehoking/Brooklyn-based comics artist and teacher. They make zines and weird queer feminist stuff, are a founding editor of Pinko *magazine and founding host of the Bluestockings bookstore comics reading series* In the Gutter, *and their work has appeared in many places, ranging from* The Holocaust in History and Memory *to the* Jewish Comix Anthology. *You can find them at www.jbbrager and @jbbrager.*

ANDREA MARCOS AND
WENDY ELISHEVA SOMERSON

CALL IN, CAST OUT

A linocut/digital collaboration, this piece was created to mark the new year of calling in justice with the shofar and casting out injustice with a Tashlich ceremony of casting rocks into a body of water.

*

Andrea Marcos is a queer printmaker, nerd, educator, graphics maker, aries-youngest-child dedicated to collective liberation and radical imagination, and is located on unceded Duwamish land, Seattle, Washington. Wendy Elisheva Somerson is a visual artist, writer, cat lover, and somatic healer in the Pacific Northwest who believes art can help us vision and create the world to come. See their work at @wendyelisheva or https://www.etsy.com/shop/TenderArt Encaustics.

MAIA BROWN

ANTIFA SHOOTING STAR

The three arrows symbol originated during the Weimar era in Germany for use in campaigns against Nazism—down with monarchy, capitalism, and fascism! The Star of David has long been a Jewish symbol, but in antiquity was not unique to the Jewish community. The star and the hexagon it creates at its center has been used by many traditions as an amulet image for protection. In this way, it is a symbol that links Jewishness to its history of interconnection with neighboring traditions and communities. Put this together and you have a meteor shower of Jewish-coconspirator antifascist action! The Yiddish reads "mir zaynen do" (we are here) from "Zog Nit Keyn Mol" (the Partisan Song)—an anthem for those Jews able to take up arms against the Nazis.

ANTIFA ALL STARS

Some of the first Yiddish I learned was the phrase "mir zaynen do" (we are here), from what many of us grew up knowing as the Partisan Song. The lyrics of "Zog Nit Keyn Mol" were written after the Warsaw Ghetto uprising by Hirsh Glick in the Vilna Ghetto in 1943. It later became an anthem for those Jews able to take up arms against the Nazis. The refrain of the song roughly translates to "our footsteps ring out, we are here." I love the resonance to the Palestinian wisdom of *Sumud* (steadfastness), understanding that to insist on living—on belonging and surviving—is a form of resistance. It is a call against erasure, an invitation across generations to choose life—a kind of life that fights until we all get free. May our footsteps be firm in our comfy punk shoes.

*

Maia Brown (she/her) is a Yiddish musician and educator on unceded Duwamish, Coast Salish land in Seattle, Washington, with a background in history and fine art. One member of the antifacist Yiddish trio Brivele and an elementary school art teacher, Maia wears different hats as a cultural worker and organizer in communities, combining research, direct action, art, education, and celebration.

GEM BEILA ROSENBERG

D Y B B U K

The dybbuk, a possession by an evil spirit in Jewish folklore, came to have some association with hysteria, an obsolete diagnosis that pathologized women's experiences. Here I reimagine an "evil spirit" as a fierce protector of women's liberation. She is a source of embodied wisdom, embracing darkness, the depths of the sea, and the glow of the moon. May we entertain our inner demons long enough to hear their message so as to deliver us to freedom. My "Dybbuk" collage is a part of a series titled *Lunar Sea* that looks at the connections between natural cycles, spirituality, and cultural mythology.

INFINITE ONE . . .

On the theme of environmentalism, this illustration revolves around the sacredness of the earth as a core Jewish value. Drawing inspiration from nature and Jewish cemetery imagery to comment on the relationship between life and death cycles, this work also depicts the equal importance of the material and spiritual realms. The quote is a recollection from ancient Jewish mystical writing (as cited in the book *Magic of the Ordinary: Recovering the Shamanic in Judaism* by Gershon Winkler). The animals represented are all threatened or endangered species in the state of New York, including the Karner blue butterfly (top left), piping plover bird (top right), and Massasauga rattlesnake. In the wild, the Massasauga eats live rodents, but is pictured here as an Ouroboros, a symbol of wholeness and infinity, with an egg, a symbol of creation. Although not an endangered plant, Myrtle is portrayed because it is sacred in our Jewish tradition.

GEM BEILA ROSENBERG

SHECHINAH

Shechinah is the feminine aspect of g-d represented here through the hamsa, a protective symbol against the evil eye adorned with pink, blue, and green eye shadow (in the original, full-color version). Ambiguous script marks the hand, representing the cross-cultural usage of this symbol throughout space and time as well as the hidden meaning behind mystical interpretations of the Hebrew alphabet. May this modern rendition of this ancient symbol be a source of protection from our oppressors' gaze and the erasure of women and gender-nonconforming people throughout history, including within Jewish text and culture.

GEM BEILA ROSENBERG

HAMSA

This hamsa plays with text as both visual and symbolic, emphasizing mind-body-spirit connection, the importance of text within Jewish religion and culture (mind), and the hand and eye as multisensory perception (body) as well as divine protection (spirit). "O," when verbalized, can be an expression of awe or release, offering reverence and gratitude for the wonders of the universe, or grounding and integrating us through vocalization or breath.

*

Gemica Beila Rosenberg is an artist based in Brooklyn, New York. Her visuals and performance explore healing, gender, and ecosystems. She received her BFA from California College of the Arts and is the curator of CARE as well as a Culture and Animals Foundation grant recipient. More of her work can be found at gemrosenberg.com and @gemica.rosenberg.

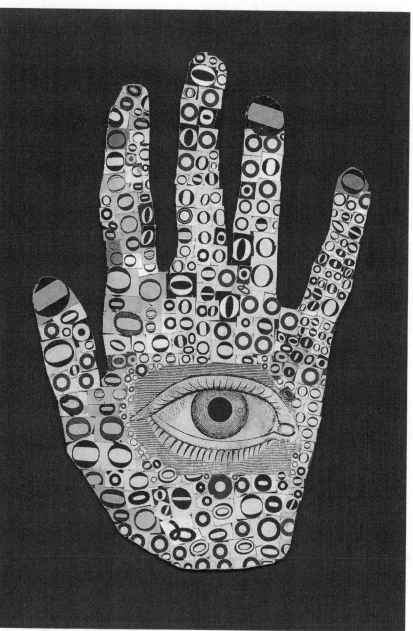

REBELLIOUS ANARCHIST
YOUNG JEWS (RAYJ) COLLECTIVE

CARE NOT COPS

This graphic was created by the RAYJ collective as a response to the Tree of Life synagogue massacre in Pittsburgh. It uses a collaboration of hand-drawn images along with text in both Yiddish and Hebrew.

*

RAYJ aims to bring people together to work for collective liberation, heal, and celebrate our culture and values.

בטיחות דרך סוליד'ריות

CARE NOT COPS

האבקו בפשיזם

BLACK LIVES MATTER! צדק צדק FREE PALESTINE!

תרדף

NO ONE IS ILLEGAL! TRANS LIVES MATTER!

As Jewish people we must continue to fight fascism, white-supremacy, and anti-Semitism.
We cannot live in fear. We cannot respond in fear.
We must build our community to resist with care, love, and bravery.
We know from history that protection of our community will not come from the reliance on the state or police system- we must support each other and build community using ritual, practices, and stories that have been given to us by our ancestors.

Let's sing, pray, dance, and grow in solidarity with all marginalized groups.

NRW

WENDY ELISHEVA SOMERSON

REPAIR

This linocut print speaks to the possibility of repairing our hearts in
the past, present, and future with the help of the crow, a messenger
between the worlds.

SHANAH TOVAH

As this linocut print suggests, on the day the world was born, Rosh Hashanah, we have the creative power, represented by the pomegranate, to shape new worlds, whether looking backward, in the here and now, or forward.

WENDY ELISHEVA SOMERSON

WE WILL OUTLIVE THEM

This linocut/digital image evokes Jewish resistance, drawing on the history of the phrase "mir veln zey iberlebn" (we will outlive them). For the story, see Ilana Sichel, "The Nazi History of This Yiddish Protest Banner," *Jewish Telegraphic Agency*, January 23, 2017, https://bit .ly/3qojjKF.

*

Wendy Elisheva Somerson is a visual artist, writer, cat lover, and somatic healer in the Pacific Northwest who believes art can help us vision and create the world to come. See their work at @wendyelisheva or https://www.etsy.com/ shop/TenderArtEncaustics.

PART II

RESISTANCE

AS

REPAIR

DIRECT ACTION

OF THE AGGRIEVED

CINDY MILSTEIN

Daily, and sometimes hourly, we are assaulted by the latest losses. It isn't simply that time and the news cycle have sped up due to so-called communication technologies. It's that we're in the crosshairs of history.

That history is being written on bodies—bodies that are piling up; sometimes our bodies, or those of people we love. It is etched onto place-names as our morbid shorthand—Charleston, Charlottesville, and Pittsburgh; El Paso, Minneapolis, Louisville, and Kenosha. That history transforms ballot boxes into the equivalent of coffins in countries like Brazil and the United States, and not only generates pandemics but also exacerbates their deadliness.

History seems to be happening to us, an increasingly out-of-control and inevitable narrative that doesn't end well, yet may end soon. For among other things, we are in a climate where even the climate itself is targeting humanity for disappearance.

There is little need, of course, to make any sort of accounting of the weight of this world. Already, in even gesturing at the enormity of this moment, we feel the fear and depression creeping in, the sorrow and hopelessness taking hold.

We've been taught by past rebels, to paraphrase Joe Hill, not to mourn but instead to organize. Today, though, given the magnitude of the new forms of brutality that we face, there's a palpable sense of despair about the possibility of organizing. All the weapons in our arsenal appear useless, outdated, futile. And even if we wanted to mourn, we come up against another contemporary conundrum: the theft of our traditions around grief—whether from colonialization and capitalism, or relatedly, Christian dominance—and thus the loss of knowing how to grieve well or at all, much less in community with others. We confront our inability to know how to share and hold our own and each other's feelings, much less the full range of them.

Yet we must.

Or rather, we don't have a choice. This crossroads is deeply impacting our hearts, whether we want to admit it or not.

Too many of us desperately try to stuff our emotions into the deepest recesses of our consciousness. Too many have been socialized to believe that feelings, especially those around grief, aren't acceptable, natural, or brave. Increasingly, the highly profitable "care industry" has convinced us that when we experience the worst of losses in our lives, we should "step back" to care for ourselves on an individual level, on our own. Our minds and bodies are turned into pressure cookers, waiting to explode in detrimental ways, further alienating us from each other in a time when we're extra isolated due to COVID-19.

We can, conversely, reclaim our capacity to be fully human in all our messy beauty and specifically as counter to this messy ugly time. We can self-determine to mourn and organize together.

This rebellious mourning begins with more questions than answers, because as anarchists and Jews, we are partial to questioning as itself a form of revolt, and because none of us knows any easy way out of this epoch. For instance, as Marko Muir, a longtime anti-eviction organizer and friend in the class war zone of San Francisco, mused, "Is it really hate we are fighting, or the system that creates haters with the power to erase us? Is it really hope we are longing for, or a collective grieving and more joyful militancy to fight back against that erasure?"

We can start with the question, Mourn what? To which we might reply, All that's being stolen from us, and all that we're told isn't grievable.

We mourn all the innumerable losses that aren't necessary to how we're structured as humans—say, to be born and die in our own good time—but indeed are the logical "collateral damage" of hierarchical forms of social organization—states and borders, heteropatriarchy and ableism, antisemitism and anti-Blackness, to name just a few. We mourn all that doesn't garner a marble monument or even a humble tombstone. We mourn all that we shouldn't have to bear losing and mourning, if we were to inhabit a far more egalitarian, humane world. We mourn all that we love.

And another starting point is, Organize what? To which we might respond, All that we need and desire, toward lives worth living, as direct actions of the grieving against the structural violences and losses that we are being compelled to suffer.[1]

We must organize everything for everyone, as mutual aid against the disasters that are battering us from all sides. We must organize forms of care and dignity that defy commodification, containment, or social control. That is, all that we can prefigure, empathetically and materially, to remain steadfastly side by side with each other, even or especially if the worst should occur. We must organize all that we love.

Mourning and organizing—not as separate moments, but as tenderly interwoven as the braids on our challah loaves and havdalah candles, as intimately attuned as when we mingle our voices in song, as hauntingly resolute as the blast of a shofar to gather us together. The voluntary conjoining of the two as a renewed promise of social love in how we go about experimenting, in the here and now, with forms of freedom against forms of fascism.

This is not mere hyperbole. It was put into practice in the wake of the Tree of Life synagogue murders, for one, when Donald Trump thought he could come to so-called Pittsburgh.

On Tuesday, October 30, 2018, just a few days after the massacre on Saturday, October 27, IfNotNow Pittsburgh, self-described as "part of a larger movement to end the Occupation" in Palestine/Israel, led a coalition of other groups in holding a shiva, a "Jewish ritual of mourning and community healing," in the streets. As IfNotNow explained,

---

1. The phrase "direct action of the grieving" is borrowed from historian Peter Linebaugh, whom I heard use it during a webinar in spring 2020.

CINDY MILSTEIN

212

"Today, President Trump will visit Pittsburgh. We do not need him. We stand with each other and mourn for our dead, and show up to protect each other.... We stand in solidarity with all the communities threatened by white nationalism."

Trump's motorcade was temporarily thwarted that day from reaching the Tree of Life by hundreds of mourners, in what one newspaper called a simultaneous act of "street protest" and "sitting shiva," noting that Trump was "turned away by the grief of a city that didn't want him anywhere near."

This is but one illustration of the power of collective grief, of ceremony and/as uprising. Or rather, the art of collective grief, when we permit ourselves to make visible and share the wholeness of our emotions, authentically, thus giving meaning to losses such as, in the span of that one week, the anti-Black murders in Kentucky and antisemitic murders in Pittsburgh, and making them more bearable. When we join hand in heart, noninstrumentally, without any effort to fix or cure what can't be undone, or pretend the loss didn't occur, or skip over our grief by leaping into action for the sake of action, but instead be witness to each other's excruciating feelings as inseparable from how we organize our lives and organizing.

Through that connection, through acts of tangible reciprocal care and active listening to each other's stories with curiosity, we form interdependent bonds. Those bonds, in turn, become co-teaching moments in how we can and should better safeguard each other, without need of state and capital, police and prisons. We remember we are not alone but rather, deeply have each other.

During a vigil in so-called Ann Arbor, Michigan, on the Sunday after the Tree of Life murders, Shira Schwartz, then a PhD student in comparative literature and Judaic studies, highlighted the notion of *shemira*: "to safeguard." As Schwartz put it, "We have many different forms of shemira in the Jewish tradition.... One example of this is the shemira for dead bodies between the time of death and burial. In this liminal space between death and burial we watch over each other. That is the time-space that we are in now."

Through such continual practices of collectively mourning our dead and collectively fighting like hell for the living, we'll increasingly find various possible answers to the many painful questions that we're being forced to ask these days. Moreover, we'll increasingly create our own time-spaces, peopled with self-organized and expansive forms of empathy, care, and love. And even if tentatively, such time-spaces will point toward a world in which our unnecessary losses are banished to the dustbin of history.

*

Cindy Milstein is a nonbinary queer Jew who aspires to the best of anarchism and fears for the entirety of fascism. They are grateful for the communal traditions within Judaism, across centuries and beyond borders, that speak to the whole of life, especially mourning. A slightly different version of this piece first appeared in Truthout *on November 6, 2018, at https://bit.ly/3q056xt.*

ON WASHING THE DEAD

JORDANA ROSENFELD

I never thought that I would be ritually washing and dressing dead Jewish people in the funeral home across from the Giant Eagle on Centre Avenue in Pittsburgh's East End. That it would become commonplace for me to gently clean the bodies of elderly women with warm washcloths—lifting the dirt from underneath their fingernails and combing their hair. That I would become conversant in the best practices for putting clothes on corpses. I never imagined that I would experience genuine love for these newly departed Jews whom I'd never met. And also for the living Jews who volunteer, like me, to spend their mornings in a cold windowless room with seafoam green walls and white tile, performing the centuries-old Jewish ritual of *taharah*.

There are more of us than ever before. Pittsburgh's independent, nondenominational Jewish burial society, the New Community Chevra Kadisha (NCCK), doubled in size in the immediate aftermath of the shooting at the Tree of Life synagogue, where three congregations—Dor Hadash, Tree of Life, and New Light Congregation—regularly held services. I am one of those who joined the chevra after the attack on October 27, 2018, seeking to displace images of violent Jewish death. I didn't know at the time that Jerry Rabinowitz, *z"l* (may his memory be a blessing), who died in the shooting, and Dan Leger, who survived it, had been founding members of the NCCK, but it soon felt meaningful that this was the space that many of us instinctively sought out in response to white nationalist violence. Over my time there, I've come to see care work and forms of mutual aid like burying the dead as deeply political activities, central to Jewish resistance to fascism in the United States.

When a Jewish person dies in Pittsburgh, we are summoned to the Ralph Schugar Chapel, the city's only Jewish funeral home. The back of the chapel resembles a large garage; its eastern wall rolls open to allow hearses to back up to an industrial cooler like the ones at the bakery where I used to make sourdough bread. Around the corner from the cooler is the preparation room—cold, stuffy, and small— where we find the *meitah*, the deceased, lying on one of two tables that look like porcelain but probably aren't, her whole body wrapped in a sheet.

We gather outside the preparation room to greet each other and read the meitah's obituary. Often, one or more of us has a personal connection to the meitah or her family, which we momentarily acknowledge. We ask the meitah for forgiveness if we fail to act according to her honor, even though we act according to our custom. We enter the prep room and remove the sheet around the meitah.

The primary responsibility of NCCK members is to perform the ritual of taharah. A Hebrew word, taharah describes a state of ritual purity. There is little halacha, or legal guidance, on performing the ritual, so the process varies from place to place, but everyone agrees it requires a lot of water. Before my first taharah, I felt most anxious about looking at the face of the dead. I worried that I would find some remnant of my mother, the only person whose death I've witnessed; it was my first time in the chapel since her funeral thirteen years ago. But in fact what I found most arresting in the face of my first meitah, and the others since, was its slackness. One rarely sees a human face making no effort to form any sort of expression. I thought of how often I hide behind my facial expressions, and was struck by both the profound intimacy of my relation to the meitah in this moment and fact that she was incapable of consenting to it.

We place a handkerchief over the meitah's face, as she is *nireh v'eyno ro'eh*, one who can be seen but who cannot see. We cut off her hospital gown and dunk washcloths in buckets of warm water at our feet. We drape her in a clean sheet, only uncovering parts of her body in order to wash them. We comb her hair, taking care to collect any strays in a linen pouch that will be buried along with her. We remove nail polish, clean up excess bodily secretions, and wipe off any schmutz left behind by medical tape. We turn the meitah on her side to wash her back; two people steady her by holding her body close, while someone else cradles her head in their hands. As we finish the washing, we recite a line from the Song of Songs: "Kulakh yafah rayati umum ein bakh" (You are beautiful, my beloved friend, and there is no flaw in you).

A warm affection blooms in my chest when we address the meitah as a beautiful, beloved friend, touching her body with the utmost care in a collective affirmation of her value. I wish that I could say I begin each taharah with love in my heart for the meitah. I arrive with little knowledge of her physical condition—whether she will have bags and tubes of bodily fluids still attached to her, open sores, or a strong unpleasant smell. The taharah calls me into an immediate physical intimacy, which forces confrontation with my learned aversion to aging, sickness, and death. The performance of the ritual challenges what I have been taught to find beautiful and valuable, based on the corporeal politics of fascism and white supremacy that dictate a hierarchy of bodies.

As I wash the meitah, it is rarely far from my mind that in her old age and perhaps sickness, she is the undesirable body; that we, in our Jewishness, are the undesirable bodies. Often, as I clean and consider her, I think of the violence inflicted on the bodies deemed undesirable. I remember the eleven Jews murdered in the building where I used to attend preschool. I remember Antwon Rose II, a Black teenager, who was shot and killed by a police officer near Pittsburgh just months before the shooting at Tree of Life. I think about Elisha Stanley, a Black trans woman, who in fall 2019 was found dead in downtown Pittsburgh. The enormity of the world's grief nearly overwhelms me, if only for a moment. I unfold a clean sheet to cover the meitah; I remind myself that this grief is not my only inheritance and I am not the only one to inherit it.

* * *

The Chevra Kadisha, meaning "sacred society," is one of the oldest Jewish mutual aid traditions still around today. K'vod v'Nichum, meaning "honor and comfort," an organization that provides guidance and support to North American chevra kadisha groups, traces Jewish burial societies back to thirteenth-century Spain. Chevra kadisha customs traveled across Europe with Sephardic Jews fleeing persecution and flourished in Europe over the next centuries, such that the chevra kadisha is most frequently remembered as an early modern Ashkenazic tradition.

Historically, in addition to performing taharah and ensuring that the deceased is never left unattended from the moment of death to the moment of burial, the chevra kadisha might help with sick care before the moment of death, or arrange for and execute the funeral process. Its members were not always publicly known; their anonymity manifested the symbolic truth that the entire Jewish community rose to support the mourners among them.

Aspects of those traditions traveled to the United States with Jewish immigrants and were once a boldly generative force in Jewish life. Early chevra kadisha groups in nineteenth-century New York City spawned comprehensive Jewish grassroots mutual aid groups that often took the form of landsmanshaften, aid societies for emigrants from the same areas of central and eastern Europe. These benevolent societies were more committed to popular participation and preventive community care than other Jewish institutions of that time, emphasizing democratic governance, offering the first opportunities for Jewish women to create and lead their own community groups, and providing financial support to vulnerable families before their need became overwhelming. Even as these organizations expanded well beyond their origins in the chevra kadisha, the funeral arrangement and financial support that they offered grieving families remained a significant draw for members. The values that Jewish communities enacted through this approach to death—among them, egalitarianism, radical compassion, togetherness, responsibility, and human dignity—allowed them to survive in a nativist, antisemitic system.

* * *

While we usually refer to the chevra kadisha's entire burial preparation process as a taharah, the word specifically applies to the ritual pouring of water. The taharah itself is rather brief. We fill our buckets with cold water and carefully pour it on the meitah, starting on her right side. We cover her in a continuous stream of water, which rolls off her body along the table's slope and into the sink, leaving her "pure."

We dry off her body and the table in order to dress her in *tachrichim*, simple white linen garments—a pair of footed pants, shirt, traditional robe called a *kittel*, long fabric belt, bonnet, and veil. According to the Talmud, in the second century CE, Rabbi Simeon ben Gamliel II asked to be buried in plain linen garments rather than the lavish, expensive burial clothing that was common at the time among those who could afford it. The use of simple tachrichim has since become customary, allowing all Jews regardless of their class or social status to be buried with dignity. The underlying principle that all are equal in death is fundamental to the chevra kadisha.

* * *

Upward mobility, suburbanization, and an increasing cultural focus on the family and individual over communal life contributed to the decline of Jewish immigrant mutual aid societies. Jews made new burial arrangements in the suburbs and gained access to private insurance coverage, diminishing the need for membership in fraternal societies.

These economic and geographic shifts fundamentally changed how we understand ourselves in relation to one another, and as a result, how we care for each other. Aspects of human life that used to be communal responsibilities, like ensuring that everyone can afford a dignified burial, became the responsibility of increasingly atomized family units. For many assimilated Jews, this move away from mutual aid as an organizing principle of community life tracks with an increased investment in white supremacist systems of power that enforce deadly hierarchies of human value.

Just as Jewish burial traditions provided a foundation for structural resistance to antisemitism, my participation in Pittsburgh's NCCK has helped me see the ways that I am invested in the logic of white supremacy. This work has pushed me to question who I deem deserving of care. To whom do I feel obligated to give my care? For whom do I show up? For whom am I willing to take a risk? So far, I have not always liked the way that I answer those questions when I'm being honest with myself. They expose the extent to which I buy into myths of self-reliance, accord value to myself and others based on what we produce, and tacitly accept the suffering of people of color within the dominant racist system.

In grappling with these questions, it is sometimes tempting to think that understanding white supremacy is the same as unlearning it. But I know that I'm not going to think my way into an antiracist practice; thankfully, the chevra kadisha has given me tools to act my way into it. Since the shooting at the Tree of Life, I have found that loving and intentional care for the bodies of people targeted for white supremacist violence is a powerful catalyst for personal and political transformation. We can unlearn hierarchies of human value by deliberately flouting them, refusing to allow the logic of white supremacy to dictate who deserves our care.

Our burial practices offer more than a way of dealing with the dead—more, even, than a connection to tradition. They are active antifascism, standing in defiance of the dehumanization of ourselves and others. Doing the seemingly mundane "care work" of feeding, burying, and loving each other, as disability justice organizer Leah Lakshmi Piepzna-Samarasinha writes, is "not a sideline to 'the real work' of activism, but the real work of activism" itself. The explosion of growth the NCCK experienced after the shooting shows that we instinctively understand that how we care for each other has great political significance and resisting fascism is about much more than tearing down our system; it's also about building a new and better world.

*

Jordana Rosenfeld is a writer and community organizer in Pittsburgh. A version of this piece originally appeared in Jewish Currents. *More of Jordana's writing can be found at www.jordanarosenfeld.com.*

JORDANA ROSENFELD

DAILY JOYS AND

TINY REBELLIONS

ELIAS LOWE

It's the middle of autumn, when the light gives ordinary objects new tones. I'm falling in love, and the whole world is vibrating. Dead leaves fall to cover the ground as I unearth the thrilling awareness of my own capacity for autonomy, through traditions that feel as familiar as they are new.

I feel as though I'm waking from a nightmare, soaked in sweat yet relieved, only to find that I'm inside another one. This nightmare is different, though; it's lucid and communal. I feel the brokenness of the world and finally understand it as the source of brokenness within me. I'm coming home to myself. I tiptoe into ritual spaces and infoshops. I mouth prayers and chants and songs.

The first time that Ami and I hang out, I sleep on their messy brown carpet. We hardly know each other, but I'm leaving a partnership and shared bedroom, and need a place to stay. I sit alone in their room, where Russian and Yiddish study sheets cling to the walls. I stare into the foreign shapes that are somehow letters. Ami gets home late, frustrated after a collective organizing meeting that turned hostile toward their unwillingness to collaborate with the university.

They sit on the floor, leaning against the bed, with flyers and clothes scattered around them, and I join them there. We talk for hours about the various worlds that we inhabit, traumas that inhabit us, and meta-analyses of our lived experiences. Our conversation is as joyful as it is serious, offering a sanctuary from the intensity of the topics. In the early hours of the morning, we both confess, hesitantly, that we believe in God and crave more ritual in our lives. I'm not even sure that *we* know why we believe in God, but it feels undeniable. God, for us, means collectivity and liberation—the power of community, the ineffable beauty and pain of life.

Less than a year later, in August 2016, Ami and I are dragging a mattress down the sidewalk in the blistering heat to move into 3210 Dawson Street. The home, like the house number, has the urgency of a countdown. *This is promising,* I think. *A whole new world,* I believe. Everything is glowing and filthy, from our bodies to the house. On the porch that night, we vow to use the enormous, dusty space to organize and grow ourselves into *true* revolutionaries. Such is the delicious flavor of youthfulness.

Our new living room is small and rodent infested, but we still gather warmly with others for our first Shabbat, bringing challah and wine and dinner. While I run back and forth from the kitchen to check on the still-undercooked potatoes, people sit on an assortment of mismatched chairs. There are six of us, and we don't know each other at all. Yet everyone, aside from myself, knows the ritual and songs. I am just starting to study Judaism, captivated by the ways that it relates deeply to the earth. I've recently learned that an ancestor of mine was a rabbi in Kiev, and my great-grandfather renounced all things ritual, erasing God from his vocabulary with World War II. Shabbat is still a mystery to me.

When the prayers begin, I don't know the words. My face flushes red, and I retreat to the couch. Oh how lonely it is in our togetherness! Closing my eyes, I listen to the new sounds and syllables, and grasp the hands of those beside me, craving a tradition that will pull me into comfort and, as a queer person, chosen family.

I lay down that night with insecurities and questions. Do blood ties to my ancestors matter? What are the ways that my great-grandparents prayed and communed? Did they speak Yiddish, German, or a language I've never considered? Did they hide and survive in order to carry on their traditions?

* * *

It's autumn again when Donald Trump is elected. Ami and I return to 3210 Dawson around four in the morning with scratchy throats from shouting, and heavy fears that supply new gravity. We lay in bed consoling each other. "You have to promise, even if it gets really bad, that you'll stay," Ami whispers. "I promise," I reply. I know that in so few words, Ami is anticipating the rise in antisemitism that's to come with Trump's presidency. I stare at the ceiling and feel the cold air seeping through the poorly insulated windows. I am afraid too, for Ami and myself, but I don't yet understand the scope of the anxiety.

Well before the election, we had planned a march at the end of November against student debt, and decide to carry it out despite the sudden change in political climate. The night of the march, we're energized even though our numbers are low. We snake through the University of Pittsburgh neighborhood using side streets and passageways to throw off the police. We approach a student building, and someone runs back and forth through the crowd, screaming "occupy!" I stand to the side below the darkening sky and look at the walkway connecting one university building to another. It's unclear if the police have locked the doors—a preventive routine of theirs during actions. My body pulses with adrenaline as the crowd rushes by me. Soon the doors open, and I find my way into Towers Lobby, described by Pitt as "a social crossroads."

We enter like a flock of birds, seemingly certain and together, although we're unsure of what to do next. Ami jumps on a table, and other queer and trans students leap up to join them. They begin to shout, "We're reclaiming this space. We are here to talk with one another, share with one another, learn with and from one another." Bodies bump against each other as more people pile into Towers Lobby. Ami continues, "It is in these slight cracks and fractures that great ideas grow. It is here that we hatch our plans for the next revolt. It is here, in unindoctrinated spaces, that we can truly meet one another, see one another, and see who we truly are, maybe for the first time in our fucking lives!" Their voice raises, and people wave black flags and dance with cardboard signs. It feels momentarily like freedom. We shout, "You can't stop the revolution." And then we start to sing, "Don't walk in front of me, I may not follow," almost intuitively turning to the same song that we do on Shabbat.

Reflecting on this action, I see how it was the catalyst for the braiding of Jewish and anarchist rituals in my life. I look at the video footage and see the joy on the faces of friends who I've since lost touch with, noting the specific words we all used, moved by the delight mixed with rage. I see relationships now broken by conflict, distance, assimilation, and loss of hope. "Don't walk behind me, I may not lead," we continued to sing.

That evening, we're able to give speeches, laugh, cheer, and sing this song before the police charge us. We had yet to reach the Hebrew verse when they pulled out their weapons, used their handcuffs, and arrested our friends. "Out!" they yell in deep tones. They push their bikes against our bodies, and we tumble on top of one another.

The rest of the night, we sit in the circle of mismatched chairs at 3210 Dawson, making tea, calling the jail, and singing. "Just walk beside me and be my friend." It's as if our Shabbats had been a rehearsal for another type of respite. We sing as we rest and wait to hear from our friends. We take care of each other the best we know how. "Together we will revolt again," our voices go on.

* * *

Following the action, there are dozens of other arrests in Pittsburgh. From noise demos to Trump's Inauguration Day, our community seems to be targeted hard. The state's crackdown feels all too palpable here, and I swallow a sense of cynicism regarding symbolic protest.

On a rainy Saturday soon after, I attend a march against climate change. It is dull, as expected, and I spend the bus ride home feeling bleak, wasted of motivation.

The next day, I'm sitting in my favorite coffee shop, watching the regulars with loneliness and tender appreciation. I strike up a conversation with Sandy, who has a way of talking excessively without self-awareness, and explain the feelings in my gut. I tell her that the repetitive, ineffective tactics have made me feel resentment toward everyone and no one in particular. I sigh and raise my hands in the air as I trail off. She responds with many random stories, long and detailed, and I almost stop listening. But somewhere between the opinions about Trump's recent tweet and details of her hometown, she mentions that marches are important *rituals* for our movements. This word grabs my attention, softening my heart. I carry the idea with me on the gray walk home.

After this conversation, the connections between anarchism and Judaism became even more evident. Direct action, such as occupying a student building, and pausing for Shabbat both speak to the need for rest—rest for the earth and its people, taking time and space back from capital.

While I felt the power of Jewish ritual in my body, I searched for answers in books too. I learned that Judaism has laws and practices that are in conversation with the land. Sukkot started as a holiday to mark the summer crops and prepare the fields for winter. Pesach began with the full moon during the month that barley was to be grown. Our ancestors ritualized the protection of the earth through creating structural intimacy with the cycles that give *us* life. The holidays I was growing to know had neither been invented nor co-opted by capital. And the ritualized resistance of marches and actions felt as important as ritual practices of prayer and rest. I didn't have to look far to see that the Torah demands rest and justice.

* * *

> *There is a realm of time where the goal is not to have but to be,*
> *not to own but to give, not to control but to share, not to subdue*
> *but to be in accord. Life goes wrong when the control of space,*
> *the acquisition of things of space, becomes our sole concern.*
> —Rabbi Abraham Joshua Heschel

I had imagined we would take over Towers Lobby for a long time. But the university could not stand the creative reuse of the space. Its police hit us hard with batons and bikes. When we stood outside the building, some of us on our knees in panic or pain, a plainclothes cop pointed a handgun at our heads. We left Towers Lobby with injuries to our bodies and minds, yet while we were inside, the tables became mountains for us to scream from, and the building's harsh white walls echoed our song. Towers Lobby, though, is not ours, nor anybody's, and keeping it was not the point.

There is something organically anarchic *and* Jewish about not needing to own any space, but instead borrowing or passing through, in ritual, in protest. This is how both traditions are able to survive. We use the ruins of postindustrial cities, the former forests that are now highways, and university buildings of the world to make temporary sanctuaries. To squat. To create. To sing together.

In Pittsburgh, the already-massive corporate university is always acquiring more and more space, moving toward a near monopoly of the city. Pitt has a twenty-year master plan that involves spending millions of dollars to stretch up the hillside, displacing entire neighborhoods of primarily Black people. The online maps show the areas that the university currently owns and those it intends to buy in bright red and blue circles.

While looking at Pitt's gentrifying maps, I'm reminded of Israel's expansion into Palestine, and think of how power consolidated can corrupt and co-opt anything it needs to. How the violent acquisition of more and more space by the Israeli state is so at odds with my community's understanding of Judaism.

Judaism offers us blessed tools for healing and fighting, but they are located amid rather than above the violence of history. Here is where communication between anarchism and Judaism becomes powerful as well as imperative. What happens when we renew Judaism with anarchism, and when we renew anarchism with Judaism?

I hope that Pitt's neocolonialist project will continue to be resisted through marches, occupations, unions, and more. Lately, when I'm in the street, I let myself shout for the ritual of shouting with other pissed off, hurt people, and understand the worth of this ritualized resistance. Sometimes, halfway through, on Shabbat or not, I feel swept back into thousands of moments that pile up and combine with other moments when the stars were in the same exact position. I can feel myself travel through time, to eras before skyscrapers, bombs, and police, or among it all, in persecution and resistance—toward all the people who have performed the same rituals, wherever and whenever they could.

As Jews, queers, anarchists, anticolonialists, and anyone else with a commitment to justice, we can find cracks and doorways—rituals leading to renewed old worlds. These cracks and doorways, handed down in whispers, act as great liberators. We enter the past as we prefigure the future, critically and collectively, holding hands and breaking bread with intention.

* * *

It's 2019, and strangers are crowded in my apartment, moving restlessly between couches and the floor. It's Friday night, Shabbat, and we're waiting to sing ourselves out of the room. My home is full of Jews, anarchists, and queers who all share the common denominator of painfully floating through a world that has othered them.

Isaac is here, a young trans boy who is three months on testosterone. He sits in his baggy blue jeans on the tattered blue sofa eagerly nodding at no one in particular. Neither Jewish nor anarchist, he has been boldly navigating his changing body in spaces void of queer people. I worry about him feeling alone in this togetherness.

Ami, confident and bashful, gets everyone's attention. We gradually form a circle with our bodies, and the chatter calms. After lighting candles and and us all uncovering our eyes, Ami leads a song that pulls us all into vulnerable comfort. Isaac sings too.

Inside the hills and houses of Pittsburgh, we've created a "third space"—not just Jewish, not just anarchist, but Jewish, anarchist, and queer. As Jews, we hold rituals that have survived through resistance and persecution. As anarchists, we erase borders between each other, even if just for a song. And as queers, we know how to love hard. In this way, boundaries of all sorts can momentarily soften.

Inside this third space, people have come and gone. Hearts have been broken, and some conflicts have hardened. The despair can feel boundless. Yet we continue to celebrate Shabbats, just like the moon continues to wax and wane, making our own container for the pain.

*

Elias Lowe is a genderqueer writer, activist, and committed friend based in Pittsburgh. They are currently working as a substitute teacher, and trying to make meaning out of daily joys and tiny rebellions. Elias helps organize an abolitionist bail fund and is deeply interested in collective healing through transformative justice. In their free time, they explore what it means to be surviving right now through intentional community building and creativity. Elias dedicates this piece to all the rebel Jews of Pittsburgh who have so often given them homes, and offers a special thanks to two people who made this essay possible: Ami, for allowing Elias to write about them, and Tahel, for holding Elias accountable to living out liberatory dreams.

ELIAS LOWE

RITUAL TECHNOLOGY FOR

A LIBERATED FUTURE

JAY TZVIA HELFAND

This is for us—we who are *timtum, feygele*, freaks, queer as fuck, trans and gender nonconforming (TGNC), and many more words that we claim, past and future.[1] Words still held in the jaw, words in the space between night and day, words saturating the soil, mineral thick with promise, words ushered in as a sigh by the waving grasses, in the gush and tumble of rushing water. Our bodies are on the body of the earth. Our bodies are woven into the web of life, into *etz chaim*, the tree of life, into our tradition. Just as resistance and longings for freedom have always existed, so have we.

For us—who have not encountered some or any of these words, we get to claim and practice belonging here. You are enough here—in your Jewishness and queerness, your transness and gender nonconformingness, your anarchism and radicalism. You are enough here.

---

1. Timtum is a Yiddish word for genderqueer, and has been reclaimed in trans and queer Jewish communities. See Micah Bazant, *Timtum: A Trans Jew Zine*, 1999, https://bit.ly/3pYjF4x.

For us—who may wonder, why ritual in these times, for us as anarchists, as Jews and revolutionaries? The answer lies in practicing ritual, in the doing, more than in the words themselves. Our rituals are tools to carry culture. They offer technologies for us to wield our power, channeling legacies of resistance. They invite us to drop into our feeling and longing, moving with precision and spirit toward the world that we're fighting for. Our questions themselves are also their own Jewish and radical ritual technology. You are enough here.

This is for us—who feel in our marrow, in our deepest gut, how our fights are connected. Jew, queer, anarchist, revolutionary, held alongside many varied and even contradictory identities, with a clarity that never again means never again for anyone. Never again for anyone.[2]

For us—for whom hope is a narrow bridge and a practice. We who experience spiraling diasporas within diasporas, as we are exiled for our anti-Zionism, our queerness, the ways that we threaten white supremacy as it moves through hegemonic Jewish religious and cultural institutions. For how we move and don't move, how we fuck and don't fuck. For how we contend with and resist what Hannah Arendt called the "banality of evil."[3]

We cultivate homefulness, *doykeit*, hereness, where we are. We

---

2. Never Again for Anyone is the name of a campaign organized by the International Jewish Anti-Zionist Network. For more information, see "Never Again for Anyone," IJAN, https://bit.ly/2V2PfzS.

3. Hannah Arendt, *Eichmann in Jerusalem: A Report on the Banality of Evil* (New York: Viking Press, 1963).

breathe into our hearts and our bellies. We nurture our depth of feeling and stretch out toward our longing. We lay claim to a lineage beyond a singular identity around suffering, beyond exceptionalism. In our clarity, tradition, and liberation, there is joy. There is radical amazement.[4]

These words are for us, all those at our backs, and those future ancestors, those to come.

Zikrona livracha; may your memory be a blessing. You are not forgotten. We remember and honor you—you who make us possible, who we make possible as we live inside of practices to honor your memory.

* * *

I offer this ritual to you, especially those of you taking estrogen (E) or testosterone (T). I do this ritual as part of taking my T shot every week. I invite you here with me, and honor specific lineages of these words and practices along the way. Thank you for your accompaniment, and also the ways that you adapt this for your needs.

SET YOUR SPACE WITH STONES AND CEDAR

Our tradition has many technologies to honor those who come before us. In Ashkenazi practice, stones are portals between worlds. We often place stones on the spaces where our dead are buried. Cedar

---

4. As Rabbi Abraham Joshua Heschel (1907–72) observed, "Our goal should be to live life in radical amazement."

has been used to invoke boundaries and protection since ancient times.[5]

If you don't already know the names of the original peoples of the land that you inhabit as you contemplate gathering stones and cedar, go find out. If you are not Indigenous, consider how you are participating in transforming the ongoing impacts of colonial genocide in which you are complicit.

If you choose to gather stones and cedar, invoke a *kavanah*, intention.

Consider: What does this kavanah mean for you, and how does it connect to what you care about? How can your invocation of portals and boundaries support your kavanah?

GATHER RITUAL OBJECTS WITH YOUR T OR E

Arrange stones, cedar, and your hormones alongside other ritual objects that hold meaning. I set mine alongside a havdalah candle made by Jonah of Narrow Bridge Candles.[6] I leave this candle unlit rather than lighting it at the end of Shabbat, as is customary for many people. I do this as a reminder that my rest is holy as a chronically ill person.

Bring your hormones and needles to that space with other medicines too, including tinctures and herbs.

---

5. I learned about stones and cedar as Jewish ritual tools to access ancestors from Taya Mâ Shere with the Kohenet Hebrew Priestess Institute. For more information, see http://www.kohenet.com/.

6. For more information, see https://www.narrowbridgecandles.org/.

LIGHT A CANDLE

Lighting candles has served as another tool used since ancient times. After the destruction of the Second Temple, marking one beginning of diasporic Judaism, lighting candles has offered a way to hold the sacred fire wherever we are.

Consider: What does homefulness look and feel like in your body, in relationships, with the land? Feel into your lived experiences or practice imagining them.

GROUNDING PRACTICE

As is most supportive for your body, sit or lay down in front of your ritual objects. For those who are able, sit with the back of your body in contact with a chair or against a wall, with the soles of your feet on the ground. Find a posture that invites more of a sense of ease and gentleness in your body. For a lot of us, this is by no means simple. Explore a posture as feels supportive to your kavanah.

Take three deep breaths, elongating the exhale. Let your jaw soften and belly get more full. Lean back if you are seated or against a wall.

With your inhales and exhales, imagine widening out to your edges, filling out from the top of your spine through the base of your feet, feeling the back of your body, and side to side of your ribs.

If it is hard to notice what is happening in your body, that's OK too.

Consider: What helps you to know that you are here right now? Sensations of warmth or coolness, movement of your breath, sounds, contact of your body against the ground, or feeling of texture, such as clothes on skin? If pain is there and it feels supportive, acknowledge that pain and the edges of it, along with the places where there is less pain.

SAY THE SHEHECHEYANU ALOUD, A BLESSING FOR THE FIRST TIME

N'vareykh et eyn hachayim shehechianu, v'kiyamanu, v'higianu, lazman ha-Zeh.
Let us bless the source of life for giving us life, for sustaining us, for bringing us to this time.[7]

Recall an ancestor, blood or chosen, or someone from your own life who helped you to feel possible, maybe from when you were a kid—a person whose gender presentation or affect invited some seedling of hope, or some question mark of what might be available to you. Feel them at your back. Imagine those who invited that sense of possibility for them.

Consider: What helps you to feel your dignity, interdependence, and aliveness? What kind of elder do you want to be? What kind of ancestor? What do the shadows of your dance with life and death teach you about arriving here in this moment?

---

7. Wording crafted by members of the International Jewish Anti-Zionist Network's liberation Haggadah. See "Legacies of Resistance: An Anti-Zionist Haggadah for a Liberation Seder," IJAN, https://bit.ly/3nQUGy8.

DRAW OUT YOUR SHOT

Feel your feet on the floor, notice the objects in front of you, invite the jaw to soften, and notice your mood.

Consider: What are the material and ongoing struggles for us now, and what were they for those before us, in order to make our access to gender-affirming medical care possible? What conditions of our lives were transformed through our fight and through fighting to win for all of us?

SING "ELOHAI NESHAMA" BEFORE, DURING, OR AFTER YOUR SHOT

Elohai neshama shenatata bi tehora hi.
The breathful soul that You, living source of life, has given me is pure.[8]

As you sing, bring your voice deep into the low belly. Sing for yourself—the present you, and the past and future you. Sing for your life, your body, your innate and unshakable dignity and belonging.[9] Sing for your hereness and any amount of awayness that moves in you. Try

---

8. To listen to "Elohai Neshama," see Let My People Sing!, "Elohai Neshama by Sol Weiss," https://bit.ly/3fBbB5e.

9. This language comes from generative somatics, a politicized healing organization rooted in growing movements for justice and transformation. For more information, see http://www.generativesomatics.org/.

to take it in, even a little. You are building a practice. As you are generous with this practice, the practice will offer generosity back to you.[10] Invite your jaw to soften and some gentleness toward yourself.

Consider: Where do you feel the vibration of your voice in the body? Are there certain thoughts, images, or sensations that show up as you sing for younger or older versions of yourself? What people, or more-than-human kin, help you feel connected to this song for yourself?

GROUNDING PRACTICE

Sit with the silence after your song, after your shot. Take three long breaths, elongating the exhale.

Consider: Where does the breath move in your body on the inhale and exhale? What does the space in between the breaths feel like?

BLOW OUT YOUR CANDLE

Recall your kavanah, your intention.

Consider: What do you feel in your body? What, if anything, has shifted? As you breathe into the space of the back of your body, offer yourself appreciation for your effort.

---

10. This concept of reciprocal generosity with ritual practice emerged from a conversation with Emiliano Lemus. They shared that when we are generous with time, time is, in turn, generous with us.

*

Jay Tzvia Helfand comes from a lineage of revolutionary queers, anti-Zionist Jews, and sick and disabled people. They honor the complex ways that their ancestors have survived and carried culture to make their life possible. Jay is a writer, plant nerd, somatics practitioner, and facilitator. They have organized inside a number of land-based racial and economic justice spaces in the Bay Area and Minneapolis, including the White Noise Collective and International Jewish Anti-Zionist Network. They also rest, garden, read poems, and walk by rushing streams in the woods. They live on Chochenyo and Karkin Ohlone land.

LAST OF ELUL

MIKVEH WARSHAW

They are called together by Rivkah, their sister. They come to dip
apples in honey and plead with their god for sweetness. A sweetness
that they know will be a creation of their own—moments they must
share in order to keep their balance in a shattered world. Miriam's
hands are covered with flour. It is her first time baking challah. She
makes a powdered handprint on her heart as she pauses in gratitude
at being surrounded by other trans women for the last of Elul, the last
month of the Jewish year.

* * *

Dear girl who belongs,

I remember the first time that I saw you. You were lined up holding
one of the too-familiar protest signs of 2009 contra the Israeli massacre in Gaza. You had long dark brown curls and were tall—as tall as
me. You had a red, green, and black Palestine bracelet on. You looked
like you knew why you were there, what you were doing, and how to
do it. I gasped. We never met. I never was good at going to protests,
but if I were to go, it would be because I want to see you again.

* * *

A few weeks earlier, Miriam sits under the full moon of Elul staring at her chipped nail polish. She still tells herself there is valor in her self-rejection. Miriam has a recognizable trans girl's gait—that of an anxious girl who knew she was not a boy, but was treated like one for decades. A girl who acquired a radical punk politics in middle school, but grew up in an assimilated family that taught her not to impose her will, not even on herself. Miriam is the kind of girl who wrote love letters at home on Friday nights with no intention of sending them. Even though she lived through the 2010s' trans women celebrity bubble, Miriam still holds onto the toxic belief that only other girls get to be girls. Even though the bubble would not last, that bubble saved a lot of her ex-bandmates lives by getting them on Affordable Care Act estrogen.

Recently Miriam hasn't gone any closer to a Jewish ritual than lighting a candle and noticing that it happens to be Friday night. As a child, she was kicked out of her conservative temple's Hebrew school for fighting. Miriam never saw any reason to return to shul. Her dismissal of all things Jewish, outside trauma and isolation, continued through the late 2010s' rise of the queer Jewish left. So when Rivkah invited Miriam to come to the trans women Erev Rosh Hashanah dinner, she initially tells her that she can't make it. She says to herself that she's too sad, too messy—a story that she worries is getting old at thirty-three. But Rivkah, the *balabosta*, knows how to get what she wants.

* * *

Can we talk about the 2010 Israeli think tank Reut Institute's leaked report revealing that a disproportionate and growing number of anti-Israel activists are gender and sexual minorities? And how the report suggested that this information could be used to delegitimize boycott, divestment, and sanctions activities globally? But also, it is 2015, and all Miriam's exes were putting little blue girl pills under their tongues every night. Pills made by Teva, an Israeli pharmaceutical company. HaShem has a morbid poetics.[1]

When Miriam pulls the challah out of the oven, the golden crust shines. Rivkah's apartment is already filled with all the girls. Ben and Bridgette smoke on the porch, Rivkah puts kugel in the oven, and Chana and Ahuva sit at Rivkah's kitchen table. Chana and Rivkah are discussing the recent Never Again protest against the internment of Samoan refugees in California. Miriam puts the challah on the table, and Rivkah covers it with a scarf.

* * *

Dear girl who grows,

I think we met at a talk about some girl's recent solidarity trip to Palestine. You wore the familiar anarcho-Jewish, anti–Israeli apartheid garb: a black Anarchists Against the Wall shirt that you cut the collar and sleeves off along with patched-up tight jeans. But you stood out in a sea of other black T-shirts. You walked like a fag. By this time in my life, I was done spending time with straight anarchist bros. I learned later you were a girl, or at least not a boy. We shared our

---

1. HaShem (the name) is one of the many words for God.

nuanced feelings of sexuality as nonbinary femmes (at the time). The only reason I stayed at the farm the summer that we lived in the same town was so I could give you fresh tomatoes for the shakshuka that your Moroccan Israeli mother taught you to cook.

* * *

Rivkah, Miriam, Chana, Bridgette, Ahuva, and Ben form a circle in the shape of the small kitchen. With their hands over their eyes, they light the candles.

Rivkah, with her motherly calmness, breaks the silence. "It can be so hard for girls like us to gather together. So before we do the ha-motzi over the bread and the rest of the blessings, I want to thank you all with so much *kavvanah* for being here tonight, for trusting me. I want you to know you are all so beautiful. I would be so honored if we could do one go around and share any *dvar* or kavvanah on your heart.[2] I know that it can feel Jew campy or goyish, so no pressure if you don't want to, but ..."

Chana jumps in first, talking about this political moment and offering a toast to the fall of Zionism. Chana ends with a short prayer for some friends of hers currently incarcerated. Miriam bites her lip and pushes her thumbnail into her palm. She doesn't like talking in front of others. She keeps her mouth shut, looks at the floor, and tries to listen.

"I hate this shit," Ben says, looking directly at Rivkah. "It reminds

2. Dvar and kavvanah refer to, respectively, speaking about the weekly Torah reading, and one's intention to carry out a precept or principle.

me of fucking check-ins during group at every janky-ass rehab in the state. But I love you, girl. So I'll give you this. Y'all know being in our bodies in this world is fucking hard, especially for a tall hairy pretransition tranny addict like me. And it feels fucking good to say that and not have some cis person jump down my throat with, 'Stop being a victim.' FUCK YOU. I began thinking about tonight and my Jewishness, which to be honest I haven't given much thought about the past many years. If there is one thing being a Jew taught me, though, it's that there is power in naming the wrongs that have been done to us and we gotta stay together. So I hope spaces like this keep happening, and may you all be written in the book of life. I'm not sure if I'll be written in the book just yet, but I'm trying."

Rivkah mouths a thank you and blows Ben a kiss.

Ahuva takes a deep breath and meets Ben's full brown eyes. "What you said feels all too real. Grateful for you speaking it, and I will just say that being around a lot of other trans girls throughout my life, when we name our hurt, it gives us room to also claim ourselves— our strengths and power. We may shatter, we may have already shattered, but don't let them take our broken pieces apart. Stay whole."

All the girls voice an amen.

Miriam, still looking at her toes, lets the other girls' words seep into her guarded brain.

Bridgette lifts her gaze to the ceiling and takes her arms out from under the scarf wrapped around her shoulders. While she is not a Jew, Bridgette has known Rivkah since before both girls knew the intricacies of curating a butch aesthetic that still kept the word "he" out of other's mouths. That was eighteen years ago, making her an elder in many trans girl circles these days.

"I can feel so many of our ancestors here with us right now. They say put your armor down when you are together. They say you can handle what comes and you won't be alone. They say keep sowing and feeling joy. Amen."

Before Miriam can say pass, tears start to roll down her face. Chana, standing next to Miriam, reaches for her hand and holds it tight. Miriam turns her head toward Chana and lifts her wet eyes just enough to meet Chana's. She whispers, "Thank you." Ahuva, on her other side, places a hand on Miriam's back and whispers, "You're OK girl. We got you."

* * *

Dear girl who loves,

I was on a dating-app date with your roommate. She brought me back to your place and introduced us, and then the next day we were on a date or something. So quickly you were vulnerable with me, sharing your problematic true story of being a gay in Israel as a young Zionist from the United States. What I remember is your clarity, how you explained your past trajectory, how you grew from the hurt that you caused and hurt that you received. We explored together the complex similarities of Jewish and tgirl trauma. How it caused you to insulate your selves from the non-Jewish and nontrans world. How it caused me to run from all community, period. We both longed for a life defined by more than our trauma. You said to move beyond, you need to first healthily self-identify. That stuck with me. You pulled me out of my shell by asking me hard questions that I thought shouldn't have been hard. How come I haven't started hormones or had surgery? Why don't I observe Sabbath or learn Yiddish (my mother's tongue)? I wanted you to teach me.

* * *

Miriam was scared of needles, but she found a pharmacy that only charged fifteen dollars for estrogen in a vial. She imagined what her ancestors would think about her dilemma. Miriam figured that they might swell with wonder like leavening bread from the possibilities that girls like her have—girls with access to a queer clinic in a state that covers "trans care." But what would they think about her? Miriam, who kvetched and refused to take oral estrogen because it would mean crossing a picket line even though it would be practically free. Miriam, a Jewish anarchist who almost faints pushing estrogen into her thigh before every Shabbot to avoid having to get estrogen made in Israel. Would they scoff, cheer, or show respect? She sometimes felt that she was confusing her trans ancestors with her Jewish ones.

* * *

Miriam breathes in and smells the kugel in the oven. She takes in gentle looks from everyone and then rests her eyes on the round challah covered with a purple scarf.

"I'm sorry. I … I'm not good at this. Being in Jewish spaces again is new for me. I don't think I would be in them if they didn't look like this and if it weren't for meeting Rivkah. Yeah, so I baked my first challah today. I realized that it was one of the only fond memories I had of being a kid. I'd watch my mom bake it. I remember she would tell me how the round challah for Rosh Hashanah was to symbolize the circle of the year. No beginning, no end. That's how I feel. Unable to start, but also already at the end and beginning all over again. It's how tonight feels. Like I have met, crushed on, or dreamed about meeting you all before. Like I plan on meeting you again."

Ben picks up a platter of apples and honey, and passes it to her right.

*

Mikveh Warshaw is a Jewish cultural/spiritual worker who helped start a liberation-oriented, anti-Zionist havurah in New Haven, Connecticut, called Mending Minyan. She is an Ashkenazi, trans woman, psychiatric nurse practitioner at a community health center. This piece is built off the brilliance of Mikveh's dear friend Zora Berman, who hosted her first ever tgirl Rosh Hashanah dinner some years ago. Thank you to Zora, and all the other brilliant, beautiful Jewish radical trans girls in her life, past, present, and future! Mikveh thanks her fiancé and gentile love of her life for encouragement to write this piece and editing help, and Cindy, whose creative and editing genius made this whole project happen.

ON MAKING AND

HOLDING SPACE

MICHAEL LOADENTHAL

Mobilized by the authoritarian nativism and outright racism of Donald Trump, on January 20, 2017, I joined hundreds of anarchists in an antifascist and anticapitalist march to disrupt the presidential coronation in Washington, DC. We were attacked by police, who kettled some 220 of us on a street corner, eventually mass arrested us, and later charged us with felonies that could have put us behind bars for decades. Our prosecution played out over the course of eighteen stressful months, yet in the end, unable to summon the credibility required for conviction, the US Attorney's Office dropped all our charges in July 2018.

The case—nicknamed J20, for the January 20 inauguration date—greatly impacted myself and my family in a litany of ways. One effect, though, was especially harmful to my spirit. Because of the legally mandated obligation to show up for court proceedings, I was unable to be present for my maternal grandmother's shiva—the Jewish practice of gathering in community for seven days of mourning. When Dorothy died in spring 2017, I flew into Philadelphia for her funeral, but had to quickly get back to DC for yet another perfunctory court date. This meant that I couldn't grieve collectively with my family, and as my extended family lacked adult-age males, the mourning period was shortened because we were unable to reach the traditional scriptural quorum of ten.

In my unsuccessful attempt to be excused from this particular court appearance, my lawyer petitioned on religious grounds, which to this day feels like a needless violation of my and my family's privacy. It also felt like a capitulation of my anarchist principles. The filing forced me to make my case to an unfeeling, bureaucratic state body that only confirmed its contempt for human life through its silence and inaction. The shame of this experience stuck with me for far longer than I could have imagined. I felt that I had betrayed my grandmother, a woman so loving, attentive, and gentle that I wanted to honor her with my presence. In turn, I realized how much the prosecution was affecting my family, and how much I was embodying the guilt of that in detrimental ways to them and myself.

Then in 2018, I went to anarchist summer school, held in a big barn-as-classroom on rural wooded land in Massachusetts, hundreds of miles away from my family. I was there to teach about state repression along with the various ways that people stay strong through counterrepression and solidarity efforts. I taught my sessions, shared facts, histories, and strategies, and engaged in a week's worth of political conversations, while pitching into the life of running a camp.

It was Friday night, the second-to-last day of our summer school, and a small contingent of us Jewish anarchists decided to host a Shabbat service in a nearby public park. There was a lunar eclipse that evening, the first new moon after my charges had been dropped and an opportunity to begin anew. We arrived before sundown and sat down to establish a small circle in the grass, but then had to continually shift ourselves outward as our circle grew and grew. It was populated by people of many genders, ethnicities, and faiths, Jewish and non-Jewish, and I sat across from two friends I've known for nearly half my life. Our service began late, delayed by the excited chatter of those who'd gathered. Each time new folks joined, not wanting them to be left behind, we invited them into the circle and backtracked a bit.

We sourced candles from the collective house that was our base camp, and carefully took turns cupping our hands around the flames as they flickered in the breeze, trying to keep them alight. Our Shabbat table was a milk crate, but holy in its own way. Juice was passed around, and challah was shared, including vegan pretzel bread on my behalf because I had mentioned that it was the practice at my house. We shared the Shabbat blessing in a tune unfamiliar to me, yet I picked back up my familiarity with the blessings over wine and bread.

Following the traditional Shabbat prayers and practices, we decided to do something untraditional: we recited the Mourner's Kaddish, a ritual that has become central to my Judaism as I age and family pass away. Despite being in the middle of a loud park, with the What Cheer! brass band setting up and tuning for a nonpermitted outdoor show, we held the space as sacred. Here in this park, I reclaimed the space of mourning stolen from me by the US Attorney's

Office and police. As anarchists, we helped each other to mourn in our own self-determined way. One of us mourned their sibling on the anniversary of their death, while others grieved more recent scars.

By happenstance, just as we concluded the Mourner's Kaddish, the band began to fiercely play. When the music reached its first crescendo, it was undeniably "culturally Ashkenazi" and klezmeresque. Friends could be seen from across the park, gathered around the band, beaming with delight. We rushed over to participate in the beauty, and I joined with a dear friend and Jewish anarchist who remarked—having to almost shout above the horns and drums—that the retaking of this park was like being transported back to the shtetl.

The music spun us into circles, another familiar cultural practice, and a crowd of hundreds reveled in a joyful dance that couldn't help but feel Jewish. Around us were tables where Iraqi men sat chain-smoking, while children of all colors twirled gleefully with sparklers. A local kid ran up to me, gifting me a cold bottle of water and a T-shirt that they had screen printed the previous day. By the end of a dozen songs, I felt transformed.

The next day, our last at that year's summer school, as we circled up to share real-world examples of how anarchism can create a community of care in an uncaring world—how we can and have intentionally done that as anarchists—I cried. I cried trying to write down parts of the previous night's park story to share. I cried thinking of our losses and the many yet to come. I retreated for a few minutes to the back of the barn to sob, and when I thought I'd regained my composure, returned to my perch in a sheltered corner of the main room and rested my head against the wall. From there I was directly across from the facilitator, an old and dear friend. They acknowledged me with loving eye contact, and my tears resumed.

In that moment, I was reminded of the metaphor that I had used the day before when presenting on building resilience and countering political repression. I spoke of our need to create dense, interconnected, yet flexible networks. I suggested that we might better resist state surveillance, infiltration, prosecution, and direct violence through solidifying our relationships, as if weaving a tight-knit blanket made of rubber—a blanket that once it's pulled and misshapen, would quickly bounce back to its original shape. I realized that the prosecution, my grandmother's death, and the hateful political climate had all conspired to mishape me, and I hadn't been able to pull myself together again—until now. I could suddenly feel myself able to stretch without breaking.

In that barn, I no longer had to hide away. I knew that being vulnerable was OK. It didn't make me less of an anarchist, less of a fierce militant (which I strive to be), or less of a man (whatever that toxic bullshit means). I felt safe, validated, heard, and healthy. I could be fully present, helping to make and hold this space in common.

Maybe this is the most that we can hope for. It seems that we're fighting for our mere existence these days in a world full of increasingly fascistic people. Creating and holding space for collective care is no easy task. But for the first time in my life, I understand the power of bringing our personal grief into our political circles, and our anarchistic politics into our Jewish circles.

*

Michael Loadenthal is an anarchist Jew, precarious professor, and constant organizer. He works to provide support, defense, intel, training, and strategic planning for regional and global social movements and networks of agitators. Michael and his partner are raising their kids to embrace and be proud of their Jewish history, culture, and customs in an age of antisemitism, fascism, and assimilation. This essay would not have been possible without a host of troublemakers and accomplices. Thank you to the beautiful anarchist hearts who created and held this space, among them Cindy, Olivia, Anne, Ami, Hillary, Naomi, Madeleine, Dom, Merc, and Payton. Michael offers this modest contribution in memory of Dorothy Rice Cohen (1924–2017), partner to the late Robert Cohen, and daughter of Masha Sher and Isadore Roseman. She will be remembered always.

ON MAKING AND HOLDING SPACE

255

PESACH SEDER

FOR FREEDOM

YAEL LEAH AND YAELLE CASPI

Australia's policies on refugees sicken the heart. The government has declared that it is illegal to seek asylum, and thus anyone who arrives on this continent hoping for refuge is detained indefinitely. Some refugees have now spent ten years in offshore detention centers, under shockingly dehumanizing conditions.

As Pesach 2019/5779 approached, a group of us—an autonomous collective of Jews—were discussing how we felt about this festival of freedom in relation to the incarceration of asylum seekers. The stories and rituals of Pesach seemed an apt expression of our struggles to help gain freedom for refugees—struggles that we could relate to as Jews too: "Passover asks us to remember the plight of refugees, from biblical times to now. As Jews we know too well the trauma of fleeing persecution and genocide. We know the sorrows of escaping only to be turned away from safe shores."[1]

So we decided to organize a seder for freedom, both to engage our

---

1. Here and below, quotes are from our Haggadah, available at https://bit.ly/33iO3gh.

own communities in taking action and bring our protests to the Australian government's doorstep. We compiled our own liberation Haggadah, gathered all the ingredients for the holiday, and linked up with the Australian Jewish Democratic Society, a well-established leftist organization that's been active on social justice issues for over thirty years.

On Pesach, we set up and circled around a seder table outside the Department of Immigration and Border Protection in Narrm/Birraranga/Melbourne—where inside the building, policies and decisions are made about refugees' lives.

We placed our table strategically at the exit of the office building, where workers would soon spill from the doors at the end of the working day. Security quickly approached us, questioning why we were setting up our trestle tables, candles, and seder plate. After explaining that we were enacting a religious obligation in solidarity with refugees and asylum seekers who were being held so cruelly by the Australian government, we were left to our seder, although under a watchful eye and curious glances.

We were a ragtag group huddling on folding chairs and milk crates around brightly colored, mismatched tablecloths. Yet warmth and connection emanated across generations, young and old. The seder began with a land acknowledgment, and an introductory round of names and pronouns. We all took turns reading from our Haggadah. Some stumbled over the Hebrew, but the group's support strengthened our collective resolve to speak up and out through Jewish ritual.

We ate matzo, drank our four cups of wine or grape juice, and sang the Pesach songs (in a rather off-key fashion). We dipped our *karpas* (parsley) into salt water to symbolize the tears of our ancestors as well as our empathy with those currently in Australia's detention centers, suffering tears and pain of their own. Most important, we used our Haggadah to highlight our concerns around freedom, liberation, and borders, and show respect for the sovereignty of the Wurundjeri people, whose land this action took place on. As our Haggadah observed,

> The festival of Passover celebrates freedom and liberation. We are here today honouring a millennia-long tradition that binds us to history, culture, ritual, and lore. In so doing, we acknowledge that we are on the lands of the Wurundjeri people of the Kulin nation. A people who, like Aboriginal people everywhere on this continent of so-called Australia, had their cultures, rituals, and lores taken away from them.
>
> We are here today to celebrate the freedoms that we have and fight for the freedoms that we don't have. We are here to say that borders and border regimes don't protect but instead oppress us. We are here to acknowledge the true sovereigns of this land that we are on: the Wurundjeri of the Kulin nation and many hundreds of clans on this continent on which Australia imposed its borders.

Every time that othered or marginalized communities confront injustice, we build and affirm our communities as well as relationships of solidarity. We also create and enact narratives that question the white supremacist logic dictating who belongs and who doesn't, who gets to possess and who gets dispossessed, and who gets to make decisions and who doesn't. In this settler colonial state, with no treaty with or restitution for Aboriginal peoples to this day, it is a logic that determines who gets to own land and profit from it, who gets to decide where the borders are, and who gets to enter those borders. In this action, if only for the duration of our ritual, we used our Jewish voices to disrupt the legitimacy of this system, with our Haggadah asserting,

The Passover story chronicles the Israelites' exodus from slavery in Egypt. It celebrates the movement from oppression to liberation, and our belief that tyranny can be overcome and justice can prevail. Every year we sit and tell this story. It is woven into a myriad of stories of our families and ancestors who have escaped tyranny and genocide—who were refugees, leaving everything to find safety. Rooted in our communal experience, the Jewish people know that our futures are bound up with those who now are forced to leave their homes due to war, genocide, oppression, climate change, and poverty.

Next year at the seder table, may we share more stories of migrant justice and decolonisation.

*

Yael Leah is an activist and community organizer for the Australian Jewish Democratic Society. Yaelle Caspi is a nonbinary queer Jew who volunteers with the Australian Jewish Democratic Society, working to dismantle settler colonialism in Australia and Israel/Palestine.

"SPILLING OUT JUICE

AND BRIGHTNESS"

ROSZA DANIEL LANG/LEVITSKY

Jewish radicalism has always been a cultural project as much as a political one.[1] We have created new ways of being jewish (from veltlekhkayt/secularism to mizrahi pan-arabism to jewish witch-craft), new jewish practices (from Yiddishist Third Seders to antifas-cist Mimounas to anarchist Yom Kippur balls), new forms of jewish education (from anarchist reading rooms to Bundist school systems to jewish queerpunk zines), and a plethora of cultural materials.[2]

---

1. The title of this piece is a phrase from Anna Elena Torres's translation of the last major poem by Peretz Markish zts"l, a Soviet yiddish poet admired as a com-rade by yiddish anarchists inside and outside the USSR. His "der fertsikyeriker man" ("The Forty-Year-Old Man") is a dense and expansive vision of revolution, hidden (in manuscript form) just before his arrest and murder by Joseph Stalin's government. Anna Elena Torres, "The Horizon Blossoms and the Borders Vanish: Peretz Markish's Poetry and Anarchist Diasporism," *Jewish Quarterly Review* 110, no. 3 (Summer 2020): 458–90.

2. Mimouna is the North African mizrahi and sefardi tradition of holding a cele-bratory dinner the night after Passover ends, generally along with muslim neigh-

Throughout the 170 or so years of modern jewish radicalism, our culture making has wrestled with how to use existing jewish cultural materials in our organizing and agitation. This piece lays out some thoughts on that, based on my experience over more than two decades as an anarchist cultural worker in jewish radical spaces in the United States. My hope is to encourage our jewish anarchist spaces to be rooted in our own specific geographies and many diasporic histories, and be increasingly culturally literate as we build new forms of radical jewish culture together.[3]

Before diving in, I want to name a few things that I take for granted.

First, there is no single jewish culture, and there are no universal jewish cultural materials. Jewish communities emerge in particular

bors and friends; it has recently been reclaimed as a time for visible antifascist solidarity among jews and muslims (and between arab jews and jews from Eastern European lineages).

3. Our choices in how we present our words are political. Like many multilingual feminists writing for anglophone audiences, I don't mark off other languages as exotic or Other by italicizing them. And like many black radicals and their comrades (especially outside the nationalist stream) going back through the twentieth century, I don't capitalize racial/ethnic/national groups; it gives these categories undue power and attributes "objective reality" to them. So throughout this piece, languages (Yiddish, Arabic, and English), times and places (Purim, Palestine, Uganda, and Central Asia), and some ideologies (Zionism, Bundism, and Yiddishism) are capitalized, while cultures and groups of people (jews, mizrahim, muslims, and austrians) are not. "Yiddish" shows up both ways, capitalized when it refers only to the language, and lowercased when it refers to the jewish culture and lineages that speak or historically spoke it.

places at particular times, primarily (today as always) through conversion and intermarriage rather than group migration, and have distinct cultures from the moment they emerge.[4] Those cultures change through time (and fissure and mix) and in many cases have been transformed by displacement from their original homes. Every recognizable form of jewishness has always been a decentralized project—not without hierarchies or elites, but always refusing a single central authority.[5] Jewish cultures differ (from each other, from themselves over time, and within themselves) on every point imagi-

---

4. This is abundantly clear from the faces of present-day jews: beta israel folks look like other people from the Horn of Africa; yiddish jews like other Eastern Europeans; bukharians like other Central Asians, and so on. The history of the abuyudaya, who have emerged as a jewish community in Uganda over the past century (see Tudor Parfitt, *Black Jews in Africa and the Americas* [Cambridge, MA: Harvard University Press, 2013]), is typical of the many less well-documented earlier community histories that Shlomo Sand assembled in his *The Invention of the Jewish People* (New York: Verso, 2009). Sand's book also demolishes the fiction of a mass expulsion from Palestine by the Roman Empire, and documents the insertion of biblical myth into the writing of jewish history by Zionist and proto-Zionist historians.

5. There have been repeated attempts to turn positions created by states and empires as points of control over jewish communities into central authorities among jews: the "exilarchs" and "gaonim" in 'Abbasid Mesopotamia, the "shtadlanim" in the Commonwealth of Poland and Lithuania, the "Judenrats" of the Nazi ghettos, the "chief rabbis" of contemporary Britain and other countries, and more. None have managed to exert authority beyond the limits set by the state regime that created them or beyond its borders.

nable, from which texts are ritually significant or legally authoritative, to what practices of everyday life are required or forbidden, to what languages are used in what spheres of life. All jewish cultural materials are specific to a particular community, place, and time.

Second, anarchist cultural work is about liberation. We aim to transform the structures of the world toward freedom, knowing (as anarchist writer Ursula K. Le Guin zts"l and many others have taught) that this means a constantly expanding practice, not a static condition that we can achieve once and for all.[6] Our tasks include (in the words of writer and organizer Toni Cade Bambara zts"l) making revolution irresistible, but also (as poet and scholar Keguro Macharia phrases it) imagining freedom and cultivating our practices of freedom. This should guide our choices of what cultural materials to use, and our uses of those materials. For jewish cultural workers, this means taking special care to avoid perpetuating the exceptionalism that comes from the myth of jewish "chosenness." This comes in many forms— from Zionism's integral nationalism, to religious assertions of superior morality, to liberals' incoherent mix of claims for inherent "good politics" and unique victimhood; none of them are compatible with working for liberation.

Third, cultural work is organizing. Our movements tend to treat cultural work as an add-on, a late addition, an enhancement of the

---

6. "Zekher tsadik livrakha" (may the memory of the righteous be a blessing) is said or written (abbreviated, in transliteration, as ZTs"L or zts"l) to honor the names of those who have died in recent memory.

"real work." But even when it is bound up within this "supplementary" model, cultural work is always organizing work. It presents a vision of the world—as it is, or as we want it to be—and demands that folks decide what they think about it. It makes clear who is invited to participate in our remaking of the world, and who isn't. It makes our goals and priorities visible and audible, giving them texture and flavor. It enables comrades to recognize each other, even when they have never met, and even if they do not yet understand themselves as comrades. Which means we always have to ask, What is this work doing? Do we want that done? Is it doing it well?

USING JEWISH CULTURAL MATERIALS IN OUR MOVEMENTS

If there is a key truth about radical jewish cultural work in the 5780s/2020s, it is this: we as a movement—or a nest of intertwined movements in the making—are barely starting to know what's out there. Many of us have been so profoundly cut off from our lineages and diasporic jewish cultures by the hegemony of Zionism in jewish life that we don't even know what we don't know. And even those of us who haven't had to fight our way out of indoctrination into the Zionist idea that our cultures (whether yiddish, djerban, bene israel, juhuri, and more) are degenerate and obsolete have come up in a jewish institutional landscape created for "shlilat hagalut" (the liquidation of the diaspora, one of Zionism's two fundamental pillars). Except in rare cases, before we start searching on our own, we've each been exposed to a small fragment of a culture, whether it is the traditions of a specific Hasidic court, the stories and songs that a particular leftist family from Tehran chose to pass on, or the practices developed by a specific Newton, Massachusetts, havurah since the 1970s.[7]

So when we first come into the spaces created by the yiddish cultural revitalization movement, developing radical mizrahi spaces in the United States, or the Svara queer yeshiva, we are stunned by what we find. After only knowing the ice cubes from our own freezer, an entire iceberg is floating in front of us! It takes some time to realize that even once we've looked under the water, what we've seen is still just a fragment of the glacier that spawned it.

I've been involved with the yiddish cultural revitalization movement since I was a teenager. By the time I was in my thirties, I felt like I had a solid hold on some parts of it—the explicitly political musical repertoire, especially, through a dozen or so albums made by the Klezmatics, Adrienne Cooper zts"l, Zahava Seewald, Josh Waletzky, Dan Kahn, and so on. Then I reached a point in my slow study of the Yiddish language where I could deal with the primary sources directly. And found books of five hundred songs that I'd never heard, about work, prison, military conscription, and revolution. And archival recordings of hundreds more. And stacks of poetry by the writers of some of those songs. And dozens of radical magazines that spread these words and musical ar-

---

7. Havurot are ritual communities not led by a rabbi (though some have rabbis as participating members) that developed as part of the late twentieth-century shift toward deinstitutionalizing and democratizing jewish ritual practice.

rangements. What I already knew was real, but now I'd seen some of what I hadn't known to imagine. I've seen friends go through the same process with the folklore of daily practice, regional traditions of piyyut/pizmon semiliturgical poetry and music, yiddish women's poetry, and much more.

There is, truly, always more out there. The main trick, if there is one, of radical jewish cultural work is always looking beyond what we know. If you think of Irena Klepfisz or Adrienne Rich for queer jewish poetry, what about Marilyn Hacker, Dina Libkes, or Yehuda Halevi? If "mir veln zey iberlebn" is a familiar antifascist song now because of the band Tsibele, have you heard Yaakov Rotenberg's Łodz Ghetto songs, or thought about how the halabi Purim repertoire from Aleppo could be used? But of course, we don't start knowing any of these names; we only find them by reaching, asking each other, and most of all, sharing what we've found.

A decentralized tradition like ours is based on sharing what we find so that all our understandings grow together. We stay connected by learning together through our webs of relationships and mutual support. And that's true even when what we're uncovering isn't obviously connected to each other's work. What I've learned about yiddish songs against military conscription in the Russian Empire may suggest something useful to someone unpuzzling the relationship between beta israel communities rooted in Ethiopia and the state of Israel. What theater maker and scholar Jenny Romaine has learned about the mourning laments of yiddish jews, tatar muslims, and baltic pagans in what's now Belarus might be able to help a sefardi comrade thinking about her relationship to the Klamath River watershed and its indigenous communities in this moment of climate crisis. I don't know; those aren't connections that have happened yet. The zines, calendars, websites, performances, chapbooks, and patches where we share what we've found are some of the most significant parts of our work.

HISTORIES, CONTEXTS, AND FORMS

What matters most for our work with jewish cultural materials is knowing what it is that we're working with. And that starts with knowing where *this* song, *this* symbol, *this* piece of commentary, and *this* ritual practice is from. Things that are familiar or meaningful to us, that resonate with our experience, that welcome some of us, do not do the same for others.

Jewishness has always been multiracial, multiethnic, and multi-lingual. Any piece of a jewish culture is particular, and what's important is knowing in what ways it is. The jewishness that we as anarchists have to offer is one that is about multiplicity rather than the forcibly homogenized religious-nationalist culture of Zionism or the single, narrow paths of religious traditionalisms. We need to be clear both when we are staying focused within a specific jewish community's culture and when we are bringing together material from different lineages. Understanding as best we can which jewish cultures, communities, and sections of society are the original homes of a song, text, or ritual—who made it, and who it was made for—makes it possible for us to know what lineages and communities we are representing, and work on representing them well.

For quite a few years, musician and educator Ira Khonen Temple has been the music director for the Purimshpil that our theater collective puts on every year in Brooklyn. Many jewish communities have traditions of carnival and performance during the spring Purim holiday. Our project grows out of the yiddish version, but serves a radical and progressive jewish sphere whose mixture of jewish communities has been becoming more visible as well as growing in scope. Ira has sought out teachers and musicians to ensure that our shows make audible our diasporist commitment to encouraging that change. In 2018, for example, the show's score included "ronu gilu," a mizrahi pizmon (paraliturgical song) from Syria sung for Purim in Levantine Hebrew; "esta noche de purim," a North African sefardi Purim song in Judezmo; "haynt iz purim," a Yiddish song often used in US Purimshpiln; and "Bulldagger Swagger," an English-language dyke anthem by jewish queerpunk legend Phranc.[8]

As well as knowing where our materials come from, we need to understand what they have been for—what they meant when they

---

8. For more about the Purimshpils created by the Aftselakhis Spectacle Committee (in cahoots with Jews for Racial and Economic Justice, though with significant political divergences from it), look for us on the internet (@purimnyc on Instagram, and @spectaclecommittee on Tumblr and Facebook) and Flickr (in albums by our longtime documentator @erikcito).

were made, and what has happened to those meanings over time. When we take up a single piece of cultural material, we are pulling on a knot in a densely woven web. What it is attached to matters, especially as we connect it to new threads and weave new patterns. This is especially significant because when these histories are not attended to, they can easily reassert themselves regardless of our intentions.

In the 1970s, a cluster of young progressive Zionist men entered jewish political and religious life—some, like Arthur Waskow, seeking a jewish version of the politicized spirituality and charismatic leadership that they saw in the "beloved community" of black churches, and others, like Michael Lerner, looking for a space where their misogyny and rape apologism was less widely known than the antiauthoritarian Left zones where they'd been based.[9] They soon seized on a theological phrase to anchor their politics: "tikkun olam." The phrase had never had a social or political resonance before; it was about reincarnation, predestination, and the individual spiritual athletics of kabbalistic and Hasidic religious leaders who sought to bring about the apocalypse by gathering the fragments of divinity scattered in an irredeemably sinful world. Waskow, Lerner, and their brethren spun out an entirely new use for the phrase, based on its English translation (repairing the

---

9. Louise Crowley's 1971 articles in Seattle's *Sabot* and then London's *Anarchy* give the backstory that Lerner tried to dodge by embracing his jewishness. They're available here: https://bit.ly/2JdbRee. Reliable gossip from the Bay Area attests to Lerner's continued sexual harassment and assault of women in his spiritual/political community.

world) and obscuring its actual history as a concept. The term caught on, becoming the preferred way for liberal NGOs to mark a project as jewish, and for jewish NGOs to mark a project as liberal. But with no political roots below its new meaning, the phrase soon drifted right back to the individualism and passivity of its historical usage, away from any action toward structural change. At this point, "tikkun olam" marks synagogue food pantry volunteer programs as opposed to efforts for wealth redistribution, energy efficiency drives rather than antifracking blockades, campaigns for more employer-controlled visas instead of open borders, and vigils for peace in place of struggles for justice.[10]

Some of the pieces of jewish traditional text that have most consistently been used for radical purposes are the ones dealing with the ger.[11] These passages, found in most jewish communities' liturgical texts, place the relationship between jewish communities and the ger at the heart of ethical action. During the period when the Talmud was

---

10. For a more detailed look at the history of the rabbinic uses of "tikkun olam," see Jill Jacobs, "The History of 'Tikkun Olam,'" *Zeek*, June 2007, https://bit.ly/3nU9zzU. Be aware, though, that her purpose is explicitly not criticism but instead to defend and justify its current uses. For a more critical analysis and interpretation of its recent history, including its function of defanging previous jewish radicalism, see Rachel Mattson, "Repairing the Idea of 'Repairing the World': Thinking Historically about Jewish Community Service" (Manhattan Jewish Community Center's 2010 lecture for Ma'ayan, December 6, 2010), https://bit.ly/362M4i6.

11. "Ger" is a term from the Torah with a dense net of meanings in the tradition: stranger, neighbor, foreigner, convert/jew by choice, or Other.

compiled (roughly the third to sixth centuries of the Christian era), they were at the heart of the debates about the future of jewishness. Would the people of Judea remain a nationality/ethnicity/race (based on parentage)? Would they follow the newly invented Christian model and become a religion (based on belief)? Or would they create something more flexible and ambiguous, an extended chosen family based on affinity? By answering that the ger (here meaning "jew by choice") does pray in the name of "Abraham our father"—that an active decision to join a jewish community creates kinship—we opted for the last choice and allowed for the emergence of everything that we would today recognize as jewish.[12] Illustrating the pull of that tradition of radical challenge to exclusionary versions of jewishness, the past two decades have seen even jewish liberal NGOs move in their invocations of the ger from supporting immigrant workers' labor rights during the 2006 Day Without Immigrants actions, to condemning the Obama administration's mass deportations, to taking concrete direct action to disrupt the concentration camp system caging immigrants and refugees across the United States.[13]

---

12. It's a bit more complicated, of course. There were divergences between different communities, and these specific debates reemerged occasionally until the 1500s. For details, see Shaye J. D. Cohen, *The Beginnings of Jewishness: Boundaries, Varieties, Uncertainties* (Berkeley: University of California Press, 1999).

13. I specify "concrete" here to distinguish those Never Again actions that materially impact the operation of the US deportation system from symbolic actions that are often—wrongly—described as direct action because they involve participants getting arrested (which itself does nothing to affect that system).

The flip side of this attention to what's behind a particular piece of material—whether it's a Talmudic passage, folk song, or recipe—is knowing who will see, hear, touch, and taste it when you use it. We shape our work to match its contexts, whether we're addressing other jews (and exactly which other jews), a mixed group of radicals, a mainly goyish environment, or a muslim space. Our choice of materials allows us to insist on our particularity, build connections, and do both along myriad different lines. It also makes it possible for us to create spaces that are actively unwelcoming to many we might want to invite in.

The six-pointed star was never a widely used emblem of jewishness until the late 1800s, when the Zionist movement adopted it as its insignia.[14] Before that, it was part of the common European and West Asian stock of decorative motifs and occult symbols, but only had a particularly jewish association in and around Prague. The Zionist movement's propagandizing of the six-pointed star as an overarching "jewish" symbol has been part of its efforts to claim that Zionism and jewishness are identical. The jewish Far Right, in occupied Palestine, the United States, and elsewhere, has used the six-pointed star as a symbol of threat and terror, emblazoning it on palestinian homes tar-

---

14. This is exhaustively documented in an article for *Commentary* by religious historian (and Zionist) Gershom Scholem. See Gershom Scholem, "The Star of David: History of a Symbol," in *On the Messianic Idea in Judaism and Other Essays on Jewish Spirituality* (New York: Schocken Books, 1971), 257–81; Gershom Scholem, "The Curious History of the Six-Pointed Star: How the 'Magen David' Became the Jewish Symbol," https://bit.ly/3fA2xoc.

geted for demolition, walls still bloody from Zionist massacres, and the uniforms of paramilitary and military murderers. Its presence marks a space as aligned with the movement and state whose insignia it is, and as hostile toward palestinians and other targets of Zionist violence.

The hamsa (in Hebrew and Arabic) or tafust (in Amazigh languages) is a widely shared symbol of good fortune and protection across West Asia and the eastern Mediterranean. Sefardi artist Tom Haviv's hamsa flag project began as a somewhat liberal gesture toward a future binational state in Palestine, centered on a "neutral" regional symbol. Since then, it has developed into a radical diasporist and decolonial vision, with the hamsa standing for both a rejection of borders and a focus specifically on Eastern Mediterranean, North African, and West Asian jewishnesses within that departitioned landscape.[15] One recent physical form it has taken is a long banner alternating hamsas with the phrase "one and many" in languages of the sefardi and mizrahi world (Arabic, Judezmo, Farsi, Turkish, and more), welcoming a specific range of communities, both jewish and non-jewish, into the spaces where it is brought.

For the past three years, I've been using a new symbol in my jewish antifascist work, incorporating a pomegranate containing the letter alef into theater costumes, banners, posters, flyers, and zines. The pomegranate has a long history in jewish cut-paper art, calligraphy, synagogue ornamentation, and embroidery, used across Europe,

---

15. For reflections on the project and its development, see Tom Haviv, "The Hamsa Flag," *Protocols* 1 (summer 2007); Tom Haviv, "The Hamsa Flag (Second Edition)," July 15, 2019, https://bit.ly/3m1rl3E. See also Tom Haviv, *A Flag of No Nation* (New York: Jewish Currents Press, 2020).

North Africa, and West Asia, but especially in Iran. The fruit invokes ideas of multiplicity and sweetness contained in tart toughness. Its circle-and-crown silhouette also hints at the explosive named for it in many languages: the grenade. Adding the alef—for antifascism, anarchism, or autonomy, as you wish—evokes the classic circle A in a jewish incarnation.[16]

Similar considerations apply when thinking about what a piece of cultural material is in itself, through its form. On one level this is straightforward: muwashshahat (an Arabic and Hebrew poem/song form with a refrain) are too long to easily fit on a banner, badkhones (wedding jesters' improvised rhymes in Yiddish) would usually be a bad choice for a memorial event, and intricate folk dance footwork may not be teachable during a street action. Yet it is important at another level as well, perhaps most strikingly when it comes to sacred texts and ritual forms, which are often used as a shorthand for jewishness in liberal and progressive spaces (and increasingly in radical ones too).

---

16. It also serves as an alternative to the triple-arrow symbol that has recently been revived in the United States. That emblem was created by the German Social Democratic Party after its parliamentary maneuverings to placate the Far Right (by criminalizing street protests and militant community self-defense, among other things) put Adolf Hitler into power and the party belatedly decided to join the antifascist resistance it had done so much to suppress. The triple arrow is a perfect insignia for the contemporary appeasers who have made "#resistance" a joke, but not for anyone who takes the history of antifascism seriously.

A substantial majority of jews in the United States (and jews world-wide) have no connection to synagogues or organized ritual practice beyond their families (blood or chosen).[17] That majority increases the further left you go: a secular jewish Right barely exists, and while the ritually observant jewish Left has been growing, it is still numerically tiny (despite the wildly disproportionate media attention it gets).[18] Cultural materials that come from traditions of observance, however beautiful, have no deep resonance for most jewish radicals. In fact, they largely serve as reminders of experiences of exclusion as well as a false standard of jewishness that makes "authenticity" dependent on observance or spirituality.

Further, throwing an isolated Talmudic citation or Torah verse into

---

17. This has been the consistent finding of polls done by the UJA-Federation, despite a methodology that (among other problems) overcounts observant and "affiliated" people by adjusting the numbers that its polls find based on the number of Federation and synagogue members in an area.

18. And much of that attention has focused on misrepresenting one group, Neturei Karta, which is in fact part of the jewish Far Right. Neturei Karta's opposition to Zionism has nothing to do with anticolonialism, antiracism, a critique of jewish nationalism, or support for the human rights of palestinians (and that's leaving aside the group's misogyny and antiqueer/antitrans bigotry, among other things). Like the Satmar Hasidim, it is anti-Zionist precisely because its messianic beliefs say that the only legitimate jewish state is a theocratic one, which will be preceded by a far more effective cleansing of non-jews from their holy land. The group has nothing in common with actual jewish liberation theology projects like Svara or actual observant progressive groups like Torah Trumps Hate.

a political event or text not only doesn't draw in most jewish radicals (and turns off many); it also doesn't do anything to appeal to those who are deeply immersed in those textual traditions. These texts have webs of interpretation and use that give them meaning in the communities that value them, in ways that rarely cling to the direct meaning of the words (especially in English translation). It's instantly noticeable—and deeply unimpressive—to folks from those communities when a passage has been harvested by someone unfamiliar with its contexts and implications.

There's nothing wrong with using ritual forms or liturgical texts in our radical jewish cultural work. But when we make them a marker of jewishness or jewish authenticity, we exclude many of our comrades, friends, and family members, pushing them further from our movements and projects. And when we use them as shorthand rather than fully exploring their meanings and complexities, we disrespect those who take them seriously as something more than that. Neither serves our work of liberation.

If, as jewish anarchists, we are striving to create radical jewish cultures that are irresistible, we cannot rely on the given forms of one strain of Jewish tradition. We need to think carefully about form— for example, to know when adding new verses to a fast-moving, doggerel street song like "daloy politsey" (down with the police), a song in Yiddish with a mostly Russian chorus, is what makes sense, and when we should be writing a version of "ashamnu" (a penitential prayer in Hebrew listing transgressions alphabetically).

In many ways, what we do as radical jewish cultural workers is to act as a channel from the static archive of existing cultural material into the active repertoire of living culture that we, our comrades, and our movements use.[19] Sometimes that is a literal process, sometimes it is more metaphoric, and sometimes it has to be done more than once.

The great singer and educator Adrienne Cooper zts"l found the song "a gutn ovnt Brayne" (good evening, Brayne) in a folk song anthology, and it became the starting point for an investigation into yiddish songs about domestic and sexual violence. Just as an earlier generation of radical cultural workers had brought "Brayne" from the ethnomusicologists' books into the classrooms of mid-twentieth-century secular yiddish schools in Canada, Adrienne introduced it into today's yiddish cultural revitalization movement. Their shared aim in keeping the song in people's mouths, was, in her words, to let the song "equip us to act in the present" against gender violence.[20]

Choreographer and dancer Hadar Ahuvia has spent the past several years creating a series of performances investigating the creation and history of the repertoire of dances that has been promoted under the name Israeli Folk Dance. This substantial repertoire was choreographed starting in the 1920s by a group of Zionist jewish choreogra-

---

19. The terminology of "archive" and "repertoire" comes from theater scholar Diana Clarke.

20. See Adrienne Cooper with Sarah Mina Gordon, "Women Sing of Family Violence," *Lilith* (Spring 2011), https://bit.ly/3fAB8eG.

phers, mainly trained in Germany in the nationalist modern dance schools that later affiliated themselves with the Nazi government. To create a new "authentically jewish" nationalist form of dance to replace existing diasporic folk and professional dance traditions, the choreographers raided palestinian, lebanese, and syrian folk forms like debke, yemeni jewish dance practices, and even yiddish folk dances like bulgarish, grabbing steps to codify into their dances, and removing the improvisation and flexibility that give these historically rooted forms their power. Hadar's work looks at this process, the bodies that it called into being, and the ways that this dance lineage has been disseminated worldwide. To me, Hadar's use of the Israeli Folk Dance repertoire in an analysis of dance through dance asks incredibly important questions about the relationships between formal choreography and vernacular dance, strategies for decolonizing our bodies, and the cultural rediasporization of jewish communities in Palestine as an embodied part of the decolonization of that land.[21]

As we think about the archives and repertoires that we work with, it's important to remember how wide both of them are. There's a tendency, absorbed from christian religious studies scholars, to think of jewishness as something whose cultures are primarily textual or at least directed by textual authorities. This has never been true, even for the small circles of elite men whose commentaries, legal opinions, and liturgical poetry form the bulk of the high-status canon in most

---

21. See the documentation and reflections on "The Dances Are for Us," "Everything you have is yours?," and "Joy Vey" at hadarahuvia.com.

jewish communities. Until the late twentieth century, the function of the canonical texts in traditional jewish communities was to justify existing embodied practices. What folks did was determined by minhag (local custom), as handed down through intergenerational observation and person-to-person instruction; the texts were used to explain why existing custom was correct, even (especially!) when it contradicted another community's practice. Observant communities have recently shifted toward the protestant christian model, changing their practice to match abstract conclusions drawn from texts and rejecting existing minhogim.[22] But we don't have to follow them in this christianizing move. When we look for material, we can choose to seek across a range far wider than just texts.

The best matzo I've ever eaten was cooked by organizer and writer Dorothy Zellner, from a reconstructed sefardi recipe dating from the time of the Spanish Inquisition.[23] A few years ago on Passover, she brought it—soft and fragrant with honey and black pepper—to my house, where it went directly onto the seder plate. There, it joined a beet (the vegetarian lamb shank, an innovation of the "liberation seders" of the 1970s), two kinds of traditional kharoses/haroset (an

---

22. This analysis (aside from naming the christian model for the cultural shift) comes from traditionally observant scholar Haym Soloveitchik in his fascinating essay "Rupture and Reconstruction: The Transformation of Contemporary Orthodoxy," *Tradition* 28, no. 4 (Summer 1994), https://bit.ly/2KFS8ot.

23. For one version of the recipe, see https://cooking.nytimes.com/recipes/8168-angelina-de-leons-matzohs.

apple, walnut, honey, and wine yiddish version and a seven-fruit sefardi version from Surinam), an orange (a feminist symbol created in the 1980s), a crust of bread (the lesbian symbol that the orange was introduced to replace and erase), and olives (a Palestine solidarity symbol introduced in the early 2000s), among other things.[24] The matzo that Dorothy brought in the name of Angelina de Leon, a hidden jew brought to trial by the Spanish Inquisition with her Passover cooking as evidence, added a new layer of history and resonance to our conversations that night about oppression and liberation, taking the taste of another jewish culture out of the archive and into the repertoire of the ritual meal.

As we think about form, archive, and repertoire, we can also look to specifically jewish approaches to cultural work to shape what we do. Here are two jewish frameworks for cultural innovation that I've found useful in my work and for thinking about other radical jewish cultural workers' projects.

---

24. Susannah Heschel claims to have invented the use of the orange (https://bit.ly/3m7eQUm), but as Rebecca Alpert has documented in her book on contemporary jewish lesbian ritual practice, this is untrue. See Rebecca Alpert, *Like Bread on the Seder Plate: Jewish Lesbians and the Transformation of Tradition* (New York: Columbia University Press, 1998); summary at "Alternative Jewish Ritual Toolkits," https://www.ivritype.com/toolkits/. The key difference between the two, in any case, is that bread on a seder plate makes a structural critique (a jewishness that excludes lesbians cannot be in any way kosher), while the orange poses only an aesthetic one (a jewishness that is open to feminism is tastier; one that isn't is still legitimate).

"Hidur mitsve" / "Hiddur mitzvah" is a Talmudic phrase that literally means "beautifying the commandment." In traditional communities, it is the explanation and justification for the myriad ways of making jewish ritual practice a sensory pleasure, from elaborate containers for the spices used in the havdole/havdalah ritual that ends shabes/shabbat to the breathtaking ornamentation of cantorial singing. In jewish anarchist work, the principle can serve as a reminder that each aspect of our organizing can be made to bring beauty into the world—and that our work is more powerful when we make that choice.

The first major New York City campaign to take up the palestinian call for boycott, divestment, and sanctions on the colonial state of Israel was Adalah-NY's work targeting settlement builder and blood diamond dealer Lev Leviev. As well as going after the charities that he used for ethical cover (all of which quickly repudiated him), we made regular visits to his New York City jewelry store, from its private soft-opening party onward. Members of Jews Against the Occupation/NYC (which was in the process of folding into Adalah-NY) and later Jewish Voice for Peace rewrote seasonally appropriate songs to serenade Leviev's customers and employees as well as to keep ourselves entertained on the picket line. From Christmas classics penned by New York jews ("Lev's dreaming about whitewashing"), to theater tunes from Tin Pan Alley scribes ("diamonds are a crime's best friend"), to kitschy Hanuka classics ("Leviev, oh Leviev / destruction you're sowing"), we threw all the resources of the jewish songbook at him, along with palestinian freedom songs and debke dancing. Some tunes wrapped political education about Israeli apartheid and the US funding that enables it in rhyme, others presented Leviev's atrocious ethics in rhythm, and still others simply wished him "a loss of business / and a poor fiscal year." In 2018, the store closed. We declared victory and printed a tenth-anniversary final edition of our songbook.[25]

One of the core forms of jewish cultural innovation in written and oral texts is midrash, which can mean either commentary or narrative elaboration. Midrash takes what has been handed down—a legal decision, story, or poetic phrase—and uses it as a beginning point for something new, which may reaffirm, complicate, or contradict its source material. It often moves between languages as it does so, or shifts genres, styles, or forms. Midrash doesn't replace what was there before, but it can render it powerless as easily as reinforce it, or add something so unexpected that the preexisting structure has to dissolve entirely. Midrashic writing travels in time and space, making both unstable and subtly intermingled.

Poet, educator, and organizer Irena Klepfisz is one of the founders of explicitly jewish feminism in the United States as well as a key figure in diasporist political thinking and contemporary yiddish culture. One of her most influential poems, "Etlekhe verter oyf mame-loshn / A few words in the mother-tongue," interweaves languages by pairing Yiddish words with English that first appears to only translate them but quickly becomes commentary. Then the English fades out, leaving

---

25. For the songbook, alongside many other Adalah-NY lyric rewrites, see https://bit.ly/3l6S9OO.

only Yiddish in the final stanzas, whose words are still infused with the meanings and feelings given to them in another language. It is a stunning midrashic adaptation of the form of a bilingual dictionary that ultimately takes the form of a midrash on its own words.[26]

The structures of midrash are easiest to see in the textual forms that the word was invented for, but they can appear in any medium. Purimshpils and folk songs are often midrashically developed from previous stories and songs. I see Hadar's work described above as a kind of danced midrash. Poet and organizer Aurora Levins Morales's textile work frequently juxtaposes source images translated into cloth in deeply midrashic ways. Lorin Sklamberg and Joanne Borts's performance of a Yiddish translation of "Edelweiss" is a particularly subtle kind of musical midrash: taking a fake austrian nationalist song written by a jewish composer and lyricist for a jewish actor, and by translation making it unclaimable by real austrian or german nationalists.

In a sense, whenever we work with existing jewish cultural materials, we are making midrash. But there is a huge difference between doing that by default and doing it on purpose, with a deliberate hand feeling out the transformations that we are enacting.

This piece is also midrash. While writing it (and for many years before), I have leaned on the manifesto that fiddle player and composer

---

26. For Klepfisz's reflections on her bilingual poetry, the full text of "Etlekhe verter oyf mame-loshn," and a recording of her reading the poem, see https://bit.ly/3fvZ96E.

Alicia Svigals wrote in the late 1990s to explain her approach to yiddish music and culture.[27] I believe the guidelines that she named are useful to diasporist jewish cultural work more generally, especially the kind of liberation-focused work that I want our jewish anarchism to embody. So I will close this with her words (in quotation marks), accompanied by my commentary.

Our jewish anarchist cultural work should place itself:

"Against Nostalgia," whether that fixation on the past takes the form of kitsch (seeing diasporic jewishnesses as always and only funny or cute) or necrophilia (taking seriously only moments of oppression and destruction);

"For High Jewish Self-Esteem," taking our cultures seriously and honoring them as they have been, even as we transform them;

"For Our Own Languages," both literal (Yiddish, Judezmo, Judeo-Malayalam, Luganda, and so on) and figurative; and

"Against Folk-Fetishism and a False Definition of 'Authenticity'"— using archives and past moments of our cultures and communities as sources and inspirations for the work that we do, not as fixed models to reproduce exactly, or as restraints on the jewish cultures and communities that we are creating.

---

27. Alicia Svigals, "Why Do We Do This Anyway?: Klezmer as Jewish Youth Subculture," in *American Klezmer: Its Roots and Offshoots*, ed. Mark Slobin (Berkeley: University of California Press, 2002), 211–20. Her manifesto is often available online, but usually not in a stable, typo-free form.

rosza daniel lang/levitsky is a cultural worker, organizer, and New Yorker. Never learned how to make art for art's sake; rarely likes working alone. Can't stop picking things up on the street and making other things out of them— outfits, collectives, performances, barricades, essays, meals. Third-generation radical; second-generation dyke; just another diasporist gendertreyf mischling who identifies with, not as. Some current projects: Survived & Punished NY (https://survivedandpunishedny.org); Koyt Far Dayn Fardakht, a yiddish anarchist punk band (https://koytfilth.band); Naye Khayes Farlag, a radical diasporist publisher/distro; and Critical Reperformance, re-bodying performance scores (https://criticalreperformance.org). Rosza thanks (and sends love to) many teachers, including Jenny Romaine, Ethel Raim, Adrienne Cooper zts"l, Irena Klepfisz, Melanie Kaye/Kantrowitz zts"l, Anna Elena Torres, and Dotty Zellner (and on the page, Ammiel Alcalay, Judy Grahn, Qwo-Li Driskill, Trish Salah, Nalo Hopkinson, and Ursula K. Le Guin zts"l, among others); to lineage roots in bikevine/Bukovina, ades/Odessa, volin/Volhynia, budapesht/Budapest, and (through colonialism and immigration) Nundawa- onoga and the northern estuary of Lenapehoking; and to collaborators and coconspirators past, present, and future.

MAKING TIME

RADICAL JEWISH CALENDAR

RABBI JESSICA ROSENBERG
WITH RABBI ARIANA KATZ
AND ELISSA MARTEL

My adult relationship to Judaism began with struggles for justice in Palestine. I learned that there was a whole history I hadn't been taught—history that flipped so much of what I'd assumed to be true on its head. I felt I needed to relearn everything I knew about Jewishness and Judaism. If I was going to fight in solidarity with Palestinians, I had to do it firmly grounded in (though not always leading with) my Jewish self. I started baking challah every week and turning off my phone on Shabbos. I woke up on below-freezing Minnesota mornings before sunrise to go to weekday davening, even though I understood little of the prayers. I tried laying tefillin (leather straps that bind boxes with verses from Torah, fulfilling the obligation in Exodus 13:9 to "bind it as a sign").

It was around this time that Josina and I began dreaming about a calendar. Jo was one of the first people who showed me anti-Zionist Jewish living: how to be both proudly and deeply Jewish as well as fiercely committed to Palestinian solidarity. I don't remember who first thought of it, but in some moment of articulating the Jewish life that we both desired, the vision emerged: we shouldn't have to mark Jewish holidays on a Christian calendar, and we certainly couldn't mark Jewish holidays on a Chabad calendar, with pictures of Israel accompanying every month. In summer 5772, we wrote a call for artists for a digital "Jewish calendar for the year 5773 that is anti-Zionist, queer, and reflects the values we strive for in each day."

That fall I started rabbinical school. The calendar project lay dormant, with occasional conversations and vague plans about it. Then, in winter 5776, my dad was diagnosed with stage four pancreatic cancer and given a one- to two-year prognosis. Suddenly all my organizing felt too slow and abstract. I wanted to make something that I could hold in my hands and could pull off in a future I could bet on experiencing.

A few months later I had a stack of art and no idea how to make it into something real. Ariana came onboard that summer, saving the day and year with incredible layout and design skills. Our 5777 Radical Jewish Calendar sold out all five hundred printed copies.

We knew two things: we had to make the calendar again and find a way to make it differently.

Elissa Martel, the most reliable artist from the first year, lived a few blocks from us. If she joined the team, we'd not only have another organized femme queen but also be able to eat soup together while we planned. Since that winter, the three of us have joyfully made three more calendars. We each have distinct roles, and yet when needed, each assist with other's tasks. We strive to align our values with the economic realities of producing something, trying to pay artists fairly while maintaining an affordable, sliding-scale calendar printed at an employee-owned union shop. We attempt to balance this labor of love with our everyday lives, so when mailing one thousand or more calendars out of Jessica's living room became unfeasible, we happily handed over distribution to Buy Olympia. And begrudgingly and of course lovingly, we allowed Ariana to move to Baltimore to launch Hinenu, a spiritual "community rooted in joy, pursuit of justice, and radical kinship," to quote from its website, but whenever we have big conversations, at least two out of the three of us need to be in the same physical room together.

During the first calendar, Jessica had to solicit specific art for those month's calendar pages that hadn't gotten any submissions. Now in our fifth year, we have received thirty-nine submissions for the next calendar, and invite former years' artists to help review and select art. We're deeply humbled by the task of selecting art that we know will be in people's intimate spaces for a whole year. We aim for a diversity of artists and imagery, in line with and aspiring to make visible our political sensibilities, while also selecting artwork for its quality, hoping that all the pieces end up being in conversation with each month and in balance with each other. We ask ourselves, Is this something that we can envision having on our walls for a whole month?

Selecting dates for the calendar is a joyful challenge of learning how to embody our leftist Jewishness. We wrestle with what radical history to include, and discerning which people's lives and what happenings shape our collective body. We struggle with how to mark

JESSICA ROSENBERG, ARIANA KATZ, ELISSA MARTEL

Jewish time; Jewish ritual time, although most actively influenced by the seasons and our ancient mytho-histories, also reflects the long-standing militarism in our tradition.

The hardest decision has been what to do with Yom HaShoah, Holocaust Remembrance Day. In the late 1940s, initial discussions of when to communally grieve the Holocaust on the Jewish calendar focused on the tenth of Tevet, a historic day of mourning, and fourteenth of Nisan, in honor of the Warsaw Ghetto uprising. In 1951, the Israeli Parliament instead decided on the twenty-seventh of Nisan, primarily so that Yom HaShoah would be eight days before Israeli Independence Day. As anti-Zionist Jews, we want to reject this overt alignment of attempted genocide with the creation of the Jewish state and violent displacement of the Palestinian people. It hurts our hearts not to be able to participate in collective mourning with worldwide and diaspora Jewry.

At the end of the day, we have to decide what to print. We've done it differently every year. We're still wrestling.

* * *

The Radical Jewish Calendar embodies multiple, intersecting political sensibilities. The anarchists among us relish this practice of proactively choosing the time that we are living in, consenting to the rules that we will be governed by.

We will not be governed by a Christian calendar named after a pope, timed around Easter, with capitalist holidays intentionally created to sell us things, or distract us from revolutionary history and militant organizing. We will not honor the triumphalist colonial histories that the United States and Zionism require. Jewish time is a calendar older than capitalism, white supremacy, and the current occupations around the world. We collaboratively grapple with and tell our own stories of where we came from along with what histories have shaped us. By doing so, we crumble the narrative that we have to fit our lives into the death-dealing and missionizing realities that the Christian calendar upholds.

Instead, we cocreate our own time, shaped by the rhythms of the earth and seasons, by the wisdom, traditions, stories, and rituals of our ancestors. We harvest anarchist and communitarian teachings from the Jewish calendar. The new month on a Jewish calendar comes with the new moon, and our tradition teaches us that one person can't declare the month on their own; it takes multiple witnesses and a collective process to keep time. We live in a calendar that invites us more fully into relationship with the earth and her seasons, the moon and her cycles, our ancestors and their stories.

At the same time, we don't conform to a joyless, patriarchal, reactive, didactic, shaming, competitive anarchism and leftism. Rather, we feed each other while we make this calendar. We make mistakes and laugh about them. We teach about Judaism and leftist history, and commit to continuing to learn and teach—telling a story of leftist Jewish life as powerful and central unto itself, not "alternative" to anything. In this way, we crowd out the institutions that seek to rule us with power over, making things in the ruins of what we hope to be ruining.

JESSICA ROSENBERG, ARIANA KATZ, ELISSA MARTEL

We adore making this calendar for our ever-growing Jewish worlds—those of us who are feminist, queer, and antiracist, and embody a Judaism opposing and beyond Zionism, toward diasporic, anticolonialist Jewish life and Judaism—so that we can find each other across cities and borders. (We've heard more than one anecdote about someone spotting the calendar on a first date's wall and sighing in relief.)

We make this calendar every year knowing that we'll make it anew next year, for as long as we can, and when we can't make it anymore, someone else will make something else in its place. And we make this calendar beautiful on purpose: as an act of *kavod*, to honor our people, our rituals, and our history.

*

Rabbi Jessica Rosenberg, content editor, makes meeting agendas, tuna noodle casseroles, and now, calendars. She enjoys getting up with the sun, organizing for the just redistribution of resources, and propagating wandering Jews of all kinds. Elissa Martel, art editor, has been a weird art kid since childhood and peaked in fourth grade when she sang with Celine Dion. Elissa's most recent high has been working on this amazing calendar with a team of babes, obvi. Rabbi Ariana Katz, layout editor, learned how to do layout from being a nerdy high schooler hiding in the newspaper office and making zines. She likes ritual, intergenerational revolutionary learning, remembering birthdays, and Hinenu Baltimore. Thank you to Nava EtShalom for conversations about the ideas in this essay, and all the many artists and friends who have contributed to and supported the Radical Jewish Calendar for five years. To find out more about the calendar, see radicaljewishcalendar.com.

NOW PLAYING

IN PITTSBURGH

GILLIAN GOLDBERG AND
BENJAMIN STEINHARDT CASE

VASHTI: Esther, the king didn't see me as a person even before I was a lizard. Don't let him do that to you. Don't let him do that to your people.

We danced until we had to kick people out of the place. We played limbo with a prop from the spiel, the king's scepter: a long, cardboard tube with a floppy dildo attached to the top, spray painted gold and dipped in glitter. It felt like the entire community's gay b'nai mitzvah. Two tiny queers made out in a broom closet. There was a three-way kiss on the dance floor. A small group of us finished the night, still in costume, at a twenty-four-hour diner, a wrap-up party for the play that we performed on the fifteenth of Adar 5778, March 2, 2018.

If you had asked any of us at the time, we probably would have said that we were just performing a goofy Purim spiel. Throwing a party. Holding a fundraiser. Now, over two years later, we know that there was so much more going on during those many hours of rehearsal and preparation. We were building trust with one another, defining and declaring our politics, preparing ourselves and our community for the violence of fascism—and our resistance to it. Our Purim spiel marked the solidification of a new Jewish movement in Pittsburgh.

About a year before the spiel, Ben hosted a Shabbat to talk about starting an IfNotNow chapter. That initial dinner brought ten young Jewish radicals together to discuss Palestine solidarity efforts. Many of us were seasoned organizers and anarchists, but few of us had experience showing up fully as Jews. We had not planned on having a minyan—the ten-person community required for observing Jewish ritual—yet our number felt meaningful; it was the beginning of something big. We'd prepped for a short ritual, meal, and conversation; we ended up staying late into the night, sharing stories, venting, and feeding one another's enthusiasm for what was possible with a liberationist Jewish movement.

Soon after, we started doing public actions together. Over the next year, we not only built a serious local political force; we forged a community that transformed us. We discovered our need for a space in which to understand our Jewishness, and for queer and trans Jews to process our experiences in Judaism. As more joined us, we taught one another, sang songs, got kicked out of the Jewish Community Center and Hillel in Pittsburgh, traveled to Washington, DC, to lock down in protest against the American Israel Public Affairs Committee with other young Jews from across the continent, invited one another into our ritual lives, fell in love, and connected our radicalism to our Jewishness and city.

The initial goal of IfNotNow, broadly speaking, was to change the conversation around the occupation in Palestine so that mainstream institutions could no longer pretend that Jews in the United States were uncritically supportive of Israel. The strategy was simple and time tested: use direct action to force the conversation in Jewish communities and institutions. We would sing songs in Hebrew, and base actions and their framing around Jewish tradition. We'd lay claim to our heritage as people fighting for justice. The mainstream institutions that support Israel's occupation, purport to speak for Jews in the United States, and allow politicians and businesses that profit from war to be able to say they are doing it for us, should not be able to get through a major event without us disrupting them.

For a couple of years, we did just that. Yet it did not take long for our approach—embodying nonhierarchical organizing, mutual aid, and solidarity and other anarchistic practices—to create tension with the national IfNotNow organization, eventually resulting in our chapter disaffiliating. But that's another story.

> **ESTHER**: Uncle-Cousin Mordechai, this is all so stupid! What am I supposed to do, go in there and oil myself up for an entire year?

> **MORDECHAI**: Listen, sweetheart. *I* know it's bullshit, *you* know it's bullshit, but it's the bullshit we're living inside of, okay? If he likes *you*, maybe he will like *us* [*motioning to his kippah*].[1] Sweetie. Be brave! And when the king walks by, shake your little tushy, he'll like it!

---

1. A *kippah* (Hebrew for "dome"), also called a *yarmulke* in Yiddish, is a cap some Jews wear on their head.

The spiel was Gillian's idea. Though unintended, it marked almost exactly a year of organizing since that first Shabbat dinner. We would invite all our communities to the performance, including non-Jews. It would be silly, fun, and political—and raunchy. We'd encourage people to come in costume. There would be a nail polish bar as well as a craft station where people could decorate their own *graggers* to make noise with during the spiel. We'd have a bar with drinks and hamantaschen by donation, and all the proceeds from that and the tickets would be split between IfNotNow Pittsburgh and the family of Mark Daniels, a Black Pittsburgher who'd been murdered by police several weeks prior. Afterward, there'd be a dance party.

There's a joke that most Jewish holidays can be summed up as, "They tried to kill us, we won, let's eat!" Purim follows this basic format, with the addition of "let's drink!" We read from Megillat Esther (the Book of Esther), a biblical story from the Jewish diaspora in Shushan (ancient Persia). The Hebrew school version goes something like this. There is a king, Ahasuerus, who has a sidekick, Haman, who is hell-bent on killing all the Jews. A Jewish girl named Esther and her parental figure, Mordechai (who in our rendition, was played with a gloriously New York Yiddish accent), scheme to get Esther chosen as the king's new bride so that she can get in his ear and convince him not to kill all the Jews. Esther and Haman battle for the king's mind, Esther wins, and the Jews are saved.

Purim's spirit is confusion, transformation, the unexpected, subversion. At the end of the megillah, we read that the Jews are not killed, but *v'nahafoch hu*—the opposite happens. There's also all kinds of nonsense structured into the story and subsequent commentary, such as the king having his former queen, Vashti, turned into a lizard. Purim celebrates raucousness and inversion; we're supposed to get so drunk that we can't tell the difference between the names of the protagonist and antagonist. We are supposed to boo and cheer, make noise, come in disguise. It was the perfect occasion for us to celebrate our process of becoming a radical Jewish community in Pittsburgh.

* * *

AHASHUERUS: Caveat: If we kill all the Jews, who will make our bagels? Who's gonna do all my dental work? Who's gonna organize my Ponzi schemes?

Writing the spiel was a playful collective process. First, we all read the Book of Esther, our source text. We imagined as a group what our version of this story world could be like, what it would include and exclude, who would live there, and what the rules were. In an email summarizing an early writing meeting, Diana, one of our members, noted, "The only thing we've decided was definitively out (so far) was linear time." We spitballed ideas, improvising into them, feeling with our bodies who was there and what they were doing in an absurdist Shushan.

Some people came on board who were involved in the DIY theater scene in Pittsburgh, and we even had a few professional dancers, but the vast majority of the people in the spiel were not practiced performers. Many of us hadn't been in a theatrical production since middle school, and some of us never had. We were making it up as we went along, playing, tapping into creativity and love for our community. We were amateur and committed, mostly unencumbered by rules of the stage. Once we had devised the concept, a group of about eight of us got together for a marathon writing session. We spent a whole Saturday in an unused university conference room that one of us had swiped the others into. Going scene by scene, line by line, throwing out ideas, saying yes, shouting and laughing, munching on pizza, we churned out a first draft. We cast the spiel with texts to our comrades and friends, cleaned up our snacks, and went home.

Over the next frenzied three weeks, we built set pieces (including an oversize copy of *The Protocols of the Elders of Zion* for Zeresh, Haman's wife, to read in bed during an intimate scene of their home life), wrote, rewrote, shuffled scenes, brought in new ideas, threw out old ones, made costumes, memorized lines, and rehearsed. A team devoted to logistics designed and posted flyers, made a promo video, booked a DJ, baked hamantaschen, bought booze, found someone to video record, and prepared the space. The spiel came together shockingly easily and joyfully, each person caring for their part with dedication and commitment to the whole project.

VASHTI: And it only gets darker from here, folks, so buckle the fuck up.

We got stuck on the ending. We rewrote it several times, unsatisfactorily, and finally revised it moments before our performance. According to the scripture, once Esther wins over the king, not only is Haman publicly executed along with all his children, but Jews go on a violent rampage, killing tens of thousands of non-Jewish neighbors in retaliation for what had almost occurred. Who knows what kind of sense this made in the ancient world, but what were we supposed to do with this today? Cartoonish as our version was, we had stuck to the plot of the megillah. Were we really going to portray Jews killing five hundred people on the first day of the bloodshed, and then massacring seventy-five thousand people in the kingdom? How could we joke about Jews killing civilians and justifying it based on what could happen to them? Our entire organization was premised on growing a radical Jewish community that reckoned with our complex position, that understood the liberation of Palestine as our own. But we couldn't ignore the ending our ancestors had written either. Ultimately we decided to break the fourth wall and bend time. A planted audience member would interrupt Mordechai during his call to arms, rejecting his logic of violence and retaliation, just as we had disrupted so many of our community "leaders" who argue that our safety could come at the expense of other people's.

MORDECHAI: Loyal Jews who have lived under the thumb of this kingdom! Now is our moment! Beat your plowshares into swords, beat your pruning hooks into spears, for now we take our revenge!

EVA: Whoa!! Holy fuck, wait a minute! I thought you, Mordechai, were our moral voice!? Our voice of the Jewish people to say: We, as Jews, do not kill other people, right? Isn't that correct? We don't kill gentile civilians?

MORDECHAI: No no no no no. You don't understand, and you will never understand. Has your family been threatened? Has your entire nation been threatened with annihilation? I didn't think so. This is a justified act of self-defense, and I will not listen to your ignorant, thinly veiled antisemitic speech any longer.

EVA: Well, I can tell you Mordechai, I have not experienced what you have experienced, but I know that what you're doing is wrong, and hateful, and immoral. And I know that we are better than that, and that we will stand on the side of justice.

Through Mordechai—the protagonist until that point—we were calling in the ways that our parents and grandparents had used our own painful histories of oppression to ignore or justify the oppression of Palestinians. In his voice, we were naming the accusations of antisemitism that get thrown at anyone, including us, who talk back to the idea that Israeli state violence is Jewish self-defense.

In our conscious minds at the time, we were having a party, we were performing a fun Jewish ritual for our Jewish and non-Jewish communities, we were ending it with our trademark point about Jewish ancestral trauma, connecting it to Palestine and the need for solidarity, and we were holding a fundraiser for our organizing work and to help support community members who had lost a family member to police violence. Now we know that through those politics, we were doing something else too. Whether or not we realized it, we were preparing ourselves for the return of violent political antisemitism.

*   *   *

HAMAN: I am Haman. And this is my Hamanologue [*pause for laughter*]. This smarmy, hook-nosed, money-grubbing, world-controlling, baby blood–drinking Jew, Mordechai, thinks he's above bowing down to me. To me, his superior in every way. It's time for some payback. He needs to die. But not just him. It's time for all his people to suffer the consequences of his insolence. If they won't bow down to me, I'll send them to the G-d they will bow down to. *I am going to kill all the Jews.*

Haman is onstage in a spotlight, wearing a dramatic red-and-black cape and three-cornered hat, tall and menacing. He growls this monologue, oozing disgust, the guttural Hebrew pronunciation of *ch* in Mordechai choked out in mockery, the sound dangerously and repulsively alien. In the recording, audience members gasp. Someone laughs uncomfortably at his extreme and sudden call for Mordechai's death, and several more voice audible shock at the line, "*I am going to kill all the Jews.*"

When we wrote this monologue and many of Haman's other lines, there was a sinking, sick feeling in the room as we put our worst epithets on the page. But we couldn't stop ourselves, as if we were sledding down a steep hill, picking up speed. The writers in the room kept piling on slurs. We remember moments when we pulled back, hesitated, then couldn't help but add more. If we were going to do it, we needed to do it all the way. We also remember asking, Can we really do this, and in public? Why does it feel so much like we're turning our rage and pain on ourselves? What is the point?

The truth is, we felt it coming. There was the federal-level gaslighting, Donald Trump's campaign, the tweeted memes, the media undermining, Steve Bannon and Sebastian Gorka, the insinuations. Then headstones in a Jewish cemetery in Missouri were knocked over. Then other cemeteries were attacked; then there were bomb threats called into Jewish Community Centers. This was only a few months before the Unite the Right rally, the "Jews will not replace us" chant. We all heard it, but who processed it? That summer, the Holocaust memorial in Boston was vandalized, twice. We felt it coming.

When we wrote Haman's lines, we were in essence saying, *Please, take this seriously*. This is what they think of us. We have been asked where our horns are. We have had pennies thrown at us. We've been jumped in school. We've been told smugly by people that they could tell we were Jewish, or they were surprised because we don't look Jewish. But all that had been during times that felt safer.

When we watch this scene in our spiel now, we can only think of how Robert Bowers yelled "All Jews must die" while killing our Jewish community members inside the Tree of Life synagogue. We had almost written it verbatim.

We want to write about Jewishness in Pittsburgh without sinking into sadness, mourning, and grief. We want to write about being Jewish in Pittsburgh without talking about violent death, our fear and hypervigilance. We want to be able to play.

In the video of our spiel, it's shocking how much younger we look.

* * *

We closed the show with a song that we would also sing in the streets after the Tree of Life massacre: "Olam Chesed Yibaneh" (we will build this world with love). That song has a remarkable capacity to be joyous or sorrowful. We've sung it when we are together, feeling powerful, feeling unstoppable. We've sung it with our hearts broken, feeling terrified and lost. We've reached for it, a ritual, like the routines of mourning that tell us exactly how to live during the moments when the normal performance of life feels impossible. It reminds us both of the possibility of loving creation and our obligation to continue the work.

The spiel invites us to play in spaces of liberation and reimagine our histories of annihilation. We feel safer when we make each other laugh. Humor is how we have survived; it is maybe our strongest coping mechanism. And let's be honest, they keep trying to kill us all, and even though they never succeed, they keep trying. How absurd.

We have a responsibility to play. We can have fun, we can be silly, sweet, and bawdy. Play has carried us through mourning. It has allowed us understanding and connection when all of our communications were twisted by grief. When we look at photos from the night of the spiel, sometimes we wonder, Will we ever feel free like that again? As we often say to one another, sometimes in jest, sometimes seriously, and sometimes toying with the delicious tension that lives in between, *keyn yehi ratzon*, may it be so.

*

GILLIAN GOLDBERG AND BENJAMIN STEINHARDT CASE

Gillian Goldberg is an organizer, food producer, and queer ex-punk from Pitts-burgh. She lives and works in Western Massachusetts, where she is in clini-cal social work school. Her interests include salad greens, interspecies com-munication, psychosis, group dynamics, unconscious processes, and collective trauma and resilience. Her favorite hamantaschen filling is poppy seed. Ben-jamin Steinhardt Case is an organizer, writer, and retired kickboxer living in Pittsburgh. He is a PhD student, organizing graduate university workers as he studies social movements. An avid anxiety enthusiast, he also writes on Jew-ish identities, decolonization, the intersections between antisemitism and white supremacy, and the many things that irk him about the movement. They are both grateful for their comrades from IfNotNow Pittsburgh and Jews Orga-nizing for Liberation and Transformation who are building a liberated Jewish community in Pittsburgh. Special thanks to all the spielers behind the scenes and onstage for inspiration, and the community that showed up to laugh with them.

RADIO613

AUTONOMOUS JEWISH

CULTURE ON THE AIRWAVES

MALCAH, SHONI, AND AVI

*I had the good fortune to be on episode 36 of Radio613 in 2010
when I spoke to Avi and Malcah about radical Jewish musical,
cultural, and political organizing happening in my hometown of
Baltimore and beyond. At the time that the show launched, there
was a fair amount of Jewish leftist and anarchist organizing in
North America, but not many cultural spaces to talk about it.
Radio613 carved out radio and web space to do just that. One thing
I appreciated about the show was that it simultaneously honored
and challenged Jewish political, religious, and cultural traditions.
So often, Jews in activist spaces have to leave certain parts of
their Jewishness behind, like their spirituality or commitment to
preserving certain ancestral traditions, in order to fit in with non-
Jewish leftists. Not Radio613. Radio613 was a space to honor
and reassess who we are, what we believe, how we dream,
and how we resist as Jews within larger movements for justice.*
—Mark Gunnery, musician and journalist

Radio613, a show dedicated to Jewish politics, culture, and religious life, was produced between 2008 and 2015. It was broadcast on CFRC 101.9 FM, a campus and community radio station located in so-called Kingston, Ontario, and podcast online at radio613.wordpress.com, where you can still listen to it. The show was collectively created and run by us: Malcah, Shoni, and Avi, anarchist Jews who were seeking to present Jewish perspectives on religious/spiritual thought and practice, race and racism, gender and feminisms, disability, antisemitism, identity politics, colonialism, and resistance, among other things.

Prior to this show, we had all been involved in community radio and met each other as university students in Kingston (pop. 135,000), the European colonial name for the Kanyen'keha:ka, Wendat, Mississauga, and Algonquin peoples' home from time immemorial. It's a small city situated where the Great Lakes meet the Kaniatarowanenneh (Saint Lawrence) River and the world's largest freshwater basin flows to the Atlantic Ocean. Always a place of importance and beauty, the land was colonized by both the French and English, and was the first capital of colonial Canada. Present-day Kingston, with an increasing yet tiny nonwhite population (10 to 15 percent) and some eight hundred nonstudent Jews, exists under a hegemonic web of Victorian WASP cultural values steeped in generations of colonial racism, Islamophobia, and antisemitism. Talk of Judaism is not welcome, and we turned to radio as a place to be openly Jewish and decentralize the idea of Jewish community.

In our desire to birth Radio613, we were influenced by Daniel Sieradski and others who had suggested that people try to create anarchist halacha (Jewish law). That project would be a massive re-interpretation of Jewish text, requiring hundreds of religious Jews coming together to find a way to make a Jewish anarchist practice. Originally we hoped our radio show would be part of a broader effort that could include, for example, online discussion boards where people were talking through Torah and hashing it all out, especially what was inspiring or challenging to our politics and ethics. Radio613 was intended to be a starting point for reconnecting anarchism and Judaism. We wanted to nourish Jewish life as well as explore Jewish ideas and ways of being as anarchists alienated from institutional spaces, synagogues, and cultural institutions.

In the early 2000s, many "radical on everything but Palestine" Jews found themselves ostracized from the Left after years of pro-Palestinian organizing had finally made a breakthrough. Then in the mid- to late 2000s, a small crop of Jews emerged from high school onto Ontario university campuses with either an anti- or non-Zionist analysis, or at the least a refreshing new open-mindedness about Israel. There was a shift among young Jews who had been raised Zionist, but who either did not have a strong bond with organized religion, or didn't associate Judaism with the Zionism/racism of their families or community. They yearned for a spiritual and ancestral connection to Judaism that broke with mainstream Zionist and nationalist, racist and colonial, and patriarchal and homo/transphobic religious communities. This willingness to question Israel blossomed (as a result of both the period we were living in and the efforts of Palestinian/pro-Palestinian educators), and we found ourselves capable of encouraging more Jews toward radicalism.

One of the greatest challenges then became the antisemitism present in the majority of Canadian anarchist scenes. These milieus were generally dominated by white settlers from Euro-Christian backgrounds and awash in antisemitic, anticapitalist conspiracy theories. These anarchists frequently projected their critique of Christianity (based on their own experiences) onto Judaism and Islam as though somehow equivalent. In our experience, this manifested in a cultural clash between settlers from Euro-Christian backgrounds and Jews as well as Muslims. For instance, we often felt that Euro-Christian anarchists reacted with confused hostility to "mouthy Jewish women" (as Jewish and other feminist women have been talking about for generations). Most anarchists seemed to have limited ways of understanding Jews, seeing them only as white passing / invisible, Holocaust victims, or conniving, brutal, and vicious occupiers of Palestine. So where did that leave Jewish anarchists, who wanted to be both spiritual and antistate, anticapitalist, and anticolonial?

Radio613 was intimately linked to AKA Autonomous Social Center, an anarchist social center that we cofounded with non-Jewish comrades around the same time we started the show. From the beginning of AKA, we asserted an anarchism inclusive of religion, which our comrades were generally supportive of. To be clear, this religious-inclusive anarchism valorized explicitly autonomous religious expression, and set out to either challenge or supplant hierarchical and authoritarian religious structures—frequently referred to broadly as "organized religion." When we started AKA, our group included religious Jews, Muslims, and secular Christians. Jewish events that happened in the space involved, for example, building Sukkot and hosting Shabbat dinners along with Tu BiShvat and Passover seders. Since 9/11, many Muslims had managed to open anarchism to working with religious Muslims, and even accepting religious Muslims who identify as anarchists, and it is because of their hard work that we were able to identify as religious Jews comfortably within some anarchist scenes and create our own anarchist space for autonomous religious people.

Radio613 was one of those affirming and positive anarchist Jewish spaces. It helped us feel less isolated and alone. Through interviews, podcasting, and livestreams, we could connect with other rad/anarchist Jews around the world. The name we chose asserted our geographic context—613 is Kingston's area code as well as the local highway exit to Sydenham Road, where the small Jewish cemetery is, and of course, 613 is the number of mitzvot (commandments) in the Torah.

In the early days of Radio613, queer Jewish artists seemed to be leading the way when it came to expressing Jewish ethics aligned with our anarchist ethics. Malcah recalls realizing that "everybody who I thought was awesome was a queer, genderqueer, or femme Jewish artist basically." In retrospect, Shoni notes that Radio613 gravitated to artists because "art gives you the space to think about an idea without having to have it perfectly hashed out, in a liberating way. You can grapple with an idea without being subject to the rigorous expectations of social theory. The ideas these Jewish artists were exploring were important even if there were no easy answers. A lot of truths and key questions were brought out, such as: What does decolonizing Judaism look like? What is a Jewish future without, say, Zionism or assimilation?"

We interviewed organizers from Jews for Racial and Economic Justice's Purim spiel; Alexis Mitchell about her film looking at camp, exile, memory, and queer understandings of diaspora that don't rely on homeland / not homeland binaries; Temim Fruchter, (then) drummer of the Shondes, a queer, anti-Zionist, postpunk band; Mark Gunnery of RiotFolk; and Noam Lerman, who performed poetry inspired by a summer of Talmud learning about Shabbat. We tried to examine political, cultural, and spiritual issues from a position of not holding all the answers. We were learning as we went, like everyone else, though we tried to honor and elevate the knowledge and experiences of each other along with the people who appeared on the show. We never set out to exclusively interview anarchists, and although we did interview some people who identified as anarchists, we also talked to many Jews who were not anarchists, yet had a lot of affinity with anarchism. We wanted to delve into what was already out there and use it to build something new.

Radio613 gave us a chance to look through a Jewish lens at anarchist projects too. For one of our Sukkot shows, we interviewed Sam Kuhn, who spoke about the organizing work of the Tenants Action Group in so-called Belleville, Ontario. This type of work relating to homelessness, capitalism, and colonization was at the top of our minds during Sukkot, so the radio show allowed us to dig into the connections. While some of us had been involved in years of solidarity work with local Indigenous peoples in many campaigns and crisis periods, we strove to understand how we might better act in solidarity. How might we hold the dichotomy that most of us are descendants of refugees running from pogroms while simultaneously occupiers of Indigenous land without an invitation? On another Sukkot show, we interviewed someone who was organizing an anticolonial Thanksgiving dinner—giving us a chance to highlight calls for solidarity in undoing this rotten so-called Canada.

There are other ways in which Radio613 helped us explore Jewish theology that strongly resonated with and opened up possibilities for each of us to use Jewish values to navigate toward decolonization. Our Tu BiShvat episodes helped us unlearn/learn so as to reclaim the holiday from its contemporary colonial iteration. We sought to highlight what Zionist education teaches—that Tu BiShvat is a holiday about planting trees in Israel—and what it doesn't teach—that this practice is part of the ongoing ethnic cleansing of Palestinians by planting trees over destroyed villages to make way for Jewish-only settlements. We attempted to expose the brutality and deception of the Jewish National Fund by making parallels with the Canadian colonial state practice of overcoding Indigenous sacred places. We also wanted to uncover and better understand Tu BiShvat's kabbalistic beauty and the ancient ecological Jewish relationship with the land.

We used the show as a platform to share our experience hosting/participating in our first Tu BiShvat seder. Through our interactions with Indigenous teachers, we were aware that Israel's settler colonialism was being exceptionalized by many Jews and other radicals, while ignoring settler lives here in these occupied territories on Turtle Island.

Radio613 also often focused on antifascism through a Jewish historical lens. Our inaugural show looked back at the Christie Pitts Riot. On August 16, 1933, in Toronto, after months of harassment by local Nazi sympathizers unhappy with Jews swimming at local beaches, the locals formed "swastika clubs." One such club unfurled a swastika banner during a baseball game between the mixed Italian and Jewish Harbord Playground team, and another Italian team, St. Peter's (which sided with the Jewish players). The game descended into a street brawl of WASPs versus Jews and Italians after a crowd of ten thousand non-Jews rallied to the cries of *Sieg Heil.*

In another show, we interviewed David Rosenberg, author of *Battle for the East End*, on the rise of British fascism as well as Jewish responses and antifascist organizing in London's immigrant East End in the 1930s. Rosenberg discussed the October 4, 1936, Battle of Cable Street, where working-class Jews, Irish, immigrants, anarchists, socialists, and communists historically stood up to fascists—and won. Radio613 talked with prolific artist Jewlia Eisenberg, whose band Charming Hostess has created art at the "intersection of voice, text, and diaspora consciousness." Charming Hostess's work, the Ginzburg Geographies, unearths the lives and geographies of two Jewish antifascist intellectuals and organizers in Italy—Natalia and Leone Ginzburg—along with Italian regional musical traditions, antifascist songs, and Italian Jewish liturgy.

Though it was an incomplete effort, we tried to honor the work of the Jewish radical mentors and movements that came before us. For example, we aired documentaries about Yiddish anarchists and partisan fighters and organizers; interviewed Arbeter Ring educator and singer Adrienne Cooper, now of blessed memory; and did an on-air reading of excerpts from *Yours in Struggle: Three Feminist Perspectives on Anti-Semitism and Racism* (published in 1984) and *The Flying Camel: Essays on Identity by Women of North African and Middle Eastern Jewish Heritage* (published in 2003).

At times Radio613 became an outlet not just for us but also for other Jews seeking to represent themselves outside the (especially in Canada) dismally conservative Jewish press. Sound artist Orev Reena Katz joined the show several times to discuss the blacklisting of their art projects due to their position on Israeli apartheid. Throughout Radio613's duration, a fair amount of content was dedicated to klezmer and Yiddish culture. Although of course not universally appealing to Jews, klezmer and Yiddish culture provided a heart-stirring and frequently revolutionary response to our own and some of our listeners' yearning for cultural and ancestral connection. We hoped that by connecting to our own diasporic culture, we would be part of a broader effort to celebrate and reclaim an array of diasporic Jewish cultures.

Another big piece of the show was our social relationships with each other as a small collective. The show was interwoven with what we were doing outside Radio613, sharing Shabbatot and *chags* (holidays) as well as integrating Jewish practice and anarchist living and ethics into our living spaces and community projects. A large part of our practice was fighting patriarchy within ourselves and our city. This led to Radio613 ending on a sour note. We had to stop the show in order to hold an accountability process, lasting years, for Avi, whose patriarchal behavior broke our collective (and impacted many in our community). Throughout that demanding process, we prioritized anarchist and feminist ethical practices while holding space open for the possibility that Avi would engage in the Jewish tradition of *teshuva* (returning). While Avi can't repair all the harm that he did, he grew over time, allowing us to grow closer again; we now practice together again in both Kingston and so-called Montreal, where Avi has become part of a vibrant anarchist Jewish community.

Looking back, we take pride in and miss how we were able to create a community with other radical or anarchist Jews through Radio613. People were brought together in conversation and felt connected, which was especially needed in that particular political and geographic moment. These days, we take great delight and *nakhes* (pride in other people's achievements) in seeing so many spiritually grounded anticolonial Jewish groups popping up, especially outside the main Jewish centers. The proliferation of radical and/or anarchist Jewish radio projects that have emerged in the last decade, such as the *Republic of Love, Kaddish, Radio Free Babylonia, Treyf,* and *Diaspora Podcast*, provides us with similarly warm feelings.

While Radio613's loftier goal of developing deep anarchist Jewish theology wasn't realized, with Hashem's help, perhaps we left behind some seeds that might allow others to do so.

*

Malcah is an Ashkenazi Jewish anarchist living in waspy Kingston, Canada, occupied Haudenausonee and Anishinaabe land. She has been active within locally based antiauthoritarian projects for the last fifteen years. Shoni is an anarchist Jewish representative of Neptune on earth. Avi is a klezmer purveyor committed to yiddishkeit, anarchism, and cooking for community. He lives on unceded Kanien'kehá:ka territory known as Montreal. Avi would like to thank the countless teachers out there who share their Torah, political and ethical analysis, and personal, communal, and ancestral truths.

MALCAH, SHONI, AND AVI

JEWISH DRAG IN

DANGEROUS TIMES

ABBIE GOLDBERG

Turmohel, a Boston-based Jewish drag troupe, emerged out of a casual conversation at a party in 2018. We were joking around about the idea until unexpectedly, we urgently pulled out our calendars to set a meeting date. At our first rehearsal, I found myself lying on the floor next to Prince Shpilkes Sad Kid the First pretending to be a latke bubbling in hot oil. "Do you like your gender better with sour cream or applesauce?" they asked. "Call me a heretic," I answered, "but I like it with ketchup." They gasped. We rolled over to let our other side cook.

Nowadays, the five of us core members—Ch'ai Treason, Prince Shpilkes Sad Kid the First, RivKilla, Meshuggemama, and Imma GoldMan—explore gender, untold Jewish histories, ableism, anti-semitism, Jewish rituals, bagels, and more with humor, care, and a fierce commitment to being our weird, full, Jewish selves.

When we initially formed, we weren't sure if there would be an audience for our niche silliness and unabashed Judaism. We auditioned for a show at a local gay bar, but the producer emailed us back to ask if we "had anything more accessible." Undeterred, we set about creating our own show, theming it around the Jewish deli. The acts included a reenactment of New York gubernatorial candidate Cynthia Nixon's controversial order of a cinnamon raisin bagel with cream cheese, capers, onions, and (oy vey!) lox, a parody of Miley Cyrus's "Wrecking Ball" as a cooking tutorial for matzo balls, a breakup song between a lactose-intolerant Prince Shpilkes and cheese, and a masked dance to the song "Dos Bisele Shpayz" (this little bit of food) that left the stage covered in beets, cabbage, fish, and other Ashkenazi specialities.

To our surprise, when it came time for our self-produced performance, we filled the room to capacity within fifteen minutes of opening the doors. People crammed in the doorways and overflowed into the halls, and we still had to turn people away, telling them that they could watch a livestream of the show on Facebook, and meet us at the after-party for dancing and shotza balls (matzo ball shots). In meeting a need for ourselves to explore Judaism through playfulness and performance, it seemed that we were meeting a need for our community too.

Dancing onstage, I felt present in my Jewishness in a way that I never had before. We have always been a people of the earth, such as basing our calendar around the cycles of the moon, and our festivals around planting and harvest. But I think as Jewish people, it's hard to feel present in our bodies. Maybe it's because we've been told that we don't meet Western standards of beauty or gender. Maybe it's because we've been told that we're "intellectuals," only living in a world of ideas and knowledge, questioning and debating. Maybe it's because we've had to leave home so many times that it's hard to feel at home anywhere—even in our own bodies. Somehow, though, embodying a character allowed me to embody myself. Somehow, my mind and body were reunited, and I felt at home in my body.

The audience also felt it. At the after-party, we danced wildly to pop songs and klezmer music. Person after person came up to me, exclaiming things like "I want to do a drag number about leaving Orthodox Judaism!" and "I want to do a number about my *bubbe* [grandmother]!" The night was wild and unrestrained. Our freedom had let others feel free as well.

For our second full-length self-produced show, we picked a date near Halloween, but decided to focus on specifically Jewish demons and monsters. Prince Shpilkes remade themselves out of clay as a golem, RivKilla did a striptease with a Shrek mask on (*shrek* is Yiddish for fear), and Ch'ai Treason possessed souls as a dybbuk, yet the biggest Jewish monster we channeled for the night was antisemitism. RivKilla wanted to perform singer-songwriter Leonard Cohen's spooky "You Want It Darker," and we thought, "Why not use the song as the backdrop for a staging of the blood libel?" Horned and winged, hairy-legged and hungry, we could be the Jews of antisemites' false accusations and nightmares, killing a (fake) baby onstage and drinking its blood. After surveying some friends about whether it seemed too dark, offensive, or an invitation to get us on the front page of some white supremacist's incendiary "news" site, we decided to go for it, and gleefully went about gluing feathers to cardboard wings.

Work on the show stalled as we reached the High Holidays. We dipped apples in honey and asked each other, "What made us think that we could plan a drag show during the busiest month of the year to be Jewish?" But we forged ahead, making fake Tinder profiles for Jewish demons and trying not to take ourselves too seriously. On Yom Kippur, I spent the day in songful and tearful release at Nishmat Shoom, the self-described "garlic eaters minyan" in Western Massachusetts. I wasn't fasting, but I felt utterly emptied out, ready to lean into the open fearlessness that drag had gifted me. In the car on my way home, I reluctantly turned my phone back on for the first time in twenty-four hours—filled with anxiety at the thought of the so-called real world shattering my serenity.

The news was all over Facebook: there was a lethal shooting at a synagogue in Halle, Germany.

I knew that I shouldn't have let my guard down. I knew that we could never be safe.

A friend, someone whom three of us in Turmohel had spent the previous year with as part of a Jewish community organizing fellowship, was one of the people inside. Our dear friend who loves prayer, ritual, and Judaism spent the holiest day of the Jewish year barricading herself inside the synagogue's holy walls.

I am so grateful that she survived.

I am so grateful that we have survived.

The show was in three days. We held an emergency meeting. Should we cancel it? Suddenly it felt dangerous to advertise our Jewishness so publicly—not to mention that we're queer and radical. Should we do the show, but cut the blood libel piece? The world felt scary, filled with demons much worse than the ones within Judaism that we'd been reading up about in order to write our show.

Not much is taught about Jewish demons, *sheydim* as they're called in Hebrew, at least in mainstream Jewish learning spaces. There are lots of them, however. According to Abba Benjamin, one of the old Talmudic rabbis, "If the eye had the power to see them, no creature could endure the demons." There's Sheyd, who guards over open books; there are four demon queens, one for each season; Alukah the vampire; Rahab the sea monster; Sulak the bathroom demon; the Nephilim, a whole class of giants; and countless others hiding in the cramped pages of the Talmud or lurking in forgotten folktales.

Demons are complicated, like so much else in the Jewish tradition. They were said to kill babies and cause infertility, but they were also said to have helped build the Temple, taught people science and magic, and even defended the Jews during the Crusades. I guess that's why I'm tempted to disagree with Benjamin. I think to live in this world is learning first how to see the demons and then how to endure them. The world is full of horrible things—shootings in synagogues, climate change, prisons, policing, and deportation, to name a few. In order to wake up in the morning and keep going, we must find a way to see and endure the demons.

There's another Jewish demon class called the Se'irim, who (and I am not making this up) are hairy-legged dancers. We endure the demons however we can. There are demons we must fight, and demons we must learn to dance with.

We did the show. "We're scared," we told our audience. "This is scary. But this is why we do this. Our strength comes through our community, our resilience through our creativity, and our survival through each other. Our joy and sorrow are among our greatest weapons because they're why we keep fighting."

"You Want It Darker," the blood libel number, was the first act of the night. We slinked onto the stage in silky black lingerie, with papier-mâché horns sprouting from our heads. We held our arms up to the ceiling and lip-synched the word *hineini*—Hebrew for "I am here"—as blood made from cornstarch and food dye dripped down our grinning faces.

*

Abbie Goldberg is a writer of musicals, maker of puppets, and dreamer of worlds to come. She lovingly dedicates this piece to her dear friend Alona Weimer as well as Turmohel: Ch'ai Treason (Emma June Yucha), Prince Shpilkes Sad Kid the First (Hannah Nahar), RivKilla (Annelise Rittenberg), and Meshuggemama (Harry Weissman).

LOVE AND RAGE

REBELLIOUS ANARCHIST YOUNG JEWS (RAYJ) COLLECTIVE

During summertimes in our youth, Camp Moshava was our idyllic utopia. We planned a revolution, and kids jumped on chairs at the end of meals screaming, "Freedom, freedom, anarchy!" It was where we got an education in structural injustice through a radical lens. Mosh —part of Habonim Dror, a socialist and Zionist youth movement— was also where we were exposed to the complexities of the Jewish community's relationship to Israel. We grew up together there, in this place of such contradiction, which itself feels so deeply Jewish.

Mosh functioned like a youth-led, socialist commune. Campers as young as eight debated the terms for a *kupa* (shared economy) to decide how to fairly divvy up their candy and toiletries with their friends. When we were eighteen years old, we were given responsibility for running the camp and used consensus to determine everything from bedtimes for nine-year-olds to the social theory that we wanted to teach our campers. We learned the values of youth empowerment and autonomy, and were encouraged to embrace our imagination and express ourselves. As children, we experienced a freedom that gave us the confidence and skills to create a world that we believed in.

We cherished the revolutionary education that we received through Mosh and Habonim Dror, but as we got a bit older, we began to question and eventually oppose the role of Zionism in this movement. Our time at camp had taught us to challenge authority and tradition. We felt like we had the right to defy our community and lead it in a new direction. So we attempted to amend Habonim Dror North America's youth-created constitution, replacing Zionism with anarchism. In 2015, we wrote a proposal called "It's All about Changing Your State of Mind," which read in part,

> Whereas:
>
> The state of Israel functions through a hierarchy of power and the centralization of power. Those running the state are more interested in maintaining this hierarchy than protecting and representing its people.
>
> In order to maintain and protect itself as a state, the state of Israel must oppress and limit the freedom of all people living within the state of Israel and Palestinians living within the Occupied Territories of Gaza and the West Bank.
>
> Whereas:
>
> Habonim Dror North America is a revolutionary youth movement that claims to be actively supporting the creation of a new social order.
>
> A new social order is built on breaking down the status quo, and dreaming past what might seem most practical or popular.
>
> Whereas:
>
> Habonim Dror North America supports the freedom of all people. True freedom will never come from a state.

Even though each "whereas" was supposed to be decided on by the entire movement, the higher-ups attempted to shut down the proposal before it was able to reach a vote from the general body. Ultimately it failed. Still hopeful, we tried to reform our movement's definition of Zionism to at least be explicitly against the occupation in Palestine. This idea similarly crashed and burned. We were startled and hurt.

Later we learned that other movement members had attempted to change, and failed at doing so, the movement's definition of Zionism multiple times before us. We realized that our lack of success was because Zionism was a fundamental part of the ideology and structure of the movement. Habonim Dror's funding and existence was dependent on Zionist organizations and grants.

While we had the dreams, tools, and relationships to create a Jewish community that was not built on Zionism, we couldn't enact our values of anarchism, free expression, and communal agency within the structure of Habonim Dror. With pain and anger, we had no choice but to leave the community of friends and mentors that we'd grown up with. Our departure from Habonim Dror, though, included discussions about creating an alternative—one that still honored the revolutionary potential of youths, and centered itself on Jewish and collective liberation. We threw around names and had goofy video calls until we finally came up with Rebellious Anarchist Young Jews (RAYJ, pronounced "rage"). As one of us wrote in an early manifesto:

> RAYJ exists because I have yet to find a space in both the Jewish community and the radical community at large where I can further understand, debate, and loudly proclaim my identity as a radical Jew.

For me, both my Jewish and radical identities are crucial to how I understand myself. My Judaism is an identity from which I gain strength, challenge my ideas, build community, and push for justice. My radical identity connects me to larger movements for change, secular social theory, earth-shattering struggles, and important friends and allies. I am tired of having to choose between my two selves. I am tired of hiding one part of who I am when I am in the company of the other. I am tired of the shame that I feel when I call myself a radical or Jew.

I need to enrich and enliven both of my identities in order to avoid the split of self that I too often feel. This inner divide hinders me in my ability to act on the most trying questions that the Jewish and radical community must face today. In order to be a healthy critical thinker, I need partnerships with other radical Jews who empathize even in the smallest way with what I'm describing.

That's why I'm in-Rayj(ed)!

At the time, we ended up drifting away from one another, picking up new organizing projects, and putting RAYJ on the back burner.

Then on October 27, 2018, the massacre in the Tree of Life synagogue took place—shattering us all. We desperately needed the fierceness and autonomy that we'd promised each other three years earlier, and regrouped to created a graphic called "Care Not Cops." The image portrayed our sentiments that the Jewish community needs to depend on tradition, ritual, and solidarity with other marginalized peoples to be safe, rather than rely on cops and state violence. It unexpectedly went viral, and people began reaching out to us, asking how they could be involved in our collective and sharing their own ideas for building a more liberatory Jewish community. We realized how many Jews were out there who believed in Jewish anarchism, but had no community within which to articulate or practice their values.

We officially became a collective that fall, with the goal of being a healing, supportive, Jewish anarchist community for each other. We wanted to create graphics and art that resonated with other people, and in turn would move them to organize their own collectives and direct actions.

Since then, we have created art and ritual guides, and collaborated with other Jewish antifascist and anarchist organizers and collectives. While we have become more widely known than we'd anticipated, we're not trying to do mass mobilization or create an umbrella organization that's representative of all Jewish peoples' needs. Our aim is to free ourselves from any Jewish institutional and state-constructed constraints that limit our Jewish expression and practice. We hope to cultivate as well as share media, art, and rituals. We dream of building a community that we believe in. We want our work to inspire other Jews to do the same—so that together we can fight for the liberation of ourselves, our communities, and us all.

Toward that goal, below are some excerpts of the writings and art that we've created from fall 2018 to winter 2020, as encouragement for you to do the same, and of course, invitation to borrow and use any of this in your own DIY practices.

PRAYER IS PUNK

Written originally in 2017, when one of us was the Jewish education director at Camp Moshava, for the introduction to a Jewish tochnit (curriculum). Adapted in 2019 in the wake of antisemitism and state violence as a way to process the power of Jewish ritual to heal and resist.

The world's immense change and disorder creates a need for collective action. We must see our identities as Jewish people as ways to fight against society's oppressive institutions and barriers. Collective responsibility and spiritual growth are central tenants in Judaism that have the power to become acts of liberation and resistance.

The term *punk* has taken on many meanings, referring mainly to the DIY music and media scene that emerged in the late 1970s. I would like to define punk as anything and anyone that is actively defying and resisting dominant mainstream culture and society. Our Judaism is punk. Its obligations, history, and practices question the underpinnings of Christian hegemony, white nationalism, and capitalism that our society is built on. Unapologetically expressing our Judaism is an act of resistance and defiance.

In this vein, the RAYJ collective sees prayer as direct action. We interrupt expected patterns of behavior when we take time out of our day to bless the act of waking up, recite blessings before we eat food, and pray daily for a year when we mourn our dead. These acts of prayer become momentary boycotts of mainstream society.

These personal acts of prayerful resistance connect us to broader communities of people who pray—either like us or in their own ways. Together, we have the power to collectively disrupt the world simply by opening a siddur (prayer book). Can you imagine a mass protest movement organized without any meetings? If all of us punk Jews prayed at the same times every day, would we form a decentralized movement of people momentarily boycotting, doing sit-ins, and resisting the spectacle of capitalism?

Prayer truly is and must be punk. As a community, let's challenge ourselves to embody our Judaism as an act of rebellion.

A PRAYER FOR RESISTANCE

Written in July 2019 in solidarity with the Never Again movement,
and those fighting against the deportation and detention of immigrants.

Stumbling, tripping. The ground breaks. My jagged edge.

"It's shattered, all shattered," my mother and hers and hers and hers cry as windows become marbles that flood the sidewalks with their rolling danger.

Somehow these broken pieces still shine—their shifting glimmer hints at the songs and faces and footsteps that they once created. My ancestors' bones in my hands. These parts once knew a home together and created something so beautiful.

"I didn't want you to walk along this fracture," the mothers shout to their babies who dangle on edges. Babies now grown, we find one another perched on the boundaries that try to separate us. I won't pretend to know the exact sharpness of your shattered parts or vivid beauty fractured within your cracks. But we can still promise each other that we will find the pieces that make these chasms whole again. We must, we must, we must.

I breathe so that a wish may come into existence.

May my body and your strength collapse these narrow places so never again will anyone be made to walk this jagged edge.

DISLOYAL ONES

Written after Donald Trump asserted in August 2019 that Jews were disloyal to the United States and Israel if they voted Democrat.

We are the disloyal ones.

We are the ones who refuse to bow down to rulers on horseback. Whose only *melech* (king) is the life-giving force of *ruach* (breath).

We are the ones who find home not in your conquered places but rather in our sacred times. We are people of the book, not the borders drawn onto your maps. We find ourselves in curling black letters etched into parchment, not in waving flags.

We are the ones who wrestle with G-d whenever we dream. While we stand and pray, we ask our ancestors, not your armies, to gather and shield us.

We are the ones who desist from domination with candles and bread and wine. We are the ones who reject your calendar so we can grow with the waxing and waning of the shimmering moon.

We are the ones who refuse your food when we remember the pain of destruction, who sit for a week as we grieve our dead. We are the ones who sing songs of joy as the flames consume us.

The disloyal ones create defiant encampments with the mixed multitudes who remain ungovernable.

Together, our beauty turns your curses into blessings.

Mah Tovu (how goodly)

JEWISH ANTIFASCIST SHABBAT GUIDE

Excerpt from a lengthy guide created for the one-year anniversary of the massacre at the Tree of Life in collaboration and solidarity with Jewish anarchist comrades in Pittsburgh. The questions at the end were intended as a way to continue conversations with friends about Jewish anarchism.

Shabbat shalom and welcome to the RAYJ antifascist Shabbat guide.

We feel that it is important to host an antifascist Shabbat on the anniversary of the Tree of Life shooting in Pittsburgh because the shooting in Pittsburgh was the result of fascist, white nationalist, and antisemitic rhetoric and policies that have grown in popularity and clout over the past several years. White nationalism and fascism have always been a threat to Jews, black and brown communities, LGBTQIA+ folks, immigrants, Muslims, folks with disabilities, women, and many, many other marginalized people. Like other marginalized communities, the Jewish community has a history of fighting back against fascism.

Even in the most challenging moments, we can learn from the choices and traditions of our ancestors to imagine what resistance and healing can look like today. We as Jews can claim our unique history of antifascist resistance, and use it to inspire our current struggle against antisemitism, white nationalism, and fascism. We hope that this weekend of commemoration offers us all space for both healing and fighting back.

How is this moment in Jewish history making you feel?

What memories and stories of Jewish antifa organizing do you want to tell?

Do you think it is important to renew and embolden Jewish antifa organizing? What makes you excited? Nervous?

What do you hope that your community's Jewish antifa resistance is up to in three months? Two years? Five years?

*

RAYJ is a new collective within the broader North American Jewish community that aims to bridge gaps between the leftist, radical, and Jewish worlds, and bring people together to work for collective liberation, heal, and celebrate our culture and values. It is intended as a space for folks to exchange ideas, practice Jewish ritual, play, and build partnerships with one another. RAYJ is learning and growing. Please reach out to us to have conversations, connect, and tell us your ideas and dreams for our collective and the Jewish world at https://rebelliousjews.wixsite.com/rayj!

FIGHTING FASCISTS
WITH FOLK ART

JAY SAPER

Wild strawberries crept across the forest floor at the edge of a pit where Nazis and their collaborators shot an entire village of Jews in a single afternoon. Those who were with me, visiting this death site, kept their distance from the fruit, seeing in its color the blood stained into the soil. With the utmost respect for their reaction, I still couldn't help myself from bending over to harvest the bounty. As I placed the fruit on my tongue, I did not taste the vast wretchedness of these Jews' end but instead the sweetness of the lives they lived before.

I feel similarly when my hand carves lines of memory onto paper with a knife. The Jewish folk art tradition of making papercuts spans centuries and continents. Intricate designs have been used to decorate *ketubah* marriage agreements, commemorate the *yortsayt* (anniversary) of a loved one's death, and protect a mother and newborn child with a *kimpetbriv* (amulet). The most common of all Jewish papercuts is the *mizrekh*, hung on the eastern wall of a home to indicate the direction of prayer. I make papercuts so that people won't be forgotten.

Papercuts are simultaneously delicate yet durable, firm yet frail. They are prone to tear at the slightest touch yet powerful enough to be entrusted with the commemoration of life, love, and loss. The form is amenable to honoring those who in their moment of greatest vulnerability, discovered and displayed unfathomable resolve. I work within this tradition in homage to the overlooked stories of Jewish women who rose up against the Nazis during the *khurbn* (Shoah), often giving their own lives in the process, so that one day fascism might fall, and we might get to taste the fruits of freedom.

Frieda Belinfante was among the first women in Europe to artistically direct and conduct a professional orchestra. When the Nazis invaded Amsterdam, she set down the bow of her cello to take up work with the resistance.

Ala Gertner smuggled gunpowder out of the Weichsel-Union-Metall-
werke factory that was used to blow up crematorium IV at the Auschwitz concentration camp.

JAY SAPER

334

Raizl Korczak-Marle helped to found the Vilna Ghetto's United Partisan Organization. She fought in the Rudninkai Forest with the Avengers partisan unit.

As part of the Jewish underground in France, Dina "Sylvie" Lipka-Krischer carried out countless acts of sabotage and assassinated Nazi officers.

JAY SAPER

336

When the Nazis at Auschwitz ordered ballerina Franceska Mann to undress and enter the gas chamber, she threw her clothes at the SS officer, stole his gun, and shot him dead. Her final dance inspired a spontaneous uprising. Jewish women, emboldened by her example, lashed back at the gruesome guards.

FIGHTING FASCISTS WITH FOLK ART

337

Tatyana Markus carried a bouquet of asters up to a balcony, where she watched Nazi soldiers march into Kiev in the Ukraine. She cheered as the brass band played and then threw her bouquet down to greet the soldiers. The grenade she tucked inside it exploded and took their lives.

JAY SAPER

338

Vladka Meed, born Feigele Peltel, helped children escape from the
Warsaw Ghetto and smuggled in weapons used by the Jewish Fighting Organization in the historic uprising.

FIGHTING FASCISTS WITH FOLK ART

Frumka Płotnicka traveled from ghetto to ghetto with news of endless atrocities along with an unwavering spirit to help foment revolt.
She led the Będzin Ghetto uprising.

Roza Robota organized the procurement of explosives used to blow up crematorium IV at Auschwitz. The moment before she was hung, along with coconspirators Ala Gertner, Regina Safirsztajn, and Ester Wajcblum, for fomenting revolt, she called out to her fellow prisoners to take vengeance.

Rachel Sacher Rudnitzky fought against the Nazis as a Jewish partisan in the Rudninkai Forest outside Vilna, Lithuania.

JAY SAPER

Jeanine Sontag stole arms for the underground in France and transported explosives used to blow up Nazi factories. She derailed trains and executed Gestapo officers, along with their collaborators.

Niuta Teitelboim assassinated high Nazi officials, blew up their cafés, and sabotaged railways vital to carrying out the so-called Final Solution. She taught women who would go on to lead the Warsaw Ghetto uprising how to shoot weapons and build bombs. "I am a Jew," she insisted. "My place is among the most active fighters of fascism, in the struggle for the honor of my people."

*

Jay Saper is an educator, organizer, and artist who lives in Brooklyn, New York.

KLEZMER PLAYLIST FOR A

REVOLT AGAINST FASCISM

AARON LAKOFF

The role of a DJ is not unlike that of an activist. Both are trying to organize people to move in unison toward a common goal. My aim here, as your humble anarcho-klezmer DJ for this playlist, is to make you dance, of course. Yet I would argue that it's also to make you think about your surroundings, the rich histories of the music filling your ears, and deeper meanings of the rhythms and hues of the notes. And it's to hopefully convince you that music, like food, water, and winning strategies for social transformation, is essential within our struggles and movements.

I'm not going to pretend that I know a lot about klezmer—because I don't. Like you, I'm here to learn. But I am a lover of music. I like to listen deeply and figure out what music is telling us about the direction of the world—good and bad. In this case, as both an anarchist Jew and DJ, I've noticed a resurgence in antifascist klezmer, and at a time when we sorely need such rebellious voices. The alt-right and neo-Nazis have reemerged in North America, antisemitic attacks are claiming lives, and Israel continues to intensify its system of apartheid against Palestinians. There is a growing urgency for Jews to speak out, or in this case, sing out, to protect not only our own communities but our beloved neighbors, friends, and comrades from other communities too.

Most of the bands and songs you'll find here are borrowing from a long tradition of anarchistic klezmer music. Our ancestors sang labor solidarity songs because they slaved away for long hours on looms and sewing machines. They sang songs about the police because they felt the wrath of batons and rifles directed at them during protests as well as strikes. And as one example below illustrates, they sang antifascist songs, sometimes even at gunpoint, because *not* singing those songs would be a total capitulation to antisemitic forces. Today we sing songs welcoming refugees and denouncing borders, recognizing that our people have had to flee their homes and seek safety in foreign lands.

The musicians featured here are all independent artists and comrades, so when possible, buy their music or catch them the next time they roll through your town. I've also put together an audio companion to this written playlist so that you can listen to these and other radical klezmer songs after you've read about them here.[1]

---

1. See Aaron Maiden, "Playlist: There Is Nothing More Whole Than a Broken Heart," Spotify, https://spoti.fi/3nTcoRK; Aaron Lakoff, "There Is Nothing So Whole as a Broken Heart," YouTube, April 6, 2020, https://bit.ly/39n3bgm. Additionally, you can watch "Anti-Fascist Klezmer from the Shtetl to the Streets," a panel discussion and performance hosted by Independent Jewish Voices on August 13, 2020, and featuring several artists from this playlist, at https://bit.ly/3fzcLhh.

BLACK OX ORKESTAR: "VER TANZT?"

I'll start with a song from Montreal, because I'm from Montreal, and the best bagels in the world are from Montreal. The same can be argued about the best music. And the best hockey players. But that's another story.

Black Ox Orkestar was a dreadfully short-lived band in the mid-2000s. It blossomed with brilliance and innovation, and then broke up. Thankfully Black Ox Orkestar left us two beautiful albums, both released on Montreal's revered Constellation Records (a label, it is worth noting, that has openly supported the boycott, divestment, and sanctions movement for Palestine). The band sang entirely in Yiddish and played music reminiscent of traditional klezmer from the early twentieth century.

"Ver Tanzt?" (Yiddish for "who's dancing?") is the band's standout song for me. I had a chance to see them play back in 2004 at the beloved Sala Rosa hall. If you've ever been lucky enough to visit Montreal and attend a show at Sala, you'll know how enchanting it is. The historic building in which it sits on Saint Laurent Boulevard was once a Jewish labor hall. The arch above the front door used to be adorned with the letters A. R. for "Arbeter Ring" (or in English, "workers' circle").

This particular Black Ox Orkestar show in 2004 was a benefit concert to raise money for Palestinian refugees living in Montreal yet struggling against deportation orders. Scott Levine Gilmour, the band's singer, said something so powerful that it has stuck with me to this day. I'm paraphrasing, but before the band started its set, he remarked, "We sing our songs in Yiddish. Yiddish is the language of refugees. It is also a language that the state of Israel refused to officially adopt because it was seen as the language of dirty refugees. Tonight we sing these songs in Yiddish, as Jews, in solidarity with Palestinian refugees."

The band launched into "Ver Tanzt?" which asks, "Who is dancing on the graves of Jerusalem?" For me, the song evokes many things, but particularly the history of the Moroccan quarter of the Old City of Jerusalem. This entire neighborhood was razed by Israeli forces following their occupation of East Jerusalem in 1967, and the destruction paved the way for the Wailing Wall plaza. Now if you visit this historic site on a Friday evening, you can see people dancing on the grave of what was once a community.

A couple years after discovering Black Ox Orkestar, I had the good fortune of being involved in one of the most dynamic anarchist projects of my life: a collectively run production of Howard Zinn's play *Emma* (about Goldman's life). We began with Zinn's original script, translated it into two other languages (French and Spanish), took the liberty of adding scenes, and put on several performances in temporarily squatted buildings, community centers, universities, and the Montreal International Anarchist Theatre Festival. We ended up using several Black Ox Orkestar songs as part of the soundtrack. The band's dark Yiddish tunes laden with social commentary provided the perfect ambiance for a play about one of the most feared women in US history.

No Jewish anarchist playlist would be complete without at least one version of "Daloy Polizei," a seminal Russian anarchist tune. I like to say that it is to the klezmer catalog what N.W.A's "Fuck the Police" is to hip-hop. In fact, it is precisely our own Yiddish "fuck the police" anthem. I think that my ancestors have always hated the cops.

The original song has roots dating back to 1905 in czarist Russia. Anarchism was still quite popular there at this time—certainly among the working-class Jewish population. This was before the Leninist purges of anarchists. The original tune was a vociferous denunciation of Czar Nicholas II's police forces and their attacks against striking workers. According to the Jewish Music Research Center, "Daloy Polizey" was considered an anarchist song because the lyrics hinted at the killing of the czar, and "anarchism by the deed" (targeted assassinations of people in the ruling class) was a popular trend among turn-of-the-century anarchists.

While several radical klezmer bands today perform this song (because let's face it, the police haven't gotten any better in the last hundred-plus years), what I appreciate about Berner's version is that he has updated the lyrics to reflect contemporary police brutality issues. He evokes Ian Bush, a man murdered by police in northern British Columbia in 2005, or the fact that in certain jurisdictions— for example, where I live in Quebec—police investigate themselves following killings by cops.

I fell in love with Berner's music at a funny moment. The first time

I saw him play, I was at a difficult point in my life. I'd just watched hundreds of my friends and comrades get arrested at the G20 summit in Toronto in 2010 (the biggest mass arrest in Canadian history). I saw Berner play a show in Montreal, and I was, well, more than a little tipsy on whiskey, so it was fitting to see the self-professed "whiskey rabbi" perform. Berner dedicated "Daloy Polizei" to everyone who had been on the streets during the G20. It felt so cathartic to sing along and yell out the chorus at the top of my lungs with the rest of the crowd:

> Hey hey! Daloy Polizei
> It means the same thing now as yesterday,
> Out of your houses, into the streets
> Everybody say "Fuck the police!"

L'chayim!

DANIEL KAHN AND THE PAINTED BIRD: "SHTIL DI NAKHT IZ OYSGESHTERNT"

In Yiddish, the title of this song means "Quiet, the night is full of stars." From the first thirty seconds of the tune, you'd think it was a simple love song. It is anything but that. As Kahn said when I last saw him perform it, this is his "antifa love song."

Indeed, originally written in 1942 at the peak of the Nazi horrors in Europe, this song celebrates antifascist resistance, especially by women. The beautiful lyrics honor Vitka Kempner, a Jewish partisan who threw a grenade at a German convoy in Lithuania, seriously damaging it. It is a powerful embodiment of the "by any means" antifascism that anarchists and other radicals have advanced for generations. It could well be about women like CeCe McDonald and Heather Heyer.

The song reminds me of a powerful quote from Mark Bray's *Antifa: The Antifascist Handbook*. Murray, from Baltimore's Anti-Racist Action, says of fascists, "You fight them by writing letters and making phone calls so you don't have to fight them with fists. You fight them with fists so you don't have to fight them with knives. You fight them with knives so you don't have to fight them with guns. You fight them with guns so you don't have to fight them with tanks." In this sense, the song provokes difficult questions. How far will you go in the struggle against fascism? How can we stop fascists from evolving from marginal underground groupings to taking power? Ultimately, there is just as much of a need in the movement for songwriters and petition signers as there are for street fighters. No role is necessarily more important than others. Our real strength, though, comes when we recognize how all these tactics can work together, from strumming guitars and blowing clarinets to bashing the fash.

BRIVELE: "OY ZIONISTS"

Brivele, based in Seattle, self-describes as "a discontented punky-klezy trio of Yiddishists." I don't think there's anything really "punky" about Brivele, since few punk bands are able to pull off painfully beautiful three-part harmonizing quite like Brivele can. I've had the pleasure of seeing Brivele play on a couple occasions in different cities, and appreciate the trio's ability to tell sometimes funny and sometimes devastating stories and Jewish folktales while working them into their musical repertoire.

I first became familiar with the amazing anti-Zionist tune "Oy Zionists" from the band Oy Division (which also features Kahn). The song speaks compellingly to the fact that there can be no utopias on stolen lands, and we must fight for liberation wherever injustice and fascism exist. Brivele does a unique a capella version of the song, delivering its biting critique in three languages: English, Yiddish, and Russian. The harmonies and haunting rhythms in Brivele's version of the song really strike to the heart of the matter, and underline its anti-colonial poignancy, as evidenced in the lyrics:

> Oh you foolish little Zionists
> With your utopian mentality
> You'd better go down to the factory
> And learn the worker's reality.
>
> You want to take us to Jerusalem
> So we can die as a nation
> We'd rather stay in the Diaspora
> And fight for our liberation

On October 27, 2018, a man walked into the Tree of Life synagogue in Pittsburgh during morning Shabbat services and shot eleven people dead. This tragedy would become part of a string of attacks on Jews and people of color—attacks all closely linked to the rise of Donald Trump's white supremacist brand of populism. The Quebec City mosque shooting. The Charleston Church shooting. Christchurch, New Zealand. El Paso. I've taken to the streets so many times to participate in vigils following these cruel acts, but now the gun was turned against my own people.

What we're learning as Jews in this era is that we are, yet again, not safe. Some of us may benefit from whiteness, class, or other shields. But make no mistake: the fascists hate us and want us erased.

So in these moments, we need music and art that speaks to the gravity of the situation, and provides us with hope in the bleakest of times.

Tsibele, a five-piece klezmer band from New York City, offers a particularly chilling rendition of the song "Mir Veln Zey Iberlebn / We Will Outlive Them," supplying hope through grief. I'm borrowing the story directly from this band, but essentially the song is about a Nazi massacre in Poland during World War II. When Nazi officers arrived in Lublin, they assembled the Jews of the village, and ordered them to sing and dance. It was to be the Jews' last humiliating act before a certain death. One of the Jews began to sing the song "Let's

All Get Along," perhaps trying to convince their would-be assassins to spare their lives. When no one else followed along, another changed the words to "we will outlive them." The villagers were all executed; this new song was their last word. The message was clear: fascism can take us from our flesh in the here and now, but our people will survive your evil.

As Tsibele puts it,

> Our resistance song comes from that night.
> It's not uncomplicated. So many of us did not, have not, outlived.
> But this is a slogan of determination.
> It's a love note to every person working to make the "we" who will
> outlive them bigger and fuller and stronger.

In the wake of the massacre at the Tree of Life, I think this song has taken on renewed importance. A decentralized radical Jewish network bearing the name Outlive Them came together quickly after the tragedy to organize a series of actions against antisemitism and fascism. The network, like the song, clearly links the courage of our ancestors' antifascism to present-day struggles against transphobia, borders, and US Immigration and Customs Enforcement, to name a few, and for the world we as Jewish anarchists want to build: a fascist-free tomorrow.

It was a rainy day in August, and I was on a trip to New York City when I got a cryptic message from a friend: "Yiddish anarcho-punk show happening this afternoon. Secret location. Private message on Facebook for location." I couldn't resist. So I sent a message to this unknown Facebook account, stating my excitement about attending the show. I quickly got a response with an invitation, but it simply had an address—right in Midtown Manhattan. I threw on my boots and raincoat, stopped at the corner deli for a coffee and delicious everything bagel with scallion schmeer (I could go on at length about how much of a life force NYC bagels are, but that's another essay), and made my way toward the address, past skyscrapers and soulless boutiques.

When I arrived, I was standing in front of a nondescript girls high school. It was noon on a Monday. I must be in the wrong place, I thought to myself, but persisted in my adventure. I hesitated, took a deep breath, and then entered, not sure if I was going to look creepier waltzing into a girls high school or lurking around outside.

Sure enough, though, as soon as I entered, I understood why I was in the right spot. It was the site of the annual NYC Rock Camp for Girls, and I was led to the basement cafeteria, just in time for the lunchtime show.

Koyt Far Dayn Fardakht (meaning "the filth of your suspicion" in English) describes itself as "a punk band that plays Yiddish anarchist and bundist songs—the soundtrack to strikes, uprisings, assassinations, and revolutionary movements from Odessa and Vilna to New York and Galveston to Buenos Aires and Havana." Fuck yeah.

It was really special to see Koyt Far Dayn Fardakht play to a packed cafeteria of enthusiastic young girls, most between seven and twelve years old. Despite the audience's age, the band didn't hold back on the intensity or heaviness of its music. The song that really stuck with me was "Mya z'fin ir arbet gegangen" ("Mya was leaving work"), adapted from a Ukrainian poem dating back to 1904, and detailing the police murder of a Jewish worker.

Much like the tradition of other songs in this playlist, Koyt Far Dayn Fardakht has taken this hundred-plus-year-old tune and remixed it for modern times, dedicating its version to Mya Hall, a black trans woman murdered by police near Baltimore in 2015. It was beautiful to watch the band introduce the piece to the young rock campers, not mincing words about the song's severity, but also being generous enough to answer questions from the girls afterward.

WE MUST DANCE—AND LAUGH AND SING

Music is interwoven with our social movements in the most profound, rhythmic, and silly ways. This is true from Black Lives Matter protesters in the United States chanting Kendrick Lamar's affirming refrain "We gon' be alright" to Lebanese anti-government demonstrators singing the ridiculously cute children's song "Baby Shark." It is hard to think of radical organizing over the years without picket line folk songs, civil rights hymns, or the do-it-yourself underground culture of hip-hop and punk. The staying power of Goldman's famous line, "If I can't dance, I don't want to be part of your revolution," regardless of whether she really said it or not, speaks to the necessity of artistic joy in striving to change the world. Music isn't just a by-product of liberation struggles; it is their heartbeat.

Such struggles, of course, are hard, often devastatingly so, with equal moments of loss and trauma alongside the beauty. Dancing, laughing, and singing can help us sustain ourselves through it all, offering community and strength. I picture our ancestors playing klezmer, gathering in living rooms or concert halls even as bombs fell around them, and fascism took their homelands by the throat. I imagine the melancholic melodies on our ancestors' lips as women died in factory fires or went on strike, because strikes were a matter of life or death.

There's long been a soundtrack to people's lives and dreams. It is a poignant, expansive, and diverse playlist, filled with anarcho-punk, rebel reggae, booty-shaking funk, and as I've sampled here, Jewish klezmer. So what are you waiting for? Pick up your clarinet, accordion, fiddle, or microphone, and get out there and destroy fascism!

*

Aaron Lakoff is a media maker, DJ, and community organizer from Montreal. He produces the Rebel Beat, *a podcast on radical music, and agitates for class war on the dance floor. Aaron is currently working as the communications and media lead for Independent Jewish Voices Canada, a national organization of*

Jews working toward peace and justice in Israel-Palestine. He'd like to thank Avi Grenadier, a fellow anarcho-Jewish DJ who has introduced Aaron to many of these bands over the years; Darya Marchenkova, for encouraging him to do everything he does; and the workers at St-Viateur Bagel in Montreal, for keeping him well fed.

FINDING OUR OWN FIRE

FAYER COLLECTIVE

The US South is a region of the world that can't be understood from any less than a hundred perspectives. It's home to over half the United States' Black population and yet is viewed, seemingly across the board, as the most racist part of said country. It's been ignored by the political establishment and wealthy for decades, then labeled as backward and unintelligent by the same ones that landed us where we are. This has put us, as anarchists, and more so Jewish anarchists, in an unfortunately unique position. We've had to fight tooth and nail against classist forces that wish us gone in the name of development and safety, and at the same time, fight those of our class who dawn white hoods and wish us dead because we don't eat pork. At the front line of both these enemies are blue and red flashing lights, excitedly ready to beat and arrest us at a moment's notice.

This is still a simplified summary, of course. To assume that the whole southern fascist movement is working class is itself classist—something that coastal liberalism has yet to (or chooses not to) understand. Many of those we face on the streets are the same ones who're raising our rents, flipping our neighborhoods, and cutting our pay. Nevertheless, for the past decade, this is the situation that we and our friends have found ourselves in.

Indeed, Klan and Nazi activity are never infrequent in our lives. For instance, a rich Klan lawyer is actively buying up property in the Atlanta, Georgia, neighborhood where some of us live. And as Jews in the South, this has never been hidden from us, whether it took the form of some of us being attacked at our homes to witnessing parents pull their kids from school when they found out that they'd learned about Chanukah that day.

As anarchists, we've been organizing, building our world, and fostering a revolutionary culture for close to ten years now—some of us for longer than that, and some of us for only a matter of months. But for most of this time, those of us who would become the Fayer Collective never thought to or saw the benefit of organizing explicitly as Jewish anarchists. While for some of us, our Jewishness may have been prominent in our personal lives, it was only a background fact in nearly all our political lives. That was soon to change.

In 2017, the National Socialist Movement, a neo-Nazi political organization, had announced that it would hold a rally in Newnan, Georgia, on April 21 of the following year. Around November, in our own various crews and groups, we began organizing with the coalition that was forming under the banner #NoNaziNewnan. One of the coalition's goals was to get marginalized religious communities, such as synagogues and mosques, to support the counterorganizing effort, so we did outreach, but not one synagogue decided to join us. At first this seemed surprising. There were two main reasons, though, that the synagogues did not want to sign on. One was understandable: the fear of being targeted by these neo-Nazis in the future. The other was frustrating: they didn't want to be associated with what they called "the Antifa" (Atlanta Antifa was part of the coalition and the most publicly associated group with the counterdemonstration). Despite this setback and with less support than hoped, the coalition forged ahead, but what we experienced in Newnan would only encourage our already-growing resentments toward what felt like another betrayal by the institutional and liberal wing of Jews in the United States.

As we arrived in downtown Newnan, we saw the full force of what we were up against. Tanks filled the streets, snipers were positioned on the rooftops, and soldiers occupied all the "public" space. The small, rural, Georgian town was militarized, ready to defend neo-Nazis against any and all threats to their "freedom of speech." The arrests began only minutes after we gathered on a corner, before the march had even started. This was simply a prelude of things to come in Newnan that day. The police targeted us, the counterdemonstrators, by tasering people, dragging folks through the streets, violently arresting others, and threatening to turn their guns on us, and this went on, nonstop, for hours. The fascist rally was held as planned, although all the news attention was on us and not the neo-Nazis. Whether this was a victory or not has since been debated, but either way, we all left demoralized. It should be noted that many of these military police had been trained by Israel Defense Forces soldiers under the Georgia International Law Enforcement Exchange program— thus Israeli-trained police had defended literal neo-Nazis.

It wasn't long before we found ourselves in the exact same situation. The International Keystone Knights of the Ku Klux Klan called for a rally on February 2, 2019, at Georgia's Stone Mountain, where a massive Confederate memorial is carved into the rock wall. Once again, we joined in the counterorganizing effort. A coalition dubbed FrontLine Organization Working to End Racism (FLOWER) was formed. And like last time, we reached out to the institutional Jewish community, only to hear the exact same reasons for refusing to join us that we'd been given for Newnan. Fortunately we had more success overall in Stone Mountain because the Klan, which was disorganized and plagued by infighting, decided at the last minute to cancel its own event, and our antifascist coalition enjoyed an arrest-free victory march in downtown Stone Mountain.

Between the two events and failing to gain support from Jewish institutions both times, we learned a harsh lesson—one that maybe we had been in denial about for some time: we needed an explicitly revolutionary Jewish organization in Atlanta. We needed, in essence, to clearly and visibly weaponize our own identities as Jewish anarchists in order to force people to understand that some of us exist and organize beyond the liberal wing of our community.

Later that same year, Fayer, the Yiddish word for "fire," went public. While many of us are often involved with other projects and don't necessarily have the time to dedicate to a new collective, it made sense to at least have a platform—a place to give our perspective as Jews as well as a banner to march under as revolutionary Jews when necessary. Still, it wasn't long before other Jewish rebels found us, and quickly a new community formed—the first one in Atlanta where diasporic, radical, and anti-Zionist Jews could actually exist together without being harassed as "self-hating." Forging a revolutionary Jewish culture in a city that has been dominated by liberalism is not an easy task, and we've only really just started. For us, the fight against fascism isn't about "allyship"; it is a personal and direct fight for our lives. And that knowledge has put a fire in our hearts, as both anarchists and Jews.

*

Fayer is a collective of artists, revolutionaries, workers, students, criminals, and free lovers—fighting for the earth, the good life, and total liberation. You can find Fayer on Twitter at @FayerAtlanta.

EVER STIR THE KETTLE

ROBIN MARKLE

"Never again means close the camps!" we screamed over and over as
the cops ordered us to disperse, then arrested and loaded us into vans.
We were a group of young, mostly queer Jews and a few non-Jewish
Latinx people and supporters who blocked Philadelphia's annual
Fourth of July parade to highlight the hypocrisy of celebrating freedom and USA "democracy" while immigrant families were being detained and neglected in camps at the border.

I'd never met most of these people before that week in summer
2019. I saw an open call on Facebook for Jews who were interested in
taking part in a direct action against the detention camps. I filled out
a form on a Monday. On Tuesday, I got a phone call from an organizer,
and on Wednesday, went to a direct action training and art build. We
blocked the parade on Thursday. I was initially hesitant to commit to
this level of risk with folks I didn't know, but I felt compelled on a spiritual level.

* * *

As a preteen, I devoured books (both nonfiction and historical fiction)
about Jewish youths' experiences of the Holocaust. While I am not a
direct descendant of anyone who was in a concentration camp, I un-

derstood at a young age that my cultural identity linked me to people who were. I developed anxiety that someday I would be arrested and forced to relocate to a camp. That fear has never left me, though I've learned to mitigate it, partly because for most of my life, such a scenario seemed highly unlikely. Then Donald Trump was elected, and I started having dreams about my family being rounded up by police. Some two-plus years later, when news stories began appearing about the horrific conditions within the US Immigration and Custom Enforcement's border camps, I knew that I needed to act.

The parade was not my first civil disobedience action, and from training and experience, I knew to be selective about what I carried with me when risking arrest. I didn't want anything to fall out of my pockets if I was handled roughly so I wore a fanny pack, tossing in a couple granola bars, my ID, and some cash. I also packed a photo of two people I consider grandmothers: Tully and Milly. Tully was my mom's mother—someone I have fond memories of despite the fact that she died when I was five. Milly was my mom's aunt, who lived into my early twenties, and taught me grandmotherly arts like my family herstory along with how to embroider and make knishes. In the photo I carried, they are twenty-one and twenty-five, respectively, posing on a sidewalk in New Haven, Connecticut, in fashionable dresses, smiling and looking proud during summer 1936. Decades later, when going through her dead parents' things, my mother would find a letter that Tully had typed to a friend that same summer but never sent, or perhaps sent another copy. Among missives about her "new heart interest" (my grandfather) and the "swell" Charlie Chaplin film that she'd just seen, Tully wrote,

History seems to be repeating itself, according to reports in the papers of existing conditions in Poland that the Jews suffer. Doesn't it seem hopeless at times like this when civilization is supposedly far advanced and above such things as pogroms, racial differences, wars, etc., which were practiced from the beginning of Time when civilization was undeveloped!! To think that today it is repeated and War looms on the horizon makes me feel that all efforts to repel, to educate, to progress is [*sic*] in vain. I've joined a movement—Anti War & Fascism. It seems to me that all endeavors in this direction are futile. For Politics and the Munitions manufacturers will ever stir the kettle.

While Tully didn't live long enough for me ask her about these things, I think we share a similar attitude toward the world. Ongoing war and racism make us feel angry and sometimes hopeless. We know that the way things are isn't an accident. The people who profit from violence are in cahoots with the government to manufacture crisis. But we join movements anyway because Jews have always resisted; it is our way.

As I blocked the parade, I thought about Tully and her "Anti War & Fascism" movement. I don't know if she was part of a particular group, nor do I know if she went to one meeting or many. Regardless, it gave me strength as well as a sense of rightness and protection to know that I was carrying on her lineage. I hoped that her spirit was with me, and that Tully felt I was doing right by her.

After being handcuffed, I was pushed into a police wagon with seven other people. We sat on benches facing each other, four to a side. As the cops slammed the doors on us, we continued to shout, "Never again means close the camps!" while stomping a beat with our feet. We screamed for several minutes, then looked at each other and simultaneously ended the chant. There was a slight pause. I don't remember who started singing, but we all joined in and were an exceptionally talented chorus for people who had been randomly selected to share a van. We sang "This Little Light of Mine," "Amazing Grace," and some simple Hebrew songs that we knew from Passover. I taught people a Jewish folk song that I'd learned from a non-Jewish person at a political training in Detroit, "Olam Chesed Yibaneh" (We will build this world with love). Another person taught us an excerpt from "I Am Willing" by Holly Near, and we sang it again and again in overlapping rounds as the cops drove us to one station, left us waiting in the van, and then drove us to a second station:

> I am open and I am willing
> To be hopeless would seem so strange
> It dishonors those who go before us
> So lift me up to the light of change

We were still singing when the police unlocked the van doors and took us into the station, where they put us in a holding area with other people from our action. Some of the other vans (there were thirty-three people arrested in total) had already been unloaded, and our comrades looked up at us, startled, then smiled when we walked into the silent room flanked by officers and singing loudly. Soon everyone joined us, and we spent the better part of our three-hour stint in the can teaching each other songs and harmonizing. It was one of the best experiences that I've ever had in Jewish community, and I knew that my ancestors were watching and protecting me.

There were about a dozen cops in the room with us, mostly lined up along one wall. When I first arrived, they were milling around talking to each other, but as we sang, more and more of them stopped and listened. Finally none of them were talking; instead, they were our audience. It felt like the power dynamics had changed. From the basic knowledge that I have of somatics, when human beings (and other mammals) move or make sounds together in groups, their breathing and heart rates can sync with each other. We as arrestees definitely synced with each other, helping to soothe ourselves as well as feel unity and protection while we were handcuffed and jailed. Without intention, some of our energy reached our jailers too.

I feel complicated about this, of course, because I don't believe that people need to appeal to cops and wouldn't advocate for doing so. That said, when we inadvertently brought the cops closer to being human/animal with us through our singing, it felt powerful. More important, regardless of the cops' reactions, singing together was a free, accessible tool to keep our morale up while we waited to be processed. In talking with others in the days after the action, everyone brought up the singing.

* * *

My Grandma Tully and her husband, Norman, my mom's parents, were proud and active Democrats; a portrait of Franklin Delano Roosevelt hung in their kitchen. I followed in their footsteps until I went to college and met communists and anarchists, eventually choosing to align myself with the latter. That was over a dozen years ago, and while at times I've been so fed up with the bullshit that can happen in anarchist scenes and I've thought about dis-identifying, I always choose to believe that I can make anarchism what I want it to be and ignore/transform what I find offensive. Plus I have a tattoo on my forearm of myself holding a flag with a big circle A on it, so I guess I'm committed!

Several years ago, I was visiting my mom in upstate New York, and we had dinner with her sister, my Aunt Laura. I mentioned something about anarchism, and my aunt asked, "You know your great-grandpa Isidore, Tully's father, was an anarchist?" I stopped chewing. "What?" My mom chimed in, "I told you that!" "I think I'd remember you telling me that your grandfather was an anarchist!" I replied, frustrated at having not known this before. I asked them to tell me more about him. I knew that he had owned an electric factory in Brooklyn in the mid-twentieth century and liked to paint, but that was pretty much it.

Laura recalled that when she was a small child, maybe five or six, her parents would sometimes send her to stay with Tully's parents in Brooklyn for a weekend. When it was time for bed, grandpa Isidore would tell her about how he left Russia and came to Europe to escape the pogroms. It was not your typical bedtime story, my aunt mused, yet Isidore knew that he was getting older and maybe passing on this oral history felt more important than protecting Laura's innocence. My aunt only remembered the broad strokes—it had been sixty-five years—but Isidore explained to her that he left Russia with a group of other Jewish men. They walked for days together to the western border, trying to keep out of sight. One of the men became sick or injured, and the group had to leave him behind, presumably to die. Eventually they reached the border, which was guarded by soldiers with guns. They waited for an opportune time and then ran across to the other side. (I don't know what country he escaped into, only that he ended up in England.) Guards shot at them, but from what my aunt recollected, they all made it out alive.

Learning this history offered depth to my understanding of my great-grandpa Isidore. I appreciate that he came by his anarchism honestly, after living under and fleeing the violence of both state repression and antisemitism. It also gave me a deep sense of gratitude. If he hadn't attempted and survived this journey, I wouldn't be here. I exist only because one of my ancestors was willing to run across a border knowing that they might be killed. I'd been active around immigration issues before hearing this story, but I now felt a much stronger connection and purpose to supporting migrants and destroying borders.

I brought along Isidore too, in spirit, on that July 4. After being released from custody, I was greeted outside by the sweetest comrades, who gave me water and snacks. I logged onto social media to look at photos from our action, took a screenshot of one, and texted it to my mom, telling her that I had been arrested and was out. Coincidentally, she was with her cousin Miriam, Milly's daughter. "Miriam and I are both proud of you!!!" she texted back, and I replied by sharing a picture of the photo of their moms, Tully and Milly, that I'd tucked in my fanny pack for ancestral inspiration, our connections coming full circle.

*

ROBIN MARKLE

Robin Markle is an artist, chandler, organizer, and witch based in West Philadelphia. They help coordinate the Philly Childcare Collective, create art for movements against incarceration, and make queer altar candles, sold at flamingidols.com. The demonstration that this piece centers around was part of a coordinated campaign called Never Again Action. Jewish organizers held dozens of direct actions at ICE detention centers, offices, and other targets during summer 2019, and as of this writing, the network is still active. You can learn more about its work at www.neveragainaction.com. Robin expresses gratitude to Lisa Fithian for teaching them (and someone else who was in the same police van that day) how to use song and play to keep people's spirits up while in police custody.

WE ARE THE
GOLEMS THEY FEAR

ZELDA OFIR

Running down my arm is a poem about my Jewish women ancestors
who concealed themselves in the shadows, turned into birds, and sent
flames down from the skies. In the poem, the borders burn, the cities
are overtaken by the ocean foam, the prisons crumble, and we—the
women, the queers, the subversives—raise our hands in defiance of
God. I composed this poem like a collage, using words and phrases
from a dozen other poems written by Yiddish-speaking Jews over the
past century. The poem contains a communal voice as if it were a conversation between many generations of Jewish people. Individually,
each piece spoke of the pain and hope that defines our experiences
as Jews. Assembled, they speak not only of our hopes and desires in
creating a new world but the power and possibilities of our collective
strength too.

The ancient myth of the golem tells us that a beast can be raised
from the earth to protect the Jewish people. This creature, formed
of mud and clay, is said to be returned to the earth by a rabbi when
its role is finished. There are other ancient stories, about how the

witches also came from the earth and were stripped of their power by men who broke their connection with the ground.

In Talmudic literature, the word "golem" literally means unformed. Unmarried women in Talmudic literature are called unformed as well. Women are not considered to be formed until they are married, reinforcing the patriarchal idea that women are complete only in relation and subservience to men. The Talmud also mentions another group of people, "men who are like women," which we know to be queers like ourselves. Queers, who live outside the rigid world of gender, remain unformed in our inherent defiance of subservience both to men and the ways that they try (and fail) to shape our bodies and minds.

The beasts of Jewish myths—the golem, the witches—have a power feared by rabbis and men, whose roles depend on the patriarchal laws of the universe handed to them by a male God. But the very existence of the golem defies God's laws. The formation of a golem from mud and clay is in direct opposition to the Second Commandment, which tells us that we will be punished for creating or worshipping graven images. The golem is not only a betrayal of God but also a betrayal of men who were created in God's image. When the golem is brought to life, it betrays another of God's powers: the power to create life. And when the golem destroys those who seek to harm us, the golem betrays God by showing us that we do not need his divine intervention.

Golems, women, and queers: the unformed ones, the monsters, the protectors. At the end of the myth of the golem, when the rabbis try to return us to the earth, they do it because our power is too great. They sense that the golem, having saved the Jewish people from their immediate harm, seeks to enact vengeance and continued destruction against the world—a world that men seek to maintain.

The rabbis return us, the golems, to the earth, because they do not want their power challenged. This is an experience that we have had our entire existence. Men try to silence us, harm us, destroy us, and demean us, all so they can keep their dominance over us.

For as long as queers have existed, we have formed and fought in collective liberation struggles. In what ways do we, as Jewish queers, have unique ways to shape our liberation? As an anarchist Jew, I spent so many years trying to sculpt my relationship with other Jews into a form that fit me, but for years I was left empty, not even sure of what I was trying to create. When I began making connections with other queer Jewish anarchists for the first time, I felt as though I was suddenly filled with a fire that I could never turn my back on—this strange, fiery love that I had been searching for yet had never been able to name. For years we had been in demonstrations together, had fought alongside each other, but without being a visible Jewish presence, and therefore without finding each other. In conversations with other anarchist Jews, I learned that so many of us were taught that our Jewishness is inseparable from Jewish nationalism, and so the symbols of Judaism became foreign and almost tainted—and so we hid this part of ourselves. Today that has changed. We have found one another, and through our reclamation of Jewish symbols and language, we continue finding one another.

ZELDA OFIR

In a black bloc, we hide ourselves in order to become as unrecognizable as the golem. It is, in many ways, similar to the power of the diaspora. Within the borders of a state, through the creation of a national identity, we lose all the power that remaining unrecognizable offers us. Defying assimilation and remaining always in the diaspora, we can simultaneously conceal ourselves and strike in the same way that we can from within a bloc.

When I bring banners to demonstrations written in Yiddish, it is a reclamation of my resistance to assimilation. Many banners exist to be read, sending their message through the meaning of their words. In a world where few continue to speak Yiddish, Yiddish banners do not exist to be read. They exist specifically to mark us as Jews while at the same time reminding them that they do not know who we are. They cannot read our banners, they cannot see our faces, but they know that we are Jews with tools in our hands. A visible presence as Jews in a black bloc sends a clear message to our enemies that we will fight them, but the power of the words on our banners is for us alone. In its creation, Yiddish speakers purposefully changed the pronunciation of German words so that the Germans could not understand them. The Yiddish language had power in being spoken and yet not recognized by our enemies, and today is no different.

Emma Goldman felt differently, saying that if she was going to speak against her enemies, she felt that her power came from being understood. But many Jewish anarchists of the twentieth century knew that it was enough to mark ourselves as Jews as we fought. Simply becoming an active threat against fascism was to be understood enough. They do not need to understand our songs, our poems, our prayers. They need only to see that there are Jews who attack them. I want to create a world in which any Jewish symbol is seen as a threat to the state, the police, and fascism, because they know that where there are Jewish symbols, there is us.

I cover my body in Yiddish words for many of the same reasons that we bring Yiddish banners to a bloc. With these symbols marking me as a Jew, I draw toward me both my comrades and enemies. I have found other Jewish anarchists among the throngs of demonstrators because of the ritual tzitzit (fringes) hanging near their hips. I have found other Jewish anarchists because of Jewish songs that they sung while marching against Nazis. (A favorite example of the latter was an anti-Nazi song sung to the tune of "I Have a Little Dreidel" at a demonstration that coincided with the first night of Chanukah.)

We saw, in Charlottesville, that glorious moment in which the importance of anarchist struggle was made clear and the general public applauded us for confronting the fascists. Although that demonstration was not specifically Jewish, we can see the parallels with the myth of the golem. Under direct attack, the liberals allowed us to protect them. Within two days, they sensed that our goals went beyond those hours in Charlottesville, that our goals were to continue attacking the white supremacy that holds society intact, and they condemned us once again, trying to force us to melt back into the earth where we could no longer threaten their power.

It is not a coincidence that so many Jewish holidays arise from our connection with the earth—Tu B'Shvat, Sukkot, Pesach, and of course each Shabbos and Rosh Chodesh, which follow the path of the sun and moon. As anarchists and queers, we also recognize that our liberation depends on the survival of the land that nourishes us. In the moments—weeks and months—following repression, when I know that I often feel hopeless and beaten down, in what ways can we use our unique Jewish connection to the earth to re-form ourselves from the mud and clay?

In an essay called "The Edge of Knowledge: Jews as Monsters / Jews as Victims," Jewish historian Lester D. Friedman asks, "There is an important relationship between normality and the monster. Why does normal society ostracize the monster, and what does the monster do to alienate society? Why does the monster attack normality, and what does normality do to repel the monster?"

We will never stop attacking normality. For as long as Jews and queers have existed, we have always been outside normality, looking in and knowing that it is exactly what we do not want to be. We know that the golem acts in vengeance against gender, against God, and against society. We know that we are the golems they fear.

*

Zelda Ofir is a strange, small animal, collector of rocks and Yiddish poems, and a believer that the half-moon is the luckiest moon of them all. The ancestral trauma that lives within us inspired them to become a nurse—a position that they take on not as a career but rather as a skill set from which they can participate in illegal resistance. They want to spread the fires of Jewish revolt until their hands are too old and too wrinkly to hold a match. On Tu B'Shvat, when the sap starts running, they will walk into the mountains and turn back into the rock golem from which they came.

between the sea and the dry land;
between the upper waters above and the lower waters below;
between jews and goyim—
let us distinguish the parts within the whole and bless their differences.
may our lives be made whole through relation.

blessed are we, who make holy the profane;
who experience the gradients between light and dark;
who build solidarity beyond nations;
who ritualize the passage of time.

may we be our own prophets, strength and song in hand.
dance with us to grow the song of the world.
dance with us to repair the world.
come with us to the waters of redemption.

—havdalah bracha, adapted by morgan holleb, pinkpeacock.gay

AK Press is small, in terms of staff and resources, but we also manage to be one of the world's most productive anarchist publishing houses. We publish close to twenty books every year, and distribute thousands of other titles published by like-minded independent presses and projects from around the globe. We're entirely worker run and democratically managed. We operate without a corporate structure—no boss, no managers, no bullshit.

The Friends of AK program is a way you can directly contribute to the continued existence of AK Press, and ensure that we're able to keep publishing books like this one! Friends pay $25 a month directly into our publishing account ($30 for Canada, $35 for international), and receive a copy of every book AK Press publishes for the duration of their membership! Friends also receive a discount on anything they order from our website or buy at a table: 50 percent on AK titles, and 30 percent on everything else. We have a Friends of AK e-book program as well: $15 a month gets you an electronic copy of every book we publish for the duration of your membership. You can even sponsor a deeply discounted membership for someone in prison.

Email friendsofak@akpress.org for more info, or visit the website: akpress .org/friends.html.

There are always great book projects in the works—so sign up now to become a Friend of AK Press, and let the presses roll!